Wa__e, D_ __ I.
__ __ radi__a_ cen_er: middle
.__ Americans and the politics of
W37 alienation.

38247

Oakton Community College

Morton Grove, Illinois

260706
609 0181gm

THE RADICAL CENTER

THE
RADICAL
CENTER

MIDDLE AMERICANS AND
THE POLITICS OF ALIENATION

DONALD I. WARREN

38247

UNIVERSITY OF NOTRE DAME PRESS

NOTRE DAME *LONDON*

Library of Congress Cataloging in Publication Data

Warren, Donald I
  The radical center.

  Includes bibliographical references.
  1. Middle classes—United States. 2. Radicalism—United States. 3. Social problems. 4. Political participation—United States. I. Title.
HT690.U6W37   301.44´1   75-19880
ISBN 0-268-01594-5
ISBN 0-268-01595-3 pbk.

Manufactured in the United States of America

To Max B. Jaslow —
    a Dedicated Teacher

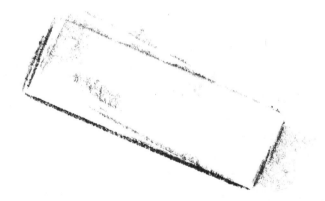

CONTENTS

PREFACE

The following memorandum was written by a research staff member during the early stages of the study of Middle Americans:

> There are some obstacles which make the study of "Middle America" troublesome for the social scientist. One is the liberal philosophy of change based on seemingly obvious evidence which sets up a conflict with the accepted picture of the values of the lower middle class. The conflict is that this lower middle class, working class, blue collar population, which makes up a large chunk of America, is seen as holding values which are antithetical to the liberal, academic community. These values are: pro-militarism; pro-Protestant work ethic (for many the highest value is their pride in the honest work they do); pro-consumerism (this includes big cars, campers and snowmobiles); and anti-black [sentiment]) especially as blacks are seen as the threatening enemy whose presence causes their schools to become battlegrounds, and their neighborhoods to deteriorate; the enemy who takes their tax dollars by devious means and the jobs they deserve by preferential treatment.
>
> Given this commonly accepted view of the "Middle American," how can a liberal, social scientist objectively study them? It is easy to study, feel sympathy for and believe in the virtue of minority peoples who have suffered unequal treatment and hatred for so many years. It is harder to come to the study of Middle America without ambiguity and moral dilemma.
>
> Another problem with the analysis of social problems of lower middle class people by social scientists is the scientists' immense social and real space distance from the problems and the people who embody them. Just comparing the numbers of people in the country with various levels of educa-

tion, the Ph.D. social scientists form a minute minority which tends to isolate them from the rest of us. The intellectual also tends to live in various centers around the country away from the working man. He lives in non-industrial university towns or in big cities, but hardly ever among the working class.

There is another problem that further confounds understanding. As long as morality and achievement are thought of as related, an American who sees himself at a specific achievement level in relation to others also assigns lesser moral value to those below him and higher to those above him. This relative view of self combined with the need to accept, explain and assign value to one's self, work together to diminish understanding between people. The dynamic of interaction becomes a contest where the interactants have defined themselves and must either hide their deficiency or assert their superiority as they have defined it. All of us have a basic human need—to justify our existence to ourselves and to any significant others. Those with the highest educational resources are best able to define themselves and their achievements in the most "moral" terms. In a country where freedom and mobility are assumed, it is easy for the best-educated to appear as the most perfect human beings, the epitome of achievement.

And indeed, how many analyses by social scientists present a view of a low-educated, low-income sub-population as a kind of moral ideal? Some articles or photographic essays do portray the "common" man in all his simplicity and strength and basic goodness. This seems value-free, but a condescending, patronizing tone is barely hidden.

It is against this background of potential misunderstanding that one comes to the study of another social group. It is across this chasm that the social scientist tries to classify, codify and communicate the vital concerns of "Middle America."

Loraine A. Reish
Research Assistant
"Middle America Project"
April, 1972

I received the following letter after an appearance on the national TV program, "AM America," February 7, 1975:

Dear Professor Warren:

Your interview on television this morning was interesting and I was impressed with your assessment of the problems many people must cope with. Some of your remarks pointed up a line of thinking that has been of concern to me for some time. Please permit me to share with you some of my thoughts.

Now obviously, people do have problems from time to time, some quite serious. These fall generally into two categories: personal and social. The nuclear family, living "cheek by jowl" with too little privacy, is hardly isolated: their lives are so invaded now that they do not have time to contemplate and arrive at common-sense value judgments. Generally speaking, the families that are able to solve their problems themselves are families grounded in traditional Judeo-Christian moral values. (Of course, there are exceptions, but I am not speaking of the extremes.) However, you probably do not come in contact with these families since they do not consult you with their problems; they are, in fact, the stable "backbone" of our whole society. And, strangely, they are the most deprecated by the behavioral scientists—strange until one examines the motives of the social planners.

In the area of social problems, one of our greatest problems is defining true grass-roots movements and movements that are masked to "appear" as grass-roots movements. Whether the problem is city planning, clearing clogged drainage creeks, solving teenage sex- and drug-related problems, or promoting genuine accountability in the public schools—we see this recurring problem of government and union agencies rushing in to "help" us, and often creating the problem in the first place, so they can perpetuate their bureaucracies, hire more "experts," confiscate more tax money and solve their own mental problem, which seems to be a lusting after personal power.

Well, that's quite an indictment, but my work in many genuine grass-roots movements convinces me that the government is almost afraid we will be self-reliant enough to solve our own problems without federal guidelines. All the sweet, soft, "caring" words do not cloak the monumental contempt for the people on the part of the government helpers. Whereas, the people who in their own efforts help each other,

*within families, within neighborhoods, WITHOUT the out-
side invasion of various agencies, do not have contempt for
each other.*

*This idea of contempt is an important element. Our na_
tional news media and various agencies and institutions bom
bard our senses with the pervasive atmosphere of doom, the
terrible problems, the insurmountable crises throughout the
world. And they really want us to believe every bit of it,
aside from the fact that crises make more sensational news
reporting. There is the perpetuation of the theory that the
present time is almost impossible in which to live, and that
we must change, change, change our whole life-styles and
attitudes in order to survive into the future. Ahhh but
"change" from what into what social order? And if change is
to be necessary, just who will make the decisions? The
people-planners or the people themselves? Since too many
people-planners have this thinly veiled contempt for the
people, I am comforted in knowing they will get nowhere,
though they do have our tax money to exploit for their own
nefarious purposes.*

*It is the grass-roots people themselves in whom I have a
growing faith, once they are truthfully informed on the
major issues. Americans are the greatest people in the world,
with a marvelous sense of humor and genuine sense of joy in
the here and now, and a faith in the future. From one
individual to another individual the great silent majority is
coming awake, and they will not be deliberately divided and
collectivized into little warring groups. They are not isolated;
quite the contrary, they need more privacy, more calm,
peace, quiet and time to think. And most of all they need a
sense of individual self-assurance that they can define and
solve their own problems with the help of God. But not with
the "help" of the government. Already, they have just about
helped us, and helped us to death. As the independent
teen-agers say to their hovering, smothering parents, so we
the people say to the social agencies: "Bug off. Get off our
backs, damn it."*

Anne V. Bowker
Tulsa, Oklahoma

ACKNOWLEDGMENTS

A number of colleagues, co-workers and participants in the various phases of interviewing and data gathering deserve more recognition that I can provide in this brief initial word of thanks. The core study owes its existence to a Ford Foundation grant and the support and encouragement of Basil Whiting, Program Officer in the National Affairs Division of that organization. His active role in the design and initial testing of field procedures is a pattern deserving of emulation in other research programs of this kind.

My colleague and friend Eugene Litwak, now of Columbia University, as co-director of the original study from which this analysis was subsequently drawn, has played an invaluable role as intellectual stimulator and sound critic in the development of this study.

In carrying forward this work I have been fortunate and privileged to work with several staff members at the University of Michigan. In particular John Musick and Nancy Hooyman served as able and dedicated field researchers in the early phases of the Middle America Project. Thanks are owed as well to Loraine Reish, who provided office coordination and personal commitment to the concerns of this study that are very much appreciated. Professor Patrick Easto of Eastern Michigan University also performed in a valuable role in the community field studies that formed the basis of the later national survey.

There are others, both at the University of Michigan and in different organizations such as the Center for Policy Research at Columbia University, who contributed to the success of this research. Their support and interest can only be collectively acknowledged.

I wish also to thank Mr. Patrick Caddell of the Cambridge

Research Center for providing the opportunity to update and confirm patterns found in the original national survey.

The present manuscript would not have emerged without critical help from several people. These include Sybil Aldridge who worked on preparation of the annotated bibliography on Middle American studies as well as on the Boston and West Virginia community controversies. Special mention of the work of present staff members in my research organization must include Bonnie Alcumbrek who labored long and hard on the revisions in this manuscript.

I wish to express a special debt of gratitude to Jim Langford who was willing to delve into a much longer draft and divine whether shining through it were nuggets of truth and insight that should see the light of day.

Yet in spite of the contributions I have cited I am very much aware that none of the individuals mentioned should be held accountable for the conclusions and interpretations expressed in this book. These are necessarily my own seeking after knowledge of the often bewildering complexity that is the social reality of America at the close of its second century.

Ann Arbor, Michigan
July 4, 1975

INTRODUCTION

March 19, 1975, was a blustery, late winter day for a Washington protest. The major newspapers and wire services largely ignored the events occurring around the emergent angry voices of Middle America. Only public broadcast radio detailed the merging of two expressions of the deep political frustration and alienation of this country: the forces of Boston anti-busing groups and the West Virginia mining-country parents had united for one day of direct action. Their organization—ROAR—marked the evolution that our earlier research had so clearly foretold: Middle American Radicalism. Ignored by the mass media and, perhaps, to a lesser degree by congressional delegations to whom they addressed their grievances, they are, nevertheless, a basic part of the social ferment in contemporary American Society.

Middle American protest has come far from its protozoan beginnings in the late 1960s. With the seismograph-like instruments of survey research we have charted its course. It is not a uniform nor neatly codified entity. Instead, this mobilization now has split what previously had been "the silent majority" into two groups: in one camp is the more content and secure portion of America's broad, middle income strata of blue collar workers and white collar functionaries. The "happiness" vote of 1972 for Richard Nixon came from this same group, as did preference for George Wallace in the period prior to his primary efforts.

But there is evidence that a second group drawn from similar social strata exists. A more militant, more aggressively dissatisfied segment of Middle America gave Wallace strong support in the presidential primary period of early 1972. In the presidential election of that year, with Wallace eliminated many of

the Middle Americans stayed home. Still others who retained
their original allegiance to George Wallace voted for Richard
Nixon. It was not with deep commitment but out of a restricted
choice that many took such a course of action. There were
other signs of hostility and frustration as well. Middle American
support of Spiro Agnew's attacks on the media prior to and
during the campaign of 1972 and the construction worker
attacks on peace demonstrators in Manhatten a few years earlier, all form the background of what we are describing. The
litany goes on. The truckers' protest in the 1974 "energy crisis"
posed basic challenges to the neat political stereotypes which
we academics often ask people to live up to. Protests over
textbooks that are offensive to parents in West Virginia, as well
as the bitter disputes surrounding desegregation of schools in
Boston, serve as more recent manifestations. The organized
manifestation of these recent confrontations is the ROAR
group (Restore Our Alienated Rights).

During recent years, the industrial worker—usually and perhaps inaccurately thought of as a blue collar "ethnic"—has
shouldered his way back into the nation's consciousness. There
he is competing for national attention with the new ecologists,
women's liberationists, anti-war activists, alienated middle class
youth, and the disadvantaged black, brown and red minorities.
Given his numbers, the white worker is a formidable competi-
tor. More than that, the nature of his complaints and the
dominant position he holds in a democracy make his role an
important one with respect to the economic, social and political
changes demanded so urgently by other groups in the society.
Some of these groups see him as a reactionary, proto-fascist
force; others cherish the hope that he may yet become a
revolutionary. Those of a less apocalyptic or romantic frame of
mind, however, agree that he might have grievances, whether
real or perceived, and that he can accelerate or frustrate change
of any kind depending upon with whom he is allied.

Our task in this book is twofold. First, we must review the
rise of concern about "Middle Americans," attempt to define
the population in question, and offer an analysis of the factors

that may be troubling this social, economic, ethnic and even "psychological" group. We will then be in a position to discuss implications for national and local social programs and policies.

Though attention to the problems of the white worker has crested during the last several years, one could find signs of trouble in the white lower middle classes as far back as the 1964 presidential election when the Governor of Alabama, George Wallace, did surprisingly well in several presidential primaries. In that same year the senator from Arizona, Barry Goldwater, seized control of the Republican Party from its eastern establishment leaders by appealing to middle class Americans living in the Middle-West, West and South. To be sure, in the election campaigns that fall, Lyndon Johnson successfully saddled Senator Goldwater with the issues of nuclear irresponsibility and social security repeal and won a landslide victory. But that victory, the subsequent eruptions in the nation's black city ghettoes, the increasing opposition to the war in Viet Nam, and the growth of what Middle Americans perceived as a drug-oriented, sexually uninhibited and revolutionary "counter-culture" only served to divert attention from what was happening in the white middle and working classes.

As the decade peaked and waned, white riots occurred in Cicero outside Chicago, in Philadelphia's Kensington district, in Milwaukee, and elsewhere where black middle class families tried to move into white neighborhoods. The phrases "black-lash," "polarization" and "law and order" entered common parlance and seemed to be used with even more frequency and fervor with respect to the suburbs, which had little direct contact with blacks, than to the inner-city white neighborhoods where black encroachment was often real.

Conservative themes dominated the 1968 and 1972 presidential elections. Union leaders and Democratic party chiefs were shocked to find in early polls that George Wallace was the choice of one-quarter of the nation's workers. True, perhaps persuaded by the unions' strenuous anti-Wallace campaign, more than half of these voters subsequently found themselves unable to vote for the former Alabama Governor, but many of them—normally Democratic—did vote for Richard Nixon and thus sent a new and more conservative administration to Washington. The identical pattern occurred in 1972.

In those same years, "law and order" mayors were elected in Los Angeles and Minneapolis; Louise Day Hicks and Anthony Imperiale led urban populist revolts in their cities of Boston and Newark. Only a split of the opposition between two middle class Italian Catholic candidates saved John Lindsey, the nation's most glamorous liberal mayor, from defeat; and conservative House and Senate candidates appeared on the ascendancy while many liberal ones were on the run.

The signs appeared to go well beyond the defeat or election of political personalities; in California voters soundly defeated open housing at referendum; in Netcong, New Jersey, a local school board defied the Supreme Court and ordered prayers in the schools; in many states legislators passed tough measures aimed at controlling student dissent; in Washington congressmen reported heavy and continuing streams of mail against pornography on the stage, screen and newsstand; and throughout the country the voters rejected bond issues for schools and other needed public facilities (and in some cities the schools simply shut down when they ran out of money part way through the year). In the work place, absenteeism, lateness and poor quality workmanship were becoming serious problems, especially in the automobile industry. At the same time, union members, especially the younger ones, increasingly rejected contract settlements negotiated by older union leaders. The annual rate of all work stoppages jumped by 50 percent from 1965 through mid-1970, while in the public sector newly militant unions of postal, transit, school, welfare, fire, police, hospital and other employees helped lift public employment work stoppages from 15 in 1958 to 254 in 1968. And on the highway bumper stickers blossomed throughout the nation urging the reader to "Love America or Leave It," billboards admonished youth to "Beautify America, Get a Haircut" and flag decals given away by the *Reader's Digest* and major oil companies appeared on millions of automobile windows.

By then the white worker had taken to the streets. If he wore a hard hat he left his construction site to march in protest against the "Philadelphia" and other "Plans" designed to broaden access to the skilled constructions trade unions for non-whites. And, while Wall Street lawyers and bankers were in Washington trying to persuade the administration and Congress to get the nation out of Viet Nam, the hard-hatted "proletariat" marched in Wall Street, attacking long-haired students along the way and carrying flag-bedecked signs that read "God Bless the Establishment" and that supported the war against communism (a spectacle that a New York magazine cartoonist noted might cause grave confusion among intelligence analysts in Moscow).

Many observers prior to 1968 saw such events as either opportunities to gain votes for reactionary causes or as evidence of unreconstructed and unpardonable racism and selfishness in the lower classes. Not surprisingly, the first to consider the problems of the white workers with some degree of sympathy were thoughtful public administrators, thoughtful politicians in both parties and some social scientists, closely followed by the press. In a little noticed speech at Lincoln, Massachusetts, in 1967, Robert C. Wood, then Secretary of Housing and Urban Development, stated, "The future of city building in America turns less on the indignation of the disprivileged (urban blacks) . . . than is commonly supposed. . . . We ignore the working American at our peril."

And in an article in the January 4, 1969, issue of the *New Yorker*, Richard Goodwin—who had seen at first hand the success of Robert Kennedy and Eugene McCarthy in appealing to different segments of middle class voters—reflected on the "Sources of the Public Unhappiness" in sweeping historical and social terms, emphasizing the loss of a sense of community and of power by the average working man in the postindustrial urban environment.

The end of the extraordinary year, 1968—an unusual election widely interpreted as the demise of the Rooseveltian coalition of the intelligentsia, the minorities and the working class—and the advent of a new administration presented considerable grist for the mills of the press, and many discovered or rediscovered the white "middle American." In 1969 and early 1970 the *New*

York Times, the *Times Sunday Magazine*, the *Washington Post*, *Newsday*, the *Chicago Sun-Times, Businessweek*, the *Nation, Fortune*, the *New Republic, New Generation, New York* and other publications presented stories on one or another of the problems of the white worker. In October, 1969, *Newsweek* presented a major analysis replete with special Gallup poll data; *Harper's* ran a series of articles during 1969 and 1970 on the middle American; and *Time* made the middle American its Man and Woman of the Year in 1969.

By the beginning of 1970 the American Jewish Committee had had a seminal program on white ethnic America going for over a year; the Catholic Church was beginning to confront the problems of this major portion of its constituency in a new way; the Ford Foundation had sponsored a Conference on National Unity and was planning an informal gathering of academic, journalistic and union experts to consider "the blue collar problem"; the Nixon Administration was organizing an inter-departmental task force on "The Problem of the Blue Collar Worker"; television public affairs shows were beginning to devote attention to the Middle American; and a movie called "Joe," which featured—for perhaps the first time in a decade—a lower middle income white American ethnic "hero" (although an aberrant one), was being prepared for release.

This transformation of the "forgotten American" into what William Lee Miller calls the "suddenly remembered American" did not occur without consternation and controversy. Some observers, fearing the tread of fascist hordes, were outraged that the press (or, depending on their viewpoint, the blacks and students) had "waked the sleeping beast." Others, including some of the blacks and students, decried the hand-wringing and guilt they perceived in the press and in liberal circles about the "plight" of the blue collar family. They regarded this new concern—like ecology—as another "cop-out" by the system, further evidence of the establishment's inability and unwilling-ness to cope with its real guilt regarding both Viet Nam and the oppression of black, brown and red minorities. Still others deplored the condescension in the new concern for the *"Other America"* and charged that the upper middle classes, who have run the country, were tiring of the intransigencies of the urban and black problems. Finally, a small but growing minority sensed the possibility of a new and powerful alliance between the poor and the lower middle class that could affect what they see as "real change" benefiting all those below the mid-point of the income scale in the United States.

But now, in the period of prelude to the 1976 presidential election, the issues of ethnic conflict, inflation, unemployment and federal government intrusion into the local neighborhood have provoked Catholic urban dwellers, Protestant small-city and suburban families and a scattering of others to form the core of a new political coalition. Racist, reactionary and Know-Nothing: these are ready epithets of the liberal establishment. But still others have described this Middle American Radical group as the wellspring of American populism: the grass-roots backbone upon which our society was founded.

Who is closer to the truth? Or must we discard our conventional dichotomization of left and right and, instead, see the rise and reality of the Middle American Radicals as a distinct phenomenon? That is the argument of this book. We are not the first to say so, nor do we declare this "movement" to be a formalized and coherent whole. But it is a presence. And the bases for it along with the distinctive "style" it manifests are some of the descriptive tasks undertaken in this book.

Historical analogies to the recent MAR are to be found in the rise and success of Father Charles E. Coughlin in the 1930s.[1] The creation of the National Union for Social Justice in 1936 was the formal manifestation of "Coughlinism." Paradox and oversimplification of America's social and economic problems were the hallmark of that movement's political life.[2] So it is with the Middle American Radical: siding first with the traditional left in opposition to the privileges and power of the rich corporations—in our day the oil companies and large federal agencies—and yet mouthing the shibboleths of the far right in its fear of the growing power of the poor and minority groups in our society.

Perhaps history tells us much about what now and in the near future will shape the destiny of the Middle American Radical.

We shall speculate about these trends—avoiding, however, the neat extrapolations of the actuarial chart-readers of previous movements. It is true that each new wave of social experience in a society is not controlled by the steady tide of well defined and calibrated forces that meteorologists use to trace the arrival and passage of a storm center. But should we, as social scientists, eschew such a forecast because we cannot obtain precise measurements or cannot summon sufficient courage?

A Technical Note on the National Cross-Section Sample

This research began with 112 in-depth interviews in Milwaukee, Detroit, Indianapolis and Cleveland during the summer of 1971. Two- to three-hour interview sessions in typical "Middle America" neighborhoods formed the first phase of this Ford Foundation supported study. Subsequent to the gathering and analysis of the initial semistructured interviews was the design of a more standardized interview conducted with respondents drawn as a profile of the American population as a whole. Through the field facilities of the Institute for Social Research of the University of Michigan, a sample design was constructed to accomplish this purpose. Field work was carried by the Survey Research Center of the University of Michigan. The procedure involves area probability sampling in which particular "segments" and representative population centers are used which provide a composite of population characteristics reflecting the entire U.S. in miniature.

When completed, the sample design for the national survey provided a total of 1,926 interviews with heads of households or their spouses—of whom 1,690 were white. The total interview completion level for all sampling segments was 79.2 percent.

The purpose of the national sample was, using a comparative and generalizable survey data base, to provide the basis for testing a series of hypotheses derived from our original study design. When the pre-test of the interview instrument—drawing heavily on the experience gained in the earlier community interviews—was completed we began actual field work. The period of November 1971 through February 1972 was utilized to complete all interviews. The average contact with each respondent involved a 75-minute personal, in-the-home interview.

A second source of survey data for this book is the "Cambridge Report" conducted in March 1975 by Cambridge Survey Research Incorporated. This national omnibus interview included a number of questions identical to the 1972 survey. A number of added analyses have been included in this discussion as well as an overview of patterns in a final postscript to the present study (see Chapter 14). A total of 1,366 white respondents constitute the sample of this 1975 survey.

A Word on the Statistical Treatment
of the Survey Data

In subsequent chapters major use of percentage figures will be made to describe trends and major differences between groups compared in our analysis. Fractions have been rounded off. We shall employ two conventions in these tabulations: the first is the use of underlining for the percentage in a given row which is "statistically significant" in comparison with other values. By this we mean that using the principle of representative random sampling the difference between two groups—allowing for "sampling error"—must be large enough that it would not occur more than 1 in 20 times simply on the basis of chance factors. Therefore if the percentage is significantly higher or lower than every other percentage in the same row it will be indicated as follows: 25.0% If a pair of such figures or possibly several are similar but significantly different from other figures in the same row, then the boxed percentages indicated for each will be connected in the following manner:

25.0%   13.6%   26.1%

Also, a number of the cross tabulation tables may contain in addition to a box or in lieu of the box a plus or minus sign to the right of the percentage. This will indicate that in comparison to an adjacent grouping (a percentage in the same row) differences in values are statistically significant *for this paired comparison only*. Such a comparison might appear as follows:

25.0%   26.1%+   13.6%−   27.4%

Clearly the size of subgroups in each table affects the size of any percentage difference which is statistically significant. However as sample size goes up it is easier to obtain statistical significance but not necessarily "substantively" important differences.

1. WHAT IS A MIDDLE AMERICAN RADICAL?

There is a distinct force in American society which is both volatile and pivotal in its activism. The word *radical* has many connotations, but its basic meaning is "going to the root of the problem." From such a denotation emerges the paradoxical reality of this potentially decisive force—the Middle American Radical (MAR).[3]

Their perspective does not fit readily the traditional molds of liberal and conservative ideologies. Moreover, the definition of this social group stems from considering ideology itself as a component in a chain of thinking in response to institutional forces on the individual. As such, ideology becomes—for the purposes of this analysis—the basis for predicting patterns of social mobilization, not simply as a means of determining the strength or coherence of social beliefs. Ideology, then, is a grouping of the elements defining how people perceive problems and then choose to act or not to act on those problems.[4]

On some issues, MARs are likely to take a "liberal" stand, on others a "conservative" one. For example, the MAR expresses a desire for more police power. He feels that granting the police a heavier hand will help control crime, i.e., Wallace's Law and Order program. However, MARs are also adamant about keeping many social reforms, often wrought by the left, such as medicare, aid to education and social security.

Often MARs feel their problems stem from the rich and the government working together to defraud the rest of the country. They blame the situation on defects in the system such as bad taxes. However, their causal analysis does not suggest what effective remedial actions they can pursue as individuals.

1

Areas in which MARs take the most individual action include local government, schools and race. Whether the issue is inflation, depression, Watergate, neighborhood racial change or crime, many people in the MAR group have highly individualized definitions of the problem. Thus crime is seen as being caused by the permissiveness of parents, and the growing welfare rolls are regarded as pampering those who are lazy and do not wish to work.

Even if a problem is a very severe one for the MAR, it is often ascribed to human nature, the inevitable failings of character, or simply the unavoidable cycles of good and bad times. Such attributions make it hard to see how engaging in political action will make changes.

What is of critical importance, however, is to understand that lack of political action stems from two major belief systems of the MAR: one is that action is useless because individuals are powerless to effect changes in society or its major institutions. The other is the MAR's unwillingness to get involved at the national level because of distrust of national leaders. Analysis of the belief system of the MAR helps to understand such enigmas as the cool reception Ralph Nader receives from the middle income group whom he so staunchly advocates.[5] The MAR cannot identify with the elitist strategies of Ralph Nader. By contrast, the meat boycott permitted individual action at the local neighborhood level. People could go to the local meat market and express concern. Ralph Nader operates at the centralized government level, putting pressure on regulatory agencies of the federal government within an elite core of professionals and academics. This style and strategy of action does not particularly respond to the consumer squeeze being felt by Middle America in their local milieu.

The 1973 Meat Boycott is an example of a local effort to strike out at a non-local offender. In this survey, we found that MARs comprised the largest participating force in the consumer "strike." They refused to purchase meat from their local merchants, thus constituting a local action. But it was really farther reaching than that. This effort can be seen as a stepping stone for action on a larger scale. MARs are beginning to strike out at the national scene, through grass-roots efforts of this type. They do not feel they have the power to jump into the bureaucratic ring in Washington, but they are discovering the influential power they have at home against their offenders.

George Wallace has expressed another important element of the MAR phenomenon: that of contact at the local level on issues that affect everyday life. The MAR often has strong roots in neighborhood and community. McGovern, with his following of the poor, affluent liberals, college students, blacks, chicanos and anti-war dissidents, was the epitome of what the MAR resented on the American political scene.

The MAR consistently sees an unholy alliance growing between the liberal and minority establishment at his expense. White efforts to end racism have forced him to carry out good deeds, through his taxes, that he never felt compelled to institute. The burden falls on *his* shoulders to carry out the "social experiment" rather than on the affluent suburbanite or on the welfare poor. The Middle American Radical sees the government—local to national—allied simultaneously with minority and idealistic doctrines against his own interests and social survival.

Alliances threatening to the MAR's existence make him an unpredictable force in American political life. As a result, he is an uneasy ally to either left or right political interest groups.

Whereas the conventional radical is likely to see the need to reduce the scale of schools and government to make them more accessible, the MAR is, by contrast, concerned with the way institutions are run and complains that many individuals are not given enough power and autonomy to do their jobs properly. To the MAR, the failure of welfare agencies to diminish poverty, of police to decrease crime and of government to increase services despite increased tax revenues substantiate this view.

Middle American Radicals see formal organizations as not holding to clear-cut rules (due perhaps to rule-bending minorities) and as not being responsive to their concerns (due perhaps to confused goals established by both government and minority influence). They do not want these organizations to become smaller or to be restructured. Instead, they want new leaders who will seek broader goals by an equal application of the rules. Out of this desire stems a strong concern for action of some type on the part of the MAR.

The Truckers' Protest in the winter of 1973–1974 is a type of action that the MAR can identify with. It occurred in an industry that is highly decentralized, it required very little local action to get underway and only in the protest sense was it part of an "organizational effort." This was evident to the negotiators on the government side who were not sure that they were dealing with real representatives of the group.

To the MAR, the alliances arrayed against them are made up of people who possess defective character traits such as laziness, immorality or hedonistic life styles. For instance, the MARs who assert that race problems have occurred because the Supreme Court consists of Justices appointed for life and is, therefore, unresponsive to popular wishes are making a "system" complaint. Those who believe racial problems are caused by blacks who are lazy, immoral or possess other such stereotyped characteristics are suggesting that personally defective individuals are responsible.

It has been found that people assign different causal factors to different substantive problem areas. Most Middle Americans indicate both system and individual components as the source of their problems.[6]

Middle American Radicals have special complaints about the way government is run, but believe that many of the solutions need to start and end with individual action, rather than in traditional channels of institutional participation such as the major political party structures. Areas in which MARs are willing to take most individual action were found in our study to be those of local government, the schools and neighborhood racial problems. Wallace's grass-roots political philosophy confirms the validity of our studies in that for the MAR to be involved action must be .linked to the local neighborhoods and communities.

This individual approach, which yields the effects of collective action, is clearly an important political force. The critical point is that MARs are no longer relying on the organizations to which they belong for representation of their grievances and desires.

In the past, the Middle American Radical was amply represented by the church and labor unions. It is interesting to note that both institutions are very large scale and committed to universal rules and procedures. They tend to operate on the notion that there is an important set of principles that apply to everyone. The MAR is particularly concerned with the need to have a very structured type of orientation to the world. As these traditional organizations and the world around them have undergone changes, Middle American Radicals no longer take them for granted as their special advocates. They now feel that they themselves—as individuals banding together—can be more effective and powerful. Yet their style of protest ultimately aims not at destroying the system but at changing its leadership and expanding its immediate effectiveness.

Recent surveys have shown an increase in independent voters and a decline in the traditional committed party voter. The Middle American Radical phenomenon fits this trend, and it may be a long term pattern. In addition, this group has become extremely volatile in terms of being more likely to participate than formerly. People in general are demanding much more from public officials in policy accountability and, unless government delivers, we can expect some very strong action. The success of our institutions is not going to depend on whether experts are advising the leaders and coming up with solutions to pressing social problems, but whether people out in the grass roots have some say in those solutions. MARs may not be radicals in the conventional sense, but they are increasingly radical in expressing their demands for participation and recognition through action.

This was clear during the impeachment proceedings against Richard Nixon. By and large, MARs did not think that impeachment would be a healthy, cleansing thing for the country since it would be an unprecedented threat to the presidency. Nixon's resignation caused no such problem in that it did not alter the structure as such. MARs viewed the Watergate mess as reflecting the character defects of individuals more than an inherent problem in the executive power of the presidency or in the interrelations of the branches of government. To some extent, media coverage of Watergate tended to focus on personal rather than structural deficiencies. Although the MAR is often at odds with the news media, in this case the media did not advocate change in the basic structures, but only asked for new, responsible leadership and the MAR did contribute to bringing about such a change. Recent congressional elections seem to support this fact.

As the education level rises, we can expect that people in some of the lower status jobs in the society are different from the people who used to hold these jobs. Their consciousness is higher and, therefore, they are much more critical and expect more from their public officials. The MAR is already participating in this revolution of rising expectations and is not likely to drop out. In addition, MARs have some very special viewpoints which are bound to clash with those of other groups who are also part of this radicalization in American society.

Much that the Middle American sees operating in the country today causes him to call the idealistic notion of democratic government into question. One might predict, therefore, an increase in political participation among this group. We would maintain that this is unlikely to happen because of the second factor involved in keeping the Middle American out of political action groups. If our perceptions and interpretations are correct, the lower middle class male defines all organizations which demand verbal skills and organized political activity as incompatible with his self-image. His "ideal self" is a physically strong, hardworking, dependable person. Social aggressiveness and verbal ability are seen exclusively as feminine attributes. This was widely observed in the earlier exploratory interviews. The wife usually took the initiative in inviting the interviewer into the home, getting seated, and also usually was the most anxious to answer the questions. The male maintained his dominance by the fact that his wife showed deference to him whenever he did wish to speak. However, his answers were almost always short and to the point, whereas the wives often went on at considerable length and with considerable articulateness. Naturally, some political activity among this group will be conducted by women. The overall level of activity is likely to be quite limited because it is only the exceptional woman who is free enough from family obligations to do much outside the home.

This is not to say that there will be no organized activity by the Middle American. We can indicate that whatever activity takes place will have the following characteristics:

1. It will be of the "ad hoc" variety—directed toward a current issue or problem, rather than designed simply to gain advantage in the political arena. There will not be continuous, on-going activity.

2. It will lack traditional organizational form. There will be no meetings, little discussion, either no leaders or only generally acclaimed leaders (no formal elections).

3. In many cases, it may even be apolitical, in the sense that it will not work through established mechanisms for redress of grievances. Vigilante-type actions are a very real possibility.

No wonder the labor union leadership, the academic liberal establishment, the new left and even former energy czar William Simon have been unable to anticipate and be responsive to the frustrations and anger that is borne of the unique self-interests of the MAR. Over the next few years no one is easily going to slip this group into his political column. Survey data in the 1971–1972 study indicated 30 percent support for Nixon when we interviewed people before the presidential primaries. What he was able to draw upon in the intervening period before Watergate and after the attack on George Wallace closely corresponds to the proportion of Middle American Radicals found in the national survey. The "mile wide and inch deep" support gained from this group has now been dissipated. The most recent data from the March 1975 Cambridge Survey shows a heavy Wallace support and a lukewarm response to the Ford administration. MARs appear to initiate and epitomize the mood of national anger and distrust of dishonest "politicians."

Some Essential Questions About MARs

What causes the perspective and ideology we have described as Middle American Radical? How contagious is this philosophy? Who is immune, who is most vulnerable to it? How deep-seated are its manifestations in American society? What are the levers for change in this orientation? How dangerous is the Middle American Radical to our society? How closely linked is this phenomenon to the serious economic deprivations which many Americans have felt in the last several years?

In subsequent portions of our analysis we shall examine fully the several distinctive facets that express what the Middle American Radical is all about. For now we can set forth the following conclusions as the keystones of our analysis: first that both rising as well as declining economic horizons can foster Middle American Radicalism. That many individual characteristics of people in our society can simultaneously produce a common perspective—a bridge across religious, ethnic and regional barriers—appears to be a response to the most important antecedent factor in the spread of this ideology. The epidemic is based not on economics alone, or intergroup conflict as such, or levels of education or job alienation, or a sense of social isolation or individual status. Yet all of these are implicated. Each is a pathway to the same conclusions about our society.

But at the very core of the MAR perspective appears a set of harsh indictments about the way formal institutions such as schools, government, labor unions, corporations, churches, the police and social welfare agencies function in our society. Thus, "organizational alienation" is the common denominator which binds together the Wallacite Georgia farmer with the Polish or Italian industrial worker of our urban centers, the low income retiree, the isolated suburban housewife, and the white collar civil servant of WASP origins who feels the pressure of minority group employment pressures. Yet, the MAR is not created in a long political socialization out of family or hometown mores and prejudices. Nor is the sting of unemployment or economic insecurity more than a partial explanation at best. The MAR perspective can arise with a sudden and shocking realization about the implications of neighborhood change and the decline of services in one's local community. Unswervingly local in orientation, the MAR does feel deeply about the quality of his environment and the state of the nation.

His anger and concern are not uniformly, nor consistently, nor even visibly, translated into effective social action. Nor can we say with certainty that any given historical moment or leader can respond to the needs which MARs have. But we certainly can and must seek to comprehend what has evolved up to this moment in the political and social consciousness of the MAR. This task is a critical challenge to those who must seek to respond to the MAR phenomenon or to measure its implications for our society.

2. WHO ARE THE MIDDLE AMERICAN RADICALS?

Demographics and the Middle American

One of the difficulties in coming to grips with the concept "Middle American" is in defining who is being talked about. Labels do not help much. According to the press, the individual who makes up the "silent majority " is a white, lower middle income, lower middle class, blue collar (but perhaps also white collar clerical or service) worker. Other descriptions suggest he is an "ethnic" and "alienated," "forgotten," "angry," "troubled," "disillusioned," "relatively deprived" and "reacting." He is the "not-quite-poor American" in the "not-althogether-affluent society."

Estimates of the number of these Americans vary widely. A Census Bureau offical in 1968 referred to "Middle America" as the 11 million blue collar families with husbands earning between $4,000 and $12,000 per year (more than a quarter of all husband-wife families).[7] Former Assistant Secretary of Labor Jerome Rosow counts those "forty percent of American families—including 70 million family members-with family incomes between $5,000 and $10,000 per year as the Lower Middle Income group."[8] Time magazine has pushed the number of those in Middle America to 100 million—50 percent of the nation.[9]

The alienated Middle American is usually thought of as being a blue collar worker, and if he is, chances are fifty-fifty that he belongs to a labor union. Although only 28 percent of the non-agricultural labor force was unionized in 1968, over four-fifths of all union members were blue collar workers. On the other hand, some analysts suggest that *white collar* workers who are locked into dull, routine office jobs may be even more

10

alienated than most blue collar workers—and relatively few such clerical and other employees are unionized. Further, while the angry, forgotten American is usually thought of as working in the private sector, public employees are becoming increasingly militant—and more and more of them are joining public employees' unions. (Indeed, the three fastest growing unions in the last decade were public employee unions.)

The "Middle American" is also frequently thought of as an "ethnic." That usually means a first, second or even third generation American of central, east or south European stock (but including some Irish and some Jews) who is often found in row house neighborhoods between the black ghetto and the white middle and upper middle class suburb.

These ethnic Americans form the bulk of the nation's non-supervisory work force. They are heavily Catholic and probably comprise a majority of the 30 million Catholics who live in central city dioceses in the northeastern states. By and large, they have not moved very far above the menial jobs first open to their parents upon arrival in this country. Instead, they have stayed in the jobs, bought houses in the same neighborhoods or nearby, and formed close-knit communities. The few social scientists who have studied such neighborhoods have found them to be very conservative, placing high value upon family, home, neighborhood and traditions.[10] These communities also tend to be insular, having little real social contact with other ethnic groups or with differing mores. Although the extraordinary urban pressures of the last two decades are softening the fringes of such communities, they have not yet merged into a general American culture. As Gus Tyler of the International Ladies Garment Workers Union has said, "America is less a melting pot than a casserole with solid chunks of ethnic ingredients flavoring one another while holding onto their distinctive textures."[11]

Although much attention has gone recently to these blue collar ethnic communities, it is hazardous to maintain that they are "where the problem is at." Though beginning to stir, these communities are, by and large, still sullen and quiet, neither organized nor yet inclined to do battle with the outside world. A case can be made that the lower middle income suburbanite, burdened by a recent mortgage, consumer debt and high taxes, might be both more active and more alienated. On the other hand, at the Ford Foundation's staff conference on blue collar problems in January 1970, pollster Louis Harris cited data depicting the most alienated Americans as older couples, living in the smaller rural towns and cities that have been declining for decades.

For purposes of our initial analysis we utilized an income distribution concept for defining "Middle Americans." In this approach we selected a family income range of $6,000 to $15,000 as the basis of what we shall call an "objective" criterion for defining Middle Americans. Going beyond a simple income concept for "Middle Americans" we drew upon other socioeconomic characteristics. The first of these is the educational level of the individual. The significant advantage which attendance at a college or university provides and the general attitudes which comprise the Middle American world view dictated that we differentiate between persons who have or who have not attended an institution of high education. On this basis we limited the original concept of the Middle American to persons who have not gone beyond the level of a high school diploma.

The third basis for differentiating "Middle Americans" from other members of the society has to do with the occupational role of the individual. In terms of those white and blue collar jobs which do not include established professions or enterpreneurial roles we have arrived at a third element in our definition. Those respondents whose employment falls into categories of clerical or sales work, skilled, semi-skilled or unskilled manual work represent persons who can reasonably be identified as members of Middle America. On this basis, 46 percent of the white national sample became "Middle Americans." (See Appendix: Table 1.)

Distinguishing MARs from "Middle Americans"

One major difficulty in attempting to describe in demographic terms the alienated and anxious "Middle Americans" is that we simply do not know who is how angry at what. It may be, for instance, that income level has relatively little to do with the present malaise of the middle class—or if it does, it is almost too simplistic to define a set of income brackets and assume that they contain the "problem." Instead, it is more reasonable to assume that there might be several very different groups of alienated "Middle Americans" defined by quite different sets of cross-cutting economic and social variables.

Obviously such gross income and occupational classifications are of little help in defining the population in question, for they probably exclude as many "alienated" "Middle Americans" as they include happy and satisfied ones. In addition, any economic definition becomes highly arbitrary, given locale and occupational levels as well as purchasing power. One analyst expanded the income range for Middle Americans from $3,000 to $15,000. This was argued on the basis that the hard working farm laborer or household worker (median incomes $4,359 and $2,751 respectively) might share the same values and be just as alienated as people in higher income occupations that the mass media and others currently presume to be alienated.[12] Further, the Italian school teacher and the Jewish shop proprietor—who probably earn more than $10,000 per year and perhaps more than $15,000—might both be spiritual "Middle Americans." Indeed, the person who has become the symbol of Middle America, the construction worker, sometimes earns well in excess of $15,000.

While the uses of a combination of income, educational and occupational levels had initially seemed an appropriate way around the problem of using a single dimension to analyze the Middle American phenomenon, our exploratory interviews in a number of communities suggested to us that, in many respects, the concept of the Middle American is a highly subjective one. We discovered a rather distinct set of views, a way of considering one's individual position, that we later came to see as perhaps the most valid and important finding of our study.

The Middle American Radical perspective was developed from interviewing numerous individuals who felt very threatened by problems which were not immediately related to their economic position in society. Such individuals, in some problem areas, directed their scorn toward, and felt threatened by, groups which they seemed to consider lower in status than themselves, such as the organized poor and minority groups. At the same time, we found that many individuals were deeply concerned about status groups above their own.

An additional element in this discussion of threats from the rich, the poor and the minorities was the role of the government as an arbitrator of group interests. Many people believe that government officials favor one group over another and that they are using different standards for giving out rewards and punishments. This meant that individual status or economic achievements could be overturned by arbitrary or capricious government regulation or policy. Thus, an "ideological perspective" seemed to emerge from our in-depth exploratory interviews. This ideological point of view does not readily fit the traditional notion of "left wing" or "right wing" convictions. Instead, it seems to embody *a distinct orientation of multiple threats of being caught in the middle between those whose wealth gives them access to power and those whose militant organization in the face of deprivation gains special treatment from the government.* Nor does this attitude apply to *all* people in the middle income range or *only* to those people. In other words, the Middle American Radicals we are describing in this book are people who share a set of beliefs, attitudes and a distinct level of alienation and apprehension.

Measuring the MAR Ideology

The national survey interview involved a one-hour contact with the adult head of household or the spouse of that person. To construct the basis for defining who is a MAR, a total of 36 different questions from the interview are utilized. From the various questions, a score of 0 to 53 could be obtained on the scale of MAR ideology. (see Appendix for questions and scoring procedures.) Items composing the scale included questions about perceived threat from minorities, unfair advantage in government programs going to the rich or the organized poor, and privileges that the rich or minorities enjoy in education, the courts and other institutions.

For the white population in the survey—1,690 persons out of the 1,926 interviewed—the average score of the MAR ideology index is 23. The range of scores was divided into quartile ranks with approximately 25 percent of the sample having a score in excess of 29 on the index. In Table 1 the score distribution by quartiles is shown. For those persons we had originally designated as "Middle American" on the basis of income, education and occupation, one-third had MAR ideology scores in the upper quartile. So did one in three low income respondents. For those with middle income but some college training, one in five persons had a "high" MAR score. For the affluents—those making $25,000 or more annual family income regardless of educational level—15 percent are high on the MAR index.

For purposes of setting a criterion for defining who are MARs, the upper quartile index range becomes our operational measure. A total of 496 out of 1,690 white respondents falls

TABLE 1

RELATIONSHIP BETWEEN OBJECTIVE SOCIOECONOMIC
DEFINITION AND SUBJECTIVE (IDEOLOGICAL) DEFINITION OF
MIDDLE AMERICANS

MAR Ideology Score	Socioeconomic Middle Americans	Low Income: Below Middle Americans	High Income Respondents	High Education Respondents
High	33%	33%	20%	15%
Medium High	25%	23%	19%	21%
Medium Low	24%	24%	32%	36%
Low	18%	20%	29%	28%
Total	100% (N=782)	100% (N=468)	100% (N=222)	100% (N=132)

into this group. This is 29.3 percent of the total white sample. Table 2 shows the way this ideologically-defined group is distributed in terms of socioeconomic levels. Almost half do not fit the "objective" demographic definition of Middle Americans.

By using the "subjective" definition of MARs, we can test the hypothesis which demands the recognition of the multiple group composition of Middle America. We have contained, then, within the group sharing the same perspective, a range of socioeconomic levels as well as ethnic, religious and other groupings whose common perceptions may disguise important differences in how each segment of the Middle America spectrum is mobilized.

Our definition of MARs goes beyond the customary approach to Middle America. Had we limited our study of Middle American Radicals only to those who fit the socioeconomic profile and scored high on the ideology scale, analytic precision and an accurate assessment of the breadth of this phenomenon would have suffered. We have attempted, rather, to go beyond

TABLE 2

HIGH MIDDLE AMERICAN RADICAL IDEOLOGY IN RELATION
TO SOCIOECONOMIC GROUPINGS

	Percent in Upper Quartile of MAR Scale
Middle Income	46%
Low Income	28%
Affluents	13%
Middle Income, High Education	8%
Income Information Not Ascertained	5%
Total	100% (N=496)

the objective criteria in an effort to zero in on the core elements of the Middle American attitude. In other words, Middle American Radicals may come from different income brackets, educational, ethnic and regional backgrounds; what is important is that they share a common set of concerns and a basic world view that is distinct from other major segments of our society. While the paradigm is the middle class American who scores high on the attitudinal scale, persons from other socioeconomic levels who also score high on the MAR ideology scale are included. This means, too, that many persons who fall into the economic status of Middle America are not ideologically Middle American Radicals. This is the basis of our distinction between "Middle American Radicals" and "Average Middles."

MARs as an Ideologically Unique Group

It should be clear by now that in our attempt to define the MARs as a group we must probe beneath the objective criteria such as social position and economic status to more subjective elements such as ideological attitudes. Given this approach, we can consider five major and distinct population segments: Low Income Americans, Middle American Radicals, "Average Middles" (i.e., those individuals meeting the socioeconomic but not the ideological criteria of MARs), High Education Middles (those whose economic level is at the middle of the social structure but whose educational level places them in a distinct position) and, finally, Affluents (those whose economic position is above that of Middle Americans and who scored low on the Middle American ideological criteria). Table 3 is a prototype for comparing these five groups. Since MARs and "Average Middles" are so similar in relative size in the population and are very similar in socioeconomic terms, subsequent tabular analyses will compare how each group reacts and we shall see how they differ in a number of crucial ways.

A key dimension of the MAR ideology is the role of government as a group arbiter. To the extent that MARs see the role of government as less than neutral we can distinguish this particular set of attitudes from those identified with the tradi-

TABLE 3

DISTRIBUTION OF FIVE NATIONAL SAMPLE SOCIAL GROUPS*

	Percent of Total White Sample	Number
Low Income ($6,000 1971 family income)	19%	314
MARs (Upper-quartile of ideology scale, no income or educational level specified)	29%	496
Average Middles (No college, not in upper education quartile, $6,000–$25,000 1971 family income)	31%	521
High Education Middles (At least some college education, $6,000–$25,000 1971 family income)	7%	112
Affluents (Family income of $25,000 or more in 1971, no educational level specified)	11%	178
Respondents with Income Data Missing	4%	69
Total	101%	1,690

*All Tables are based on white respondents only unless otherwise noted.

tional left or right. In Table 4 we have defined a set of responses to questions having to do with the role of the government in aiding various groups. In particular, the question asked the respondents was:

Thinking about the help different kinds of people get from the government, do the following groups get the right amount of help; less than the right amount of help; or more than the right amount of help?

TABLE 4

TYPES OF "RADICAL" IDEOLOGY AND FIVE POPULATION
GROUPINGS BASED ON GOVERNMENT HELP TO VARIOUS GROUPS

	"Left Wing" Government Gives Too Much to Rich	*"Right Wing"* Government Gives Too Much to Poor	*"Radical Middle"* Government Gives Less to Middle Income Groups
Low Income	18%	16%	13%
MARs	24%	20%	45%
Average Middles	32%	29%	27%
High Education Middles	10%	6%	5%
Affluent	12%	19%	7%
Incomplete SES Data	4%	9%	3%
Total	100%	99%	100%

In turn, a series of seven groups were listed: rich people,
"middle income blacks," "middle incomes whites," "black workers," "white workers," "poor whites," and "poor blacks."

Those people who said that the rich received too much help
but did not say this about any of the other social groups
mentioned were grouped under the heading of "left-wing" ideology. Those individuals who said that the poor were given more
than the right amount of help from government but did not say
this with regard to any other groups were placed under the
"right-wing" category. Finally, those who responded that
middle income groups, either white or black, are given less help
than is justified and who say this about no other social group
were regarded as espousing a "Middle American Radical" position.

Table 4 indicates that of the three radical ideologies the most
frequently held is that of the left-wing perspective. Approx-

imately 1 in 3 Americans in the white sample hold this view. Of
the white sample 7 percent falls into the right-wing group,
whereas approximately 17 percent of the population takes the
radical middle perspective. If we then examine who tends to
take this radical position, almost 1 out of 2 of the respondents
who do so come from the MAR ideology group.

With regard to the left-wing view, we find that High Education Middles contribute disproportionately to this orientation in
relation to their taking the radical middle or right-wing position.
The Affluents contribute almost 1 in 5 of the respondents who
hold a right-wing position. This is about twice the proportion of
Affluents in the total sample. Average Middles tend to dis-
tribute themselves rather evenly among the three ideologies.
Low Income Americans make up a larger percentage of the left-
or right-wing ideology groups than they do of the radical
middle.

Overall, then, Table 4 indicates that, in the more traditional
political sense, holding the Middle American ideology implies a
distinct kind of radicalism vis-á-vis government's role in society.
The kinds of groups which we would ordinarily identify with
the traditional political philosophies do, indeed, tend to cluster
accordingly; the poor tend to be "left," and the Affluent
"right." But what is important is the comparison between the
group we have called MARs and the group we call "Average
Middles." Thus, while having many similarities in terms of
objective socioeconomic attributes, these two groups differ significantly in terms of their political stance vis-á-vis the performance of government.

MARs are a distinct group partly because of their view of
government as favoring both the rich and poor simultaneously.
Such a view, while concentrated among people actually in the
middle of the social structure, can also be shared by those in the
low status as well as high status positions. More importantly,
MARs are distinct in the depth of their feeling that the middle
class has been seriously neglected. If there is one single summa-
tion of the MAR perspective, it is reflected in a statement which
was read to respondents:

The rich give in to the demands of the poor, and the middle income people have to pay the bill.

What this assertion implies is that there is implicit coalition, a kind of unholy alliance or, in the view of some, a conspiracy, in which groups who otherwise might seem to be at odds have joined together against the interests of the middle. It is this attitude, then, which we sought to measure.

As Table 5 indicates, MARs do, indeed, hold the view of the rich and poor joined in a coalition. It is important to note the small degree of difference among other groups. Thus, Low Income Americans are no more disposed to see the rich and poor as allied than are Average Middles. Moreover, the difference between High Education Middles and Affluents is extremely minimal in terms of responses to this particular question.

The MAR response is a dramatic expression of the distinctive alienation felt by an entire segment of our society. The recent busing dispute in Boston provides vivid illustration and validation for the portrait of MARs which emerged from our 1972

TABLE 5

THE ESSENCE OF THE MIDDLE AMERICAN RADICAL IDEOLOGY
"The rich give in to the demands of the poor,
and the middle income people have to pay the bill."

	Low Income	MARs	Average Middles	High Education Middles	Affluents
Very True	15%	60%	12%	8%	9%
True	34%	30%	39%	36%	39%
Not Very or Not At All True	22%	7%	33%	43%	46%
Don't Know	30%	2%	16%	12%	6%
Total	100%	100%	100%	100%	100%

national survey. It predicted the class conflict endemic to the Boston controversy:

> *We have a Boston Wall, only it is invisible—it is not made of brick and iron, but of snob zoning laws that keep the blacks walled in," says Daniel E. Vonishuk, a tall sheet-metal worker and father of five, who assailed federal judges and other do-gooders who sneak back to their suburban community at night.*
>
> New York Times, 7/8/74

> *Too many people allowed the mass exodus to the suburbs, havens for segregated education, to happen without offering support to METCO and other proposals for suburban involvement. Too many people have supported an economic system that places the burden for curing social ills on a working class and on ethnic communities which, while they share the responsibility for the ills, simply lack the resources for the constructive and fair solutions to the problems.*
>
> *Rev. Thomas D. Corrigan, Letter to the Editor,* Commonwealth: *199, November, 1974*

Nor is the Boston scene an isolated istance. The boiling controversy in West Virginia provides a second clear expression of the MAR sense of class isolation and threat:

> *Usually in the vocational tract the rural kids experienced snobbery by the nouveau riche, middle class town kids which was the least subtle of any I witnessed since.*
>
> *The rural citizens who live around or near West Virginia towns, often miners or ex-miners, have endured all of the legendary abuses of Appalachia, including absentee landlordism, inequitable tax structures and strip mining of the property. In addition, however, they have been recipients of the most vicious, exclusive, small-minded city and county policies of anywhere in the nation. County buses never seem to serve the rural areas and the roads never seem to get paved. Rural coal miners and their families are excluded from decision making in West Virginia towns.*
>
> Washington Post, 10/17/74

In summarizing its views of the Boston situation a local committee of citizens presents a statement of "taxation without representation" and a manifesto for protest with clarity and force:

> *Most likely, the absurd percentage by which the act defines imbalance is merely an attempt by suburbia to "lock in" the minorities of the hard-pressed core city. Suburban legislators have fashioned a law to ease pharisaical consciences, as the law postulates that a Boston school with a 51% non-white student population is in violation of the Racial Imbalance Law while a school in Scituate, an affluent Boston suburb with up to 1% of non-white students, is in complete compliance with the law.*
>
> *The Racial Imbalance Law punishes the citizens of Boston by using a statistical absolute and allows suburbia the luxury of escape mechanisms by snobbish zoning ordinances and moratoriums on low-income housing existing outside the scope of the law.*
>
> *Until this country is well on the way to achieving equality through equal job opportunities, zoning ordinances and mortgage policies, the Boston School Committee will not allow the public flogging of its members or constituents to be offered as a substitute for a broad attack on the real factors denying the advancement of America's minorities.*
>
> *Boston School Committee,*
> New York Times, 7/24/74

Correlates of the MAR Ideology

We believe the perspective of the MAR is one that has grown in response to a variety of problems facing our society. And yet there are several universal social attributes of individuals which help to specify where and among which circumstances it is concentrated and, to a degree, the nature of its social roots.

For purposes of subsequent analysis, we must examine a wide range of correlates of the MAR ideology. Table 6 describes the geographical dimensions of our national sample. We see that 37 percent of those respondents living in southern states are in the

TABLE 6

GEOGRAPHICAL CHARACTERISTICS AND MIDDLE AMERICAN RADICAL
IDEOLOGY (PERCENT OF TOTAL POPULATION IN EACH GROUP WHICH
SCORED HIGH ON THE MAR IDEOLOGY SCALE)

Region:	Southern States	Northeastern States		Western States	North Central States
	37%	33%		27%	20%

Size of City Where Raised:	Small City	Large City	Suburb	Small Town	Rural Country Farm
	32%	31%	30%	28%	27%

Now Live in:	Central City of Largest Metropolitan Areas	Suburb	Small Cities and Towns	Medium Size Cities
	38%	35%	30%	22%

MAR category. By contrast, those living in the north central
states of the country (here we are including such states as
Michigan, Illinois, Indiana, Ohio, North and South Dakota)
show a significantly lower proportion of respondents with a
high score on the MAR ideology. Thus, nearly twice as many
persons from one region of the country have a high score on the
MAR ideology compared to another region. At the same time,
we should note that persons residing in northeastern states of
the country are much more similar in MAR scores to those
residing in southern states than they are to persons living in
western and north central states.

In terms of the kind of community in which a person was
raised, we find relatively little difference occurring. Persons who
were raised in small cities, large cities or suburbs are slightly
more often in the highest Middle America ideology group than
are those brought up in rural areas or small towns.

Turning to the present size of the community in which a
person lives, those in the central cities of the twenty largest
metropolitan areas are most likely to hold the MAR ideology.

This is closely followed by those residing in the suburbs of these same major metropolitan centers. Respondents who lived in medium sized communities, that is those of under 100,000 population, are the least likely to be high on the MAR ideology scale. At the same time, those who now live in small towns or rural areas are about midway between residents of central metropolitan cities and medium sized cities in terms of the MAR ideology.

On an overall basis, the most significant differences in ideology are related not to the size of the community, length of residence or to the kind of community in which one was born and raised, but in terms of the regional location of the respondent.

Tables 7 and 8 reflect sex and age factors. Men are more likely than women to have a high MAR ideology score.[13] We find there is a relatively small variation between MARs and others in terms of age distribution. Those in the age group 30–39 and those in the age group 60 and above are somewhat more likely to be MARs. Persons under 21 in the sample are least likely to be high on the MAR ideology scale.[14]

In terms of such characteristics as marital status, family life cycle and employment, we again find some differences of note.

TABLE 7

SEX OF RESPONDENT AND MIDDLE AMERICAN
RADICAL IDEOLOGY

MAR Index	Women	Men
Highest Quartile (MARs)	28%	32%
Second Highest Quartile	19%	30%
Third Highest Quartile	27%	24%
Lowest Quartile	27%	14%
Total	100% (N=976)	100% (N=714)

TABLE 8

AGE DISTRIBUTION OF MARs AND
OTHER WHITE RESPONDENTS

Age	MARs	Others
Under 21	2%	3%
21–29	17%	20%
30–39	22%	18%
40–49	17%	19%
50–59	17%	18%
60–69	14%	12%
70 or Older	11%	10%
Total	100% (N=496)	100% (N=1194)

These tend to be concentrated in the employment area, with the small group of disabled persons in the sample being highest in terms of holding the MAR ideology, followed by the retired and unemployed persons.[15] Working males are next in order, with working women showing a slightly lower proportion. The difference between working women and housewives is a relatively small one. The lowest number in terms of holding the MAR ideology is found among persons reporting their work status as that of a student. (See Appendix: Table 2.)

Catholics are more likely to be strong in the MAR ideology than are Protestants. Jews are similar to Catholics. The difference between Jews and Protestants is statistically significant, while that between Catholics and Jews is not. In the 1972 survey we find that those persons indicating no religious preference are least likely to hold a MAR ideology.[16] (See Appendix: Table 3.)

In regard to the specific Protestant sects, we find that Mormons and Baptists are most likely to have a high MAR ideology score, while Presbyterians, Methodists, Lutherans and those indicating no particular denominational ties are lower on the MAR score range. (See Appendix: Table 4.)

Some nationality differences are reflected in adherence to the MAR ideology. Individuals who identified themselves as Italians were most likely to be high on the MAR ideology score, with those of Polish, Irish and French extraction also showing significantly large proportions of respondents with a high score on the MAR index. Individuals who, when asked about nationality, chose to say "American" were relatively low on the MAR ideology score, and this is true as well of those indicating a German or Scottish nationality. (See Appendix: Table 5.)

The educational level of the white respondents in the 1972 study show important differences between MARs and others. We note that 43 percent of the MARs have completed only 11 grades of schooling or less, compared to 32 percent of other white repondents. By contrast, 1 in 5 MARs attended college

TABLE 9

EDUCATIONAL LEVEL OF MARs AND OTHERS

	MARs	Others
0–8 Grades	22% ⎫ 43%	16% ⎫ 32%
9–11 Grades	21% ⎭	16% ⎭
High School Graduate	37%	32%
1–2 Years College	9% ⎫	14% ⎫
3–4 Years College	7% ⎬ 20%	13% ⎬ 37%
More Than 4 Years College	4% ⎭	10% ⎭
Total	100% (N=496)	100% (N=1194)

and only 4 percent have graduated. This compares to 37 percent attendance and 20 percent graduation figures for the other survey participants.

In terms of occupational patterns, Table 10 reveals the very high percentage of MARs who are skilled and semi-skilled blue collar workers (for those who are employed at all). MARs are slightly less likely to be employed in clerical, sales and other white collar technical jobs than are others in the survey. They are significantly less likely to be professional or managerial workers.

At the time of the national survey, family incomes were generally lower than at present. The MAR was more often found in the $3,000 to $13,000 family income range than other whites—48 percent versus 41 percent. But, overall, MARs are found throughout the income spectrum.[17] (See Appendix: Table 6.)

TABLE 10

OCCUPATIONAL LEVEL AND THE MAR
(FOR THOSE IN THE WORK FORCE)

	MARs	Others
Professional	14%	23%
Managers, Proprietors (including farm)	11%	18%
Clerical, Sales and Related	22%	25%
Skilled Workers	19% } 40%	10% } 22%
Semi-Skilled, Operatives	21% }	12% }
Service Workers and Laborers	13%	12%
Total	100% (N=307)	100% (N=691)

Summing Up

If the socioeconomic definition of "Middle America" is that group whose income range is $6,000 to $15,000 for persons without college education and whose occupational roles exclude professional and managerial positions, then about one half of the white population of the United States falls into this category.

Preliminary in-depth interviews conducted prior to the national survey led us to consider a second definition of "Middle America" based on a set of shared attitudes about groups such as the poor, blacks and the wealthy. MARs see them as all receiving special benefits or moving ahead more than they are in terms of economic and social well-being.

Overlap between the subjective and the objective definition of "Middle America," while clearly present, leaves wide room to define individuals with extensive or limited education, high or low income, blue collar or white collar occupations as holding some very similar views about the threat from minorities, the rich and low income groups. Yet we have also found that a majority of the persons who are MARs have individual characteristics matching the group we have called "Average Middles." Although demographically similar, they are in fact far apart in basic world view. By identifying the basis for such divergence we abandon the conventional stereotype of the lower middle class individual that has equated a fixed economic strata with a state of mind. Instead, our approach focuses on reasons people with differing social positions share significant attitudes while others of the same strata do not. Where we find differences we must view them as a product of the particular variable we are dealing with. At the same time, the pattern shown in Chapter 2 underscores the research question that we must continue to probe: why is it that the ideological sense of the MAR is not correlated with objective socioeconomic characteristics? What are the factors underlying the probability that a skilled blue collar worker, for example, will have the MAR ideology or not?

The use of a subjective definition of Middle America brings

to light important facts about the dispersion within the social structure of America of those whose attitudes seem to reflect a common set of concerns: the sense that blacks, the poor and the wealthy are in some ways sources of threat and have undue access to political favoritism. That such a set of attitudes should emerge among a wide variety of individuals raises an important theoretical as well as social policy question. The use of an index which is built upon how people perceive their situation in society allows us to examine questions of the origin, prevalence and significance of a shared set of orientations. It seems clear that to understand the Middle American Radical one must go well beyond the statistical placement of people according to objective socioeconomic data.

3. THE CONCERNS OF THE
MIDDLE AMERICAN RADICAL

The Concerns of the Middle American Radical

If a single ideological perspective is shared by a cluster or coalition of people representing various socioeconomic strata in our society, it is urgent that we discover as much as we can about their concerns and their attitudes. This chapter is an effort to present, mainly in tabular form, what we found to be the major pressing problems perceived by this group. It is well to note that the questions dealing with economic matters were asked prior to the inflation and subsequent recession, the oil embargo and the disengagement from Southeast Asia.

Economic Squeeze

We began our probe into MAR attitudes toward their present situation by asking in our 1972 survey:

In general, compared with five years ago, would you say that things for you (and your family) are better, the same or worse?

It is not surprising that Low Income people were most likely to say that things were going worse for them compared to five years earlier. Yet, twice as many MARs as Average Middles chose this response to describe their life situation. About five times as many Average Middles said things have been going better than worse in the past five years. Table 11 shows that the ratio for MARs is only about 2 to 1—better over worse. At the same time, the ratio for High Education Middles is about 7 to 1.

31

TABLE 11

HOW THINGS HAVE BEEN GOING FOR YOU
COMPARED TO FIVE YEARS AGO

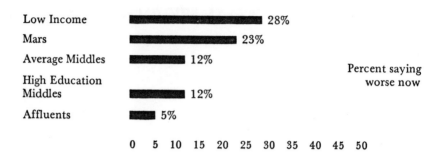

Low Income ████████████████████ 28%

Mars ███████████████ 23%

Average Middles ███████ 12%

High Education
Middles ███████ 12%

Affluents ███ 5%

Percent saying
worse now

0   5 10 15 20 25 30 35 40 45 50

In many respects, MARs are very close to Low Income Americans in terms of evaluating the way their life has been going in the recent past: 23 percent and 28 percent respectively reported things going worse in 1972 compared to 1967.[18]

One specific indicator of the way people have experienced economic distress is the general consumption pattern of their family. In 1972, 2 out of 5 Low Income Americans said they had been cutting back on buying things. At the same time, we found that over 3 out of 10 MARs indicated the same response. These patterns are significantly higher than for Average Middles (1 in 5 had cut back), for High Education Middles (17 percent cut back), or Affluents (8 percent cut back). In terms of economic conditions, MARs more closely resemble Low Income Americans than they do Average Middles.

Table 13 describes the particular ways in which people responded to the economic squeeze. Erosion of savings was the most common response. Here 3 out of 5 MARs report using up savings or saving less. MARs are the highest of all five groups in reporting that they have cut back on vacations and on hiring someone to do home repairs, that they go out less often to shows, sports events and restaurants. Both Low Income respondents and MARs are similarly higher than others in reporting that they have reduced expenditures for clothing. Finally,

TABLE 12

HOW FAMILY BUYING HAS CHANGED

"COMPARED TO FIVE YEARS AGO ARE YOU AND YOUR FAMILY ABLE TO BUY MORE AND BETTER THINGS THAN YOU DID THEN, ARE YOU HAVING TO CUT BACK ON WHAT YOU BUY, OR ARE YOU LIVING THE SAME AS YOU DID THEN?"

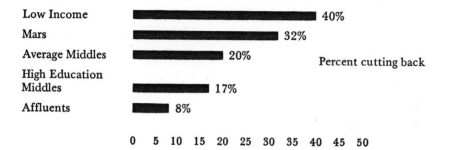

Low Income	40%
Mars	32%
Average Middles	20%
High Education Middles	17%
Affluents	8%

Percent cutting back

0 5 10 15 20 25 30 35 40 45 50

MARs are most likely to indicate that they have tried to economize on food bills. Overall, for MARs the economic downturn was felt as far back as 1967 and is not just an experience of the mid-1970s.

Personal Impact of Societal Problems

Given the MARs perception of their own situation, we asked an open-ended question which permitted respondents to describe in their own words the kind of issues they saw as most central and most pressing:

Let us talk about the problems in the United States. What do you see as the most important problems we have in this country?

The MAR problem agenda accents a set of concerns that tend to run counter to the presumed dominant issues of American society over the past several years. On the twin problems of the economy and the Viet Nam war, fewer than 1 out of 3 MARs made these their first-mentioned problem. This contrasts with almost 1 in 2 of the Low Income group and more than 2 out of

TABLE 13

TYPES OF ECONOMIC SQUEEZE AND MAJOR POPULATION GROUPS
(PERCENT INDICATING YES)

	Low Income	MARs	Average Middles	High Education Middles	Affluents
Used up savings or unable to save as much as before	49%	60%	51%	60%	37%
Cut back on vacations and travel	40%	44%	31%	24%	17%
Did more things yourself rather than paying someone for housework, repairs, etc.	57%	64%	59%	59%	40%
Went out less often to things like shows, restaurants, sports events, etc.	48%	53%	40%	35%	27%
Cut back on money spent for clothes	53%	49%	37%	39%	17%
Tried to economize more than usual on food bills	54%	58%	51%	39%	29%

5 Average Middles and Affluent Americans mentioning this pair of problems.

Given the relatively high level of economic distress being felt by MARs, their lower mention of this as the "most important problem" is significant. But the ideological focus of the MAR helps to explain why and what other issues are even more pressing. Thus, race concerns are mentioned more often by MARs than by Average Middles, Affluents or Low Income groups. High Education Middles refer to race concerns as often as MARs but for different reasons. In sharp contrast to MARs, High Education Middles mention as most important such issues as the "social fabric" of society—polarization and intergroup hostility—and ecological problems. MARs are significantly lower in their mention of such problems. Actions of the federal government and "law and order" problems are listed more by MARs than by others as the most important problems. Crime as a major problem is viewed more in terms of permissiveness as the cause (72 percent of MARs agree, compared to 64 percent of other respondents.)

Aside from the elaborate list of problems collated from our interviews, we can describe the problem focus of respondents in other terms: for example, by volume and intensity.

On the first point, since respondents could list as many problems as they wished, we had a very significant difference in the numbers actually mentioned. Unfortunately, to some extent, the number of problems listed by individuals is a function of formal educational level. MARs list an average of 2.8 problems; Average Middles indicate 2.6 problems; High Education Middles, 3.2 problems; and Affluents, 3.0 problems. (See Appendix: Table 7.) The differences are not very large and, as we note, can be viewed as a function of verbal skills, the interviewing role, and the extent to which individuals are familiar with the interviewing process.

But if we take the question of personal involvement in problems, we begin to find a new pattern. MARs are more likely than Average Middles to report that they feel some personal involvement in the problems they mention. This is measured by the interviewer in terms of whether there was any reference to personal experiences on the part of the respondents to the overall question about problems in the United States.

By taking the proportion of people mentioning at least one problem and, of this group, the proportion who indicated some personal involvement in the problem, we can devise a measure of the "intensity" of problems as experienced by individuals (See Appendix: Table 7). The higher the ratio, the more often the respondent mentioned at least one problem, but without personal involvement. The lower the ratio, the more often we find that when a problem is mentioned there is personal involvement. Comparison of these ratios for the five population groups shows that MARs have a ratio of 11 to 1. This is the lowest of all groups. That is to say, when a problem is mentioned MARs are more likely than other groups to view it in personal terms. This is less true of Average Middles, where the ratio is 14.2 to 1; and Low Income Americans, where the ratio is 14.9 to 1. The least personal involvement is found among Affluent Americans, where the ratio goes up to 22.2 to 1.

For High Education Middles, the personal involvement ratio begins to approach that for MARs—it is 12.5 to 1. This pattern suggests that, despite major value differences between MARs and High Education Middles, they do share some important attributes: both groups seem to be more personally involved in problems. This would seem to suggest, perhaps, that these are groups whose stance toward American society is likely to be somewhat more "mobilized." We may recall that on the characterization of ideology scale we found that High Education Middles were more likely than other groups to have a left-wing form of radicalism. In further analysis, we shall be concerned with following up on the notion that, of the five population segments, these two (MARs and High Education Middles) may share a rather similar stance toward direct political action.

Personal Well-Being

We have presented some of the economic and social problems which MARs and other participants in the 1972 study felt were of concern to them. At this juncture we may ask: "How do the external issues relate to individual health and stress?"

The first such indicators were the replies we received to the simple question: "How is your health?" A vast majority of those interviewed said "good" or "excellent." At the same time, a substantial minority said their health was only "fair" or even "poor." Table 14 shows the pattern of response for those feeling "poor" or "fair." Of all the survey groupings, Low Income respondents had the lowest level of self-reported

TABLE 14

HOW IS YOUR HEALTH?

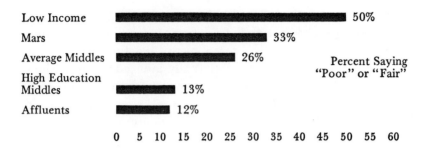

TABLE 15

WHEN HAVE YOU HAD TENSION HEADACHES?

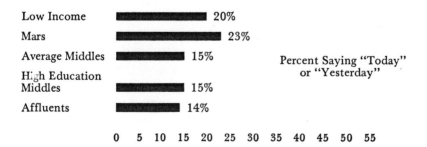

health—half said "fair" or "poor." MARs show 1 in 3 with this perception, compared to about 1 in 4 Average Middles and 1 in 8 High Education Middles and Affluents. Once again, the MAR group had greater affinity for the Low Income portion of our society than for the Middle or Upper Income groups.

What about reported tension and stress? We find that there are some significant differences in the frequency and recency with which individuals report tension headaches. MARs are more likely to indicate that either "today" or "yesterday" they felt this way. Twice as many MARs as Average Middles reported having a tension headache "today."

The tendency for MARs to report the expression of tension, which might be inferred to reflect a psychosomatic dynamic, provides yet another clue to the diversity of what might be termed MARs' "alienation." To define MARs merely as a politically active group is to ignore a range of reactions which might involve the turning inward of externally induced social tensions. The findings in Table 16 offer at least a suggestion that such an alternative response to socially induced stress may, indeed, characterize a segment of the MAR population group. Thus, if MARs are angry at the way things are going in society, we have some evidence that they manifest this in their own physical and psychological state.

The Quality of Life: An Examination of the Local Environment of Respondents

Let us pursue several indicators of various dissatisfactions in the immediate settings in which they are found and in which they function. We asked respondents to describe, in effect, their local "life space" in terms of the following introductory statement:

> Now let's talk about things that may give a person a feeling of satisfaction. Would you tell me if you are very satisfied, satisfied, dissatisfied or very dissatisfied with the neighborhood, housing, amount of time spent with family and relatives, safety and security, the community, amount of spare time, air pollution, moral standards in the community and the education of children.

In Table 16 we have listed each of these areas of concern in the order that MARs expressed the greatest amount of dissatisfaction. Compared to Low Income respondents, MARs are significantly more dissatisfied with six of the eight areas including safety and the morals of the community. Compared to Average Middles, MARs are more concerned about 5 out of 8 areas. These include the safety and morality of their community, its education, and the local neighborhood and family

TABLE 16

TYPES OF DISSATISFACTION WITH THE LOCAL ENVIRONMENT
QUALITY OF LIFE INDICATORS
(PERCENT DISSATISFIED OR VERY DISSATISFIED)

	Low Income	MARs	Average Middles	High Education Middles	Affluents
Amount of Spare Time	18%−	33%	33%	29%	34%
Quality of the Air	24%−	31%	29%	42%	32%
Morals of the Community	15%	31%+	20%	24%	21%
Time with Family	20%	27%+	20%	22%	20%
Safety of Community	12%	25%+	18%	18%	12%
Education of Children	21%	22%	14%	8%	21%
Housing	11%	17%	14%	19%	5%−
Neighborhood	11%	15%	10%	8%	3%

ties. In fact, there is only one instance—the case of air pollution—where another group has a unique and significantly higher level of dissatisfaction. On an overall basis, the pattern shown above suggests that while the concerns expressed are not always unique to MARs, there is a tendency for MARs to have a somewhat higher level of dissatisfaction on most of the issues mentioned.

In Table 17 we have added up all eight of the items of possible dissatisfaction and then show the percentage of people with three or more expressed dissatisfactions. Nearly 1 out of 3 MARs, compared to 1 in 5 Average Middles and High Education Middles, are dissatisfied with three or more items on the list. Only 4 percent of Low Income Americans and 5 percent of Affluents have this many dissatisfactions.

To pursue further the role of the local environment as the focus for the quality of life, we examined several institutions

TABLE 17

DISSATISFACTION WITH THE QUALITY OF LIFE INDEX

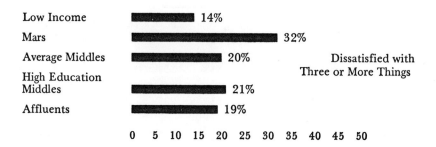

with which the local community is closely identified. The first of these is local government. The eight criticisms listed in the interview reflect the fact that MARs are significantly more critical than other population groups. MARs stress that local government "treats certain kinds of people better than others." This kind of criticism is markedly higher than any other type made by MARs or other groups. At the same time, the view that local government "does not follow clear-cut policies" or "they don't pay attention to what people like me want" are also made by a majority of the MAR population group.

MARs are also significantly more likely than other groups to feel local government has "too much power" and is "too big and complicated to run well." Moreover, if we then look at an overall evaluation in which people could indicate whether an organization is doing a good job or not, we find that nearly 2 out of 5 MARs feel that local government is not doing a good job. This is almost twice the proportion found for Average Middles and is significantly higher than any other population segment. Thus, for every type of criticism, MARs are distinct in their indictment of their local communities' political institutions.

The second proximate social institution we examined was the local school. Here again, MARs are significantly higher in their

TABLE 18

DISSATISFACTIONS WITH LOCAL INSTITUTIONS: GOVERNMENT

	Low Income	MARs	Average Middles	High Education Middles	Affluents
Treat People Differently	41%	65%	45%	43%	41%
No Clear-Cut Policies	32%	52%	32%	28%	19%
Don't Pay Attention	35%	51%	32%	28%	19%
Interfered With	27%	35	29%	28%	24%
Too Much Power	23%	33%	18%	14%	10%
Don't Treat People With Respect	15%	31%+	16%	21%	10%
Too Big	14%	26%	15%	13%	12%
Not Doing a Good Job	19%	39%	22%	28%	22%

level of criticism, particularly in the case—once again—of organizations treating people differently and not paying attention to their concerns. MARs are also very distinctive in the strength of their feelings that the local schools do not have clear-cut policies. Only in the case of Affluents do we find a fairly similar perspective. When we turn to the issue of local schools not showing respect toward people, we find that MARs are about twice as likely as other groups in the national sample to level this criticism.

On an overall basis. MARs are not as critical of local schools as they are of local governments. Considering the level of discontent with regard to particular dimensions of the local schools, MARs' total assessment of the local school is not excessively negative. Only 23 percent say the school is not doing a good job compared to 39 percent who feel this way about local government.

TABLE 19

DISSATISFACTIONS WITH LOCAL SCHOOLS

	Low Income	Average MARs	Middles	High Education Middles	Affluents
Treat People Differently	34%	45%	29%	31%	24%
Don't Pay Attention	31%	39%	24%	16%	20%
Interfered With	28%	38%	32%	32%	23%
No Clear-Cut Policies	23%	36%	24%	23%	29%
Too Big	25%	32%	22%	21%	21%
No Respect	14%	22%	12%	13%	10%
Too much Power	19%	22%	17%	9%	15%
Not Doing a Good Job	14%	23%+	15%	18%	20%

The third institution focused in on the local environment is that of the police. Even though MARs are more critical of the police than are other respondents, they are less critical of the police than they are of local government and local schools. In fact, their most significant criticism relative to other groups' complaints is that the police are interfered with and the people in charge are prevented from doing their jobs. If there is any institution with which MARs feel a sense of identity, it is the police.

By contrast, High Education Middles are significantly more likely than MARs to be critical of police for having too much power and for not showing respect to people. The fact that MARs and High Education Middles are the most critical of the local police for treating people differently may disguise the other evaluations of police on which the two groups are sharply differentiated. For the one group, the implication is that the police may be favoring minorities; and for the other, it is that police single such groups out for punishment.

TABLE 20

DISSATISFACTIONS WITH LOCAL POLICE

	Low Income	MARs	Average Middles	High Education Middles	Affluents
Treat People Differently	34%	42%	35%	44%	31%
Interfered With	31%	41%	32%	26%	25%
No Clear-Cut Policies	19%	28%	21%	23%	12%
Don't Pay Attention	18%	22%	15%	13%	7%
No Respect	14%	20%	13%	28%	10%
Too Big	5%	8%	7%	5%	5%
Power	7%	8%	5%	13%	9%
Not Doing a Good Job	10%	11%	11%	13%	7%

Primary Group Ties

One of the most pervasive social institutions is that of the family. We asked of respondents: "Aside from those who live in your house, how often are you in touch with family members and relatives—either visiting in person, by telephone or mail?" Across the major population segments of the sample there is no major difference in the frequency of contact with relatives. If there is any trend evidenced at all by the data, it is that persons who are in the High Education Middle or Affluent categories tend to have less daily or almost daily visiting with relatives. Only one in four of the High Education Middles report contact almost every day, in contrast to 42.1 percent of MARs. In terms of family contact occurring once a week, three out of four MARs have at least this level of contact with relatives. A similar proportion is found among Low Income Americans and Average Middles, as compared to only about two out of three High

Education Middles and Affluents. But these differences are not really significant and MARs do not represent a distinct group in terms of their frequency of interaction with relatives not living in the household.

In terms of wives working, male MARs are somewhat more supportive than Average Middles—50 percent thought it is a good idea "in a situation like yours" for their wives to work compared to 44 percent. (See Appendix, Table 8.)

MARs are twice as likely as others to report that the "generation gap" is a "serious problem." Overall, 2 out of 3 in the total national sample rate this "not very" or "not at all" serious. (See Appendix, Table 9.) From the 1975 Cambridge survey we find 62 percent of MARs compared to 54 percent of the other population sample believe a teacher should "be allowed to use physical force—spanking—to discipline children." (See Appendix, Table 10.)

Neighborhood as a Critical MAR Institution

Our study found another form of significant primary group interaction which focused on the neighborhood. We asked respondents the following question: "Not counting relatives who live around here, how often do you and your neighbors get together?" Relatively few Americans in the national sample have as frequent contact with neighbors as they have with relatives. But both MARs and Low Income individuals have a slightly larger proportion (which is statistically significant) of individuals who report seeing neighbors every day. This is true of 1 in 7 of these two groups, as opposed to only about 1 in 20 Affluent Americans and High Education Middles. In the Average Middle grouping, only 1 in 12 have daily contact with a neighbor.

Related to the question of the role of neighboring, we sought to measure the sets of attitudes people had toward new members of the local community. Because data from census statistics has indicated a very high rate of geographical mobility among Americans—nearly one in five persons moving in an average five year period—it is important to assess how different population segments respond to newcomers. In order to tap this attitude, we asked the following question:

If a new neighbor moved in how many of the people now living here would almost certainly do something to make the new family feel welcome?

Some important differences exist between how one group of respondents anticipates the reaction of their neighbors compared with another. Thus, among the Affluent about nine out of ten respondents feel that at least a few of their neighbors would help the new family. By contrast, among the High Education Middles this is true in 7 out of 10 cases. Among MARs we find that nearly 1 in 4 say that no neighbor would help the new family. This contrasts with 19 percent of the Low Income group and only 12 percent of the Affluent. The differential between MARs and Average Middles is extremely small in terms of helping the new family.

An important index of the role of neighborhood is the frequency of visiting. Authorities on the change processes in the urban setting have pointed out the declining role of the local community. We found that 15 percent of MARs versus 7 percent of Average Middles visit with neighbors "almost every day." MARs and Low Income individuals are similar in terms of the frequency of neighbor contact. At the same time, most MARs—as well as other groups—report visiting neighbors less often than once a week (see Appendix, Table 11). Yet in the 1975 Cambridge Report, MARs were significantly more likely than other whites to report that they knew their neighbors "quite well"—54 percent versus 45 percent.

What characterizes the MAR group, in comparison with Low Income and Average Middle respondents, is the relatively larger number who describe their neighborhood as one in which newcomers may not be welcomed or where intense visiting occurs. A vignette description of these factors can be seen in the following remarks about Boston's Southside, where busing has been such a volatile issue:

The neighborhood has never welcomed outsiders—residents who have lived there more than a decade are still referred to as newcomers. Nor, for that matter, has the rest of Boston seemed especially hospitable to Southie. Railroad tracks and a six-lane expressway cut it off from downtown Boston; the bay isolates it on the remaining three sides. Only five bridges lead in and out of Southie—not that anyone is particularly anxious to cross them. The Irish, who settled in after the Great Famine, make no secret of wanting to be left alone.

"Southie is My Hometown,"
New York Times, *11/15/74*

Here is yet a second portrait of "Southie":

"Are any of you Southies?" asked the woman in the middle. She was smiling all the time, sure that her neighborhood antennae had accurately detected outsiders. "We don't recognize any of you."

One young city worker volunteered that he had been born in Southie. But that didn't count. In fact, maybe it was even worse. The natives of Boston's parochial neighborhood are suspicious of an outsider's intentions, and with good cause. If they find an outsider who used to be an insider, they suspect his motives. Neither upward mobilization nor suburbia are idealized in Southie's wards and precincts.

"School Uproar in South Boston,"
Los Angeles Times, *9/22/74*

One journalistic account emphasized that Southie "considers itself a self-contained unit, and it is."

If Southie is an example of the traditional ethnic enclave—one that can be viewed as the "parochial"[19] type of neighborhood—it is also true that MARs reside in many other types of urban settings as well. Perhaps what unifies these different neighborhood settings is the perceived and actual decline in their environmental quality. As part of the 1972 study we asked each interviewer to rate the public services in the neighborhood in which the interviewee lives. Table 21 shows the ratings for the five survey groups. MARs virtually match Low Income respondents with 1 in 5 rated as living in "poor" or "fair" neighborhoods—where streetlights are inadequate, litter is in evidence, the street signs are poor and defective public equipment is to be found.

TABLE 21

"HOW WOULD YOU DESCRIBE THE GENERAL QUALITY OF PUBLIC
FACILITIES AND SERVICES IN THE IMMEDIATE VICINITY OF
RESPONDENT'S HOME?"

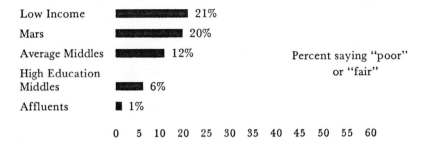

Low Income	21%
Mars	20%
Average Middles	12%
High Education Middles	6%
Affluents	1%

Percent saying "poor"
or "fair"

0   5   10   20   25   30   35   40   45   50   55   60

The following are the choices interviewers could pick from:

Poor: Broken and defective public equipment is quite evident and
           typical of the area, litter is scattered in the street and the over-
           all appearance of the street is unclean.

Fair: Some street lights are inadequate, street signs are in poor con-
           dition, there is some litter in the alleys or streets. Streets and
           roads need repair.

Good: Public services appear to be maintained, streets and roads are
           in good condition. There is little damage to street lights, gar-
           bage is not scattered around, although some equipment may
           need replacement.

Excellent: Street lights, utilities, street signs are new or in perfect condi-
           tion and lack of rubbish in alleys and street is outstanding.
           Streets and roads are in excellent condition.

In addition to the problems of the physical environment,
MARs also report more frequently than others that their neighborhood is economically mixed. Thus, 35 percent report neighbors having higher or lower incomes than themselves. This is
significantly more than is the case for Average Middles or Low
Income respondents (see Appendix, Table 12).

MARs, whether of Low, Average, or High income, place special value on being in a social environment where life style is uniform. In fact, less often than for other population groups do they find this to be a fact. There is a strong sense that racial, economic and ethnic similarity is important, yet fewer MARs than Average Middles—69 percent versus 76 percent—now live in all white neighborhoods (see Appendix: Table 13). When the question was asked of those living in all-white neighborhoods: "Is there a good chance, some chance, or a poor chance that your neighborhood will be racially mixed in the next few years," 36 percent of MAR respondents said there was a "good chance" or "some chance." This contrasts with 30 percent for Average Middles. Table 22 shows the percentage of persons saying they now live or will probably live in a racially mixed neighborhood. High Education Middles are most likely to indicate such a pattern, MARs are significantly more likely than either Low Income or Average Middle respondents to say they do already or are likely to live in a racially heterogeneous neighborhood.

Although both MARs and High Education Middles may both be seen as confronting heterogeneity in their neighborhood environment, the role of the neighborhood is much stronger in the lives of the former group. MARs are far more involved in their local area, with more frequent visiting and a greater likelihood of attempting to integrate newcomers; that is, to socialize them to the area's values and norms.

MARs and Personal Character

Middle Americans have been portrayed in the media as having certain negative characteristics, such as lack of intellectual sophistication, quasi-fascistic orientations, racism, and a whole gamut of personal, close-minded biases. One can view MARs from a different vantage point, one which stems from the high value MARs places on rugged individualism, self-reliance and autonomy. For example, in a 1975 survey 72 percent of MARs agreed that "general permissiveness of our society today is the

TABLE 22

REPORTED RACIAL MIXTURE IN NEIGHBORHOOD

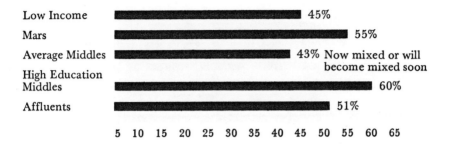

Low Income	45%
Mars	55%
Average Middles	43% Now mixed or will become mixed soon
High Education Middles	60%
Affluents	51%

5 10 15 20 25 30 35 40 45 50 55 60 65

major cause of rapidly increasing crime, while 64 percent believe a guaranteed income "will weaken America."

One of the items that we have already alluded to in our discussion of MAR ideology has to do with the need for a hierarchy of authority. Table 23 shows the distribution of responses to the statement "a job is done best when one person is in charge." We note that the majority of MARs react to this statement by saying they "strongly agree." This is a significantly higher proportion than that found in any of the other population groups. Those who are least likely to respond in this way are the High Education Middles. Thus, in terms of emphasis on what might be termed "authoritarianism" or, perhaps more accurately, a tendency to suggest reliance on hierarchical authority relations, MARs far surpass the other population segments in our study.

To reflect the MAR pride in self-reliance, we asked for responses to this statement: "Nowadays too many people think society owes them a living." Not surprisingly, MARs are significantly likely to agree strongly with this statement—nearly 4 out of 5—compared with only 1 out of 2 of the Low Income and 56 percent of the Average Middles. The group least likely to "strongly agree" with this statement are the Educated Middles. Affluent Americans are also far less likely to concur with MARs

TABLE 23

EMPHASIS ON HIERARCHICAL AUTHORITY:
"A JOB IS DONE BEST WHEN ONE PERSON IS IN CHARGE."

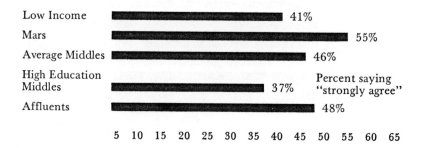

on this particular statement. In the 1975 Cambridge study, 58 percent of MARs indicated "most people on welfare could support themselves and are on welfare because they are lazy" came closest to their point of view; 28 percent chose a statement saying "most people on welfare are children or old people or sick and couldn't work anyway." For other whites 45 percent picked laziness and 34 percent said welfare recipients "couldn't work anyway."

TABLE 24

ATTITUDES ABOUT WELFARE:
"TOO MANY PEOPLE THINK SOCIETY OWES THEM A LIVING."

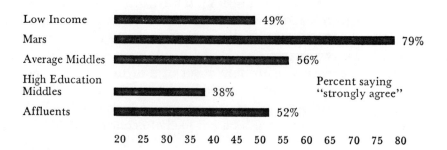

Race Tensions and the MAR

In the earlier response to the "most important problem facing the nation today" MARs mentioned race problems more than any group except High Education Middles. Throughout the survey we sought to clarify what the specific components of the race problem were as viewed by different groups. In response to a statement concerning the urban riots of the 1960s (see Appendix: Table 14), MARs more than any other group "strongly agree" that agitators were the cause—65 percent indicate this view compared to 44 percent of Average Middles and 21 percent of High Education Middles. In the 1975 Cambridge survey, MARs are significantly higher than other whites in seeing race tensions as greater than "a few years ago," 26 percent versus 14 percent.[20]

In Table 25, we obtain further insights about MARs' attitudes toward race issues. Here the question had to do with how to deal with the history of racism in American society. The particular question asked was the following: "How much responsibility do white people today have to make up for wrongs done to blacks in the past?"

TABLE 25

ATTITUDES ABOUT RACE INJUSTICE:
"HOW MUCH RESPONSIBILITY DO WHITE PEOPLE TODAY HAVE TO
MAKE UP FOR WRONGS DONE TO BLACKS IN THE PAST?"

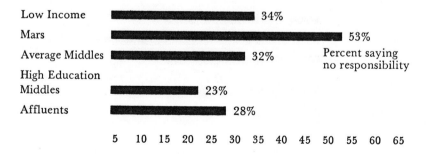

We find that the majority of MARs say that whites have no responsibility for these past wrongs. This contrasts with nearly two-thirds of the Low Income group, who feel that whites have at least a little responsibility, a view shared by a similar proportion of the Average Middle group, and by more than 3 out of 4 of the High Education Middles. Moreover, Affluent Americans are twice as likely as MARs to suggest that whites bear at least some responsibility for past patterns of discrimination.

Race perceptions relative to interaction at the personal level play a critical role in social tensions. When asked about changes in "race contact" in the five years up to the time of our survey, MARs had the largest proportion of perceived increase: 61 percent report more contact than earlier, while only 11 percent indicate less. Table 26 also shows that Average Middles are significantly less likely to report an increase in bi-racial contact (46 percent).

Summing up the Intensity in the Problem Focus of MARs

In terms of responses to the open-ended question about problems facing the United States, MARs gave greater weight to

TABLE 26

SELF REPORT OF RESPONDENTS' CHANGE IN
RACE CONTACT IN PAST FIVE YEARS

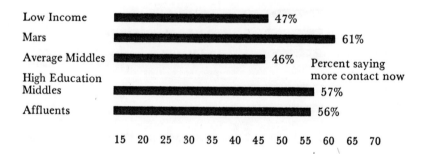

race, law and order, and less to the economy and to the war in Viet Nam. At the same time, High Education Middles and Affluents stress ecological issues more than did MARs. Affluents stress problems of the economy and morals. MARs stress concern about actions of the federal government more than do Average Middles or High Education Middles.

While the number of problems mentioned by MARs was not greater than that of other groups, when the ratio between personal involvement in problems and the number of times at least one problem was mentioned, we found that MARs have the lowest ratio of problem mentions to personal involvement. Also, the MAR ideology stresses that the cause of problems is individual—such as laziness—in regard to welfare programs.

In terms of physical health, tension and economic distress, MARs resemble Low Income respondents more than they do any other group.

The picture which emerges from our data gathered in 1972 relative to the economic squeeze felt by MARs is of interest more as a forecast than as an expression of economic crisis. Our data suggests that MARs may have telegraphed the economic recession/depression that many other Americans have experienced since the mid-1970s. This line of argument, in turn, leads to the intriguing speculation that MARs may have been one of the key groups in *triggering* the steady decline in consumer confidence and spending which has occurred since 1973. Perhaps a more conservative interpretation of the data we have presented would point out that MARs felt the economic squeeze earlier than others. Quite clearly, however, the MARs have been experiencing both real and perceived declines in their economic position since 1967. Perhaps such a prolonged drop in standard of living, following earlier gains, is the catalyst for the growth and emergence of the MAR ideology.

A perceived decline in the quality of the local community and neighborhood social and physical environment is one major distinguishing attribute of those we have grouped under the heading of Middle American Radicals. Dissatisfaction about safety, morality and the neighborhood are key elements in this perspective.

MARs were vehemently critical of local government. Here they voiced the greatest amount of criticism and to a degree that was statistically significant compared to other groups.

If there is any situation in the nation which was presaged by the findings of our study, it would be the determined resistance to busing by residents of Hyde Park in Boston. The following description of the social forces surrounding that neighborhood echoes many of the conclusions we have drawn about the concerns of the MAR.

> *Hyde Park on the edge of the city is a refuge from the central city slums for thousands of bus drivers, policemen, construction workers, sales clerks and other workers, male and female. They live in modest but comfortable frame houses behind tiny lawns and cyclone fences. According to the 1970 census, the median family income was $10,670. Most own their own houses which sell for about $20,000 to $25,000. They are full of pride in their community and in their many children who they hope to give the education they themselves could not get.*
>
> *They now feel put upon and threatened—by inflation, rising taxes, the encroaching black population, deceiving politicians and suburban liberals who expect them to pay the full cost of the social change. All of this has crystalized into fierce opposition to the busing order.*
>
> "Two Boston Areas Point Up School
> Dilemma," New York Times, 7/8/74

In this chapter we have discussed the problems and pressures felt by MARs in their family, neighborhood and local community milieu. Now we must investigate the experiences and perceptions which influence MARs in their assessment of the larger social institutions and, in turn, how the individual confronts the larger world. To what extent is the proximate social world of the MAR a cause or an effect of the larger social system, economic and political? We now turn to such considerations.

4. THE WORLD OF WORK
AND THE MAR

Debate Over the Blue Collar "Blues"

In the past few years, a great deal of attention has been paid to the so-called blue collar "blues." Articles, books and reports have focused on the growing problem of work dissatisfaction and alienation, particularly among workers in the low and middle income brackets.

In remarks made in a speech before the Tax Foundation of New York, Richard C. Gerstenberg, former GM Chairman, has lifted the sometimes esoteric debate over the blue collar "blues" to a new prominence. Gerstenberg is quoted as saying: "The current wave of public concern for the automobile worker may not be fully warranted" and that the media's composing the blue collar blues "occurs at a time when the builders of our cars earn more than the teachers of our children."[21]

Typical of the nature of this "debate" over blue collar workers is the perception by Mr. Gerstenberg that "news stories have swayed public eyes to the dehumanizing of the American worker when the average hourly worker is in the top one-third income bracket in the United States." Ironically, this view— supported by such well-known analysts of economic and labor policy as Dr. Sar A. Levitan—became the basis for the negotiation in the auto industry in 1973. The jacket of Levitan's book states: "The persuasive though partial evidence gathered in this volume suggests that the position of blue collar workers has not deteriorated. . . . Although no formal poll was taken, the verdict of most of the contributors seems to be that there is no real blue collar crisis."[22]

S.M. Lipset, in his recent review of extremist movements of the Right in the United States, analyzes the Wallace phenomenon as partly the expression of white workers "whose affluence and comfort" have been threatened by urban riots:

> The reasons for the greater participation in the Wallace movement by white trade-union members ... are inherent in the fact that the former are more likely to live inside the central cities relatively close to black ghettoes. Hence they are also most likely to be directly and personally concerned with consequences of efforts to integrate schools and residential neighborhoods.[23]

In defense of Middle American workers, Patricia Sexton argues that blue collar unionist workers are not uniquely identified with the Wallace movement and that "the political alienation of 'middle America' is consistently expressed in the failure to vote."[24] Sexton places far less stress on the protection of past gains than does Lipset and argues that, in fact, blue collar families have a large number of grievances that have not been dramatized and so have not drawn public attention.

In introducing the special theme of the disaffected hard hats, a concept of classical Marxist and industrial sociology is revived: "work-focused alienation" Sexton's argument is summarized in the following passage:

> A hidden assumption in all the talk about the alienation and participation is that there is a massive and homogeneous body in the middle of America that is content with its lot. ... The symptoms of the alienation are found in voting behavior, work habits, absenteeism on the job, strikes, hard hat disturbances, backlash, antagonism to students and feelings of distrust and antagonism. ... [25]

The ascendancy of the idea of the workplace as the crucible for political alienation is shown in its most pristine form in the recent study by Sheppard and Herrick.[26] In this review of survey findings from blue collar workers in two cities, the authors argue that the decline in traditional "working class authoritarianism" results in an increased discontent with the boredom and lack of self-fulfillment of blue collar jobs. In turn, this leads to the kind of political alienation expressed in support for George Wallace. Moreover, they argue, this is especially the pattern for the young blue collar worker.

In a survey sampling of white residents of Los Angeles, Edward H. Ransford finds that the explanation for "blue collar anger"—in this case directed at blacks and students—is rooted in "the actual or perceived social situation."

> *From this perspective much of the workingman's anger is a rational response to tangible strains, independent of personal bigotry. A lack of decision-making power on the job, the fact of hard earned dollars going for tax programs to aid blacks with no comparable programs for working class whites, a power structure unresponsive to the needs of the working-man—these stresses probably effect working class anger as much as personal prejudice.*[27]

The studies which we have cited move well beyond racism and status quo conservatism in explaining both the Wallace movement and the special issue of the blue collar blues. They share the view that blue collar workers are victims and that their victimization is directly tied to the job situation.

The fact that our national survey examined five population groups allows us to provide some comparative data on different segments of society and to see whether MARs are more alienated than others in terms of their work.

In the stereotyped version, Middle Americans have been portrayed as firm believers in the so-called Protestant Ethic of hard work. Thus, we might have expected MARs to strongly disagree with the statement: "There are many things more important in life than working hard." Table 27 suggests a much milder pattern.

There is a tendency for MARs to strongly disagree with this statement more than other groups, but not to the extent one might have expected.

Another basic approach to the question of the world of work focuses on the issue of job satisfaction. This has been used in a number of surveys and generally shows a fairly constant pattern over the last decade or two in which roughly 4 out of 5 persons interviewed generally expressed satisfaction with their current work.

In Table 28 we have included the response patterns on a

TABLE 27

ATTITUDES ABOUT WORK:
"THERE ARE MANY THINGS MORE IMPORTANT IN LIFE
THAN WORKING HARD."

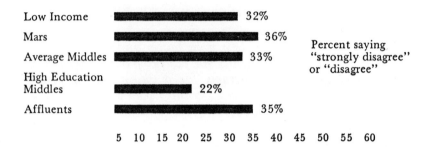

standard question dealing with overall job satisfaction. The specific question asked was: "All things considered, how satisfied are you with your job?" The multiple choice responses indicate that the level of dissatisfaction is not significantly greater for MARs than for other groups. However, if we focus on the response "very satisfied" we find that significantly fewer

TABLE 28

JOB SATISFACTION FOR THE FIVE MAJOR SEGMENTS
OF THE WHITE NATIONAL SAMPLE

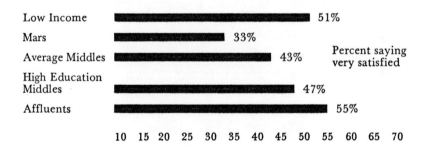

MARs choose such a response. In effect, MARs qualify their enthusiasm for the job more than do other respondents.

If we then choose as a summary measure of the differences in overall work satisfaction between different populations the ratio between those who express the view of being very satisfied and those who indicate either a "dissatisfied" or "very dissatisfied" response, we can get a rather basic view of work attitudes. Thus, for Low Income people, 5 times as many say they are very satisfied as expressed dissatisfaction. For Average Middles this ratio is 3.5 to 1. It is 5 to 1 for High Education Middles and 9 to 1 for Affluents. However, for MARs the ratio is only 2 to 1. Overall, MARs revealed a lukewarm attitude toward their work.

Let us now zero in on the nature of the particular job setting by analyzing a series of questions which asked people to describe the attributes of their job and, in particular, to indicate whether they felt that a number of characteristics—both good and bad—were true or not true of their work.

First we asked respondents to evaluate various elements and degrees of dissatisfaction with their jobs. On five of these ten dimensions, MARs are significantly more likely than Average Middles to express the negative aspects of their job. These include the chance for promotion, safety hazards, the amount of pay, how often a person comes home from the job "so tired that you can't really spend time with family or friends," and "not having the chance to do what I do best." These dissatisfactions or negative qualities of the job are shared in three instances with Low Income Americans.

We find a general pattern in which the MAR has a view of the work setting which is, in a number of instances, quite similar to that of the Low Income person. The areas in which MARs are distinct and have a significantly different perspective than any other group include two: safety hazards and not getting the chance to do what they do best. In both instances, MARs are significantly more likely than either Low Income, Average Middles or other groups to say that these drawbacks are present.

Since much recent discussion of job alienation has been focused on the right to participate in decision-making on the

TABLE 29

TYPES OF JOB DISSATISFACTIONS AND MAJOR POPULATION SEGMENTS
(PERCENT "VERY" OR "SOMEWHAT" DISSATISFIED)

	Low Income	MARs	Average Middles	High Education Middles	Affluents
Chance for Promotion Not Good	69%+	62%+	56%	50%	45%
Safety Hazards	34%	53%+	43%	22%	30%
Amount of Pay Not Good	34%	27%+	17%	20%	13%
Often Fatigued by Work	23%	26%+	17%	13%	12%
Not Have Time to do a Good Job	8%−	17%	14%	22%	28%
Not Have a Say in the Job	27%	24%	25%	8%	1%
Job Security Not Good	22%	22%+	12%	16%	10%
Not have a Chance to do Many Different Things	22%	21%	18%	12%	5%
Not Get a Chance to do What I do Best	14%	23%+	13%	13%	5%
Not Have a Chance to Make Friends	11%	15%	17%	9%	16%

job, the findings in Table 29 may have particular relevance. The question as actually phrased was: "I have a say in deciding how the job gets done." We find that MARs as well as Average Middles and Low Income Americans share a common sense that this is not particularly true of their work. However, for the High Education Middles and Affluents, there is a virtual absence of this criticism. The lack of input into decision making is not a uniquely MAR phenomenon, but one that seems to be a direct function of having a limited level of education together with a low to modest or only moderately high level of income.

Another dimension of work which also has been discussed extensively is the concern over variety or monotony in the work place. We find that once again it is not MARs alone, but Low Income and Average Middles as well, who complain about the fact that they do not do "a lot of different things on my job."

One of the important findings in Table 29 is the fact that more "traditional" issues such as safety or health hazards and fatigue are among the paramount MAR discontents. Pay, promotion, and security are a cluster of concerns that distinguish MAR's from Average Middles and, in turn, link MAR's to their low-income working peers.

Using the number of job criticisms made by our respondents, we can measure the "extensivity" of work alienation or dissatisfaction. We can see that MARs are significantly more likely than Average Middles, High Education Middles or Affluents to mention four or more job dissatisfactions. At the same time, this high level of discontent is shared by Low Income Americans. But MARs are significantly more likely than Low Income respondents to have three or more criticisms.

TABLE 30

INDEX OF TYPES OF WORK DISSATISFACTION

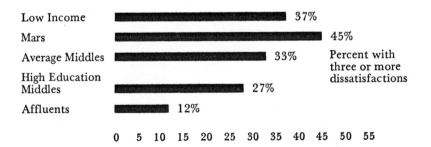

Low Income	37%
Mars	45%
Average Middles	33%
High Education Middles	27%
Affluents	12%

Percent with three or more dissatisfactions

0 5 10 15 20 25 30 35 40 45 50 55

Yet another measure of the overall pattern of work alienation has to do with the intensivity of job complaints. Several steps were employed in constructing such an index. First, we scored the concerns that people expressed on a four point scale. For positive attributes of the job, the statement "not at all true" had a weight of four, "not very true" a weight of three, "somewhat true" a weight of two, and "very true" a weight of one. By reversing this scoring when dealing with negative attributes, we may then add the total number of points scored on the ten areas of job discussion contained in the interview. This overall index of work dissatisfaction then serves as an "intensity" measure.

Although it was possible to have a total point range of 0 to 33, we found that half the population had a score of 9 or less. On this basis, a score of ten or more indicates high intensity of job dissatisfaction.

A significantly larger proportion of MARs are above the median on the job dissatisfaction scale, with 63 percent having a score of 10 or more on the index, in comparison to 39 percent of Average Middles, and only 19 percent of the Affluents. The measure of intensity seems to sharpen the kinds of differences noted for the extensivity of job discontent. The number of complaints and the depth of concern indicate that MARs are a distinct group and that they approach their job with a lower

TABLE 31

INDEX OF WORK DISSATISFACTION

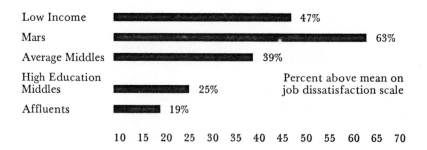

Low Income ████████████████ 47%

Mars ████████████████████ 63%

Average Middles ████████ 39%

High Education Middles ████ 25%   Percent above mean on job dissatisfaction scale

Affluents ██ 19%

10 15 20 25 30 35 40 45 50 55 60 65 70

level of satisfaction than do other groups in the society, including Low Income respondents.

Thus far we have focused on the more "traditional" measures of work alienation. However, since a major proportion of our interview dealt with the individual's view of social institutions, we included among those institutions the respondent's own work place. This allowed us to measure not only the discontent or satisfaction with a specific job, but also with the organization in which he works.

While MARs are more critical on each of the organizational dimensions than are other respondents, in only two instances is this at a level which reaches statistical significance. These are the view that the work organization "does not pay attention to what people like me want" and the belief that the organization does not treat people with respect. In the case of the organization not having clear-cut policies, MARs are significantly higher than Average Middles, but not markedly different from

TABLE 32

TYPES OF COMPLAINTS AGAINST THE WORK ORGANIZATION

	Low Income	MARs	Average Middles	High Education Middles	Affluents
No Clear-Cut Policies	28%	38%+	30%	35%	32%
Treat People Differently	24%	38%+	31%	35%	31%
Pays No Attention	21%	33%	24%	24%	20%
Interfered With	18%	27%+	20%	31%	22%
Too Much Power	12%	23%+	17%	12%	15%
Doesn't Treat People with Respect	10%	23%	13%	10%	9%
Too Big	8%	20%	15%	17%	.18%
Not Doing a Good Job	16%	18%	13%	18%	13%

the level shown for High Education Middles or Affluents. In regard to treating people differently, MARs share a high level of criticism with all groups, except Low Income respondents. On the issue of outside groups interfering, MARs share the view of High Education Middles. In general, MARs are also more likely to say that the work organization has too much power and they feel this much more strongly than do Average Middles or Low Income Americans. In terms of the organization not doing a good job, MARs and High Education Middles tend to be slightly more critical than other groups.

Overall, MARs tend to be less differentiated in their criticism of their work organization than they are in their criticism of their specific job. But the percentage of MARs having three or more complaints about the organization where they work indicates a greater alienation than that felt by other groups.

Work Attitudes of MARs: An Overview

For several years now, manpower experts have suggested that many white workers might be alienated because they are locked into dull, dirty, uninteresting, low status jobs.

Recent media accounts have highlighted how absenteeism on older, more routine, tedious and noisy automobile lines has increased to approximately 10 percent on some Fridays and

TABLE 33

EXTENT OF ALIENATION FROM THE WORK ORGANIZATION

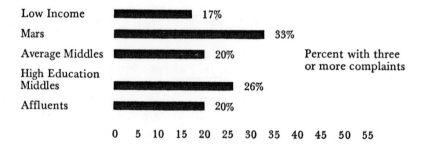

Low Income — 17%

Mars — 33%

Average Middles — 20%

High Education Middles — 26%

Affluents — 20%

Percent with three or more complaints

0   5   10   15   20   25   30   35   40   45   50   55

Mondays. Reportedly, auto workers sometimes complain about excess overtime and even decline higher-paying but duller jobs. Quality of work performance has declined, employee turnover and tardiness are up, bickering and grievances have increased.

These phenomena seem to be concentrated disproportionately among the younger workers (40 percent of the auto workers are now under 35). Increasingly well educated and aware, such workers—regardless of the color of their collar—may be less likely to accept autocratic workplace discipline, more prone to status dissatisfactions, and more likely to value leisure time and job satisfaction over more pay for more hours or less interesting work. At the same time, they want rapid advancement in title and pay, and chafe under union seniority provisions.

How Valid is this Perspective?

About 1 in 4 MARs are union members, with 75 percent in blue collar jobs. Both management and union leaders are now accepting a common ground of argument: that work dissatisfaction is at the heart of blue collar alienation. We believe this premise is dangerously incomplete, regardless of who wins the debate. Our study shows that workers may indeed show great alienation from their work; yet they *still* feel "satisfied" with their job. They may see the need for more autonomy, more respect, and more chances to do what they are best at, but— unlike their older peers—these values no longer need to be exclusively or largely played out in the work setting. Leisure, community and special interest groups, and outside interests provide broader opportunities for the young worker to achieve satisfaction. Consequently, many see their work place as only one of a number of arenas where they can seek prestige and respect, and more and more they are devaluing its role and potential for providing such sources of gratification.

There are many forces in working-class life which sustain a value system in which authoritarianism flourishes. Among these is, first, *the insecurity of upward mobility based on income alone and not on education or occupational prestige.* Greater contact with more affluent middle class groups only heightens this insecurity, as does the threat that a decline in income means a drop to a lower class status. A second element in the authoritarian environment is the boredom of work relieved only by *stimulation from authoritarian of conflict-oriented interpersonal relations*. A third is the traditional *emphasis on individualism and autonomy*. These elements are fundamental in the blue collar philosophy. Blue collar workers know that the upper classes have more freedom of choice than they, yet they see no connection between success, power, freedom of choice and a democratic administrative structure. They need to have clear-cut rules and to "know where they stand." This authoritarian stance does not indicate indifference toward self-realization. Their authoritarian attitudes are independent of issues of dignity, autonomy and work satisfaction. Recognizing income as the only ladder they can climb, their attitudes are engendered by the ever-present threat that, with a loss in income, they might slip back even further. But blue collar life for young workers is not focused only on the work setting. Once they have a foothold on that income scale, what really counts is the capacity to be independent of others and to be able to act with an assurance of what the outcome will be.

Especially for the blue collar worker, the work setting is like a sieve, with larger community forces—his neighbors and his friends—passing through and across a highly permeable boundary. With such a wholeness to the environment, many of the positive and negative elements of the community come to be played out in the work setting. In this sense, race tensions, alienation from government and the sense of denied prestige are reflected in the work setting as much as they are generated there.

The deadening and dead-end character of many blue collar jobs become sources for maintaining traditional values among unchallenged minds and unrecognized bodies. Although sheer monotony alone does not generate a desire for rebellion, it does stimulate conflict within the authoritarian work setting. In other words, the very restrictiveness of a traditional work setting serves to maintain values of authoritarianism via a mechanism which Bruno Bettelheim described as the "identification with the aggressor process." And in this special milieu, political reaction is triggered as much by the sustaining role of alienation-generated authoritarianism as by the discontent with the job itself.

The MAR blue collar worker operates within a tradition of individualistic revolt in which group political action is atypical, even though such action may focus on specific leaders such as George Wallace or specific protest actions like those in the busing controversy. Clinging to tradition and alienated from his work, the blue collar worker is seeking action, but not necessarily to make his job "meaningful."

Our findings cast doubt on the proposition that modifying the characteristics of the job setting will either restore to many a central life interest in work, or provide a balanced work/leisure equilibrium. Image manipulation will not convince young blue collar workers that they have garnered real respect, power and economic security in the work environment; moreover, job satisfaction is not their main ambition.

Job "enrichment" must be viewed in terms of changing the individual's relationship to the total work organization, either by providing real opportunity for mobility to those who want it or by reducing job insecurity for the young worker whose interests lie elsewhere.

In this chapter we have reviewed a series of measures, first of general job satisfaction and then the specific attributes of the job and work organization. In a number of instances we have found that MARs are significant in their discontent and alienation from work and from the organization in which their job is performed. Therefore, we must add to our array of factors to be considered in the MAR syndrome a clear confirmation that the arena of work may be a source of affects which express themselves in other institutional spheres or the reverse may be true, namely, that the discontents and expectations developed from other community and institutional spheres find their way into the work place as an expression of discontent and alienation.

5. ORGANIZATIONAL CRITICISMS: MAJOR TARGETS AND GRIEVANCES

Institutional Alienation

We now come to the point of examining one of the major topics which was pursued in our national survey interview. As we have already indicated in the chapters dealing with the local environment and with the world of work, we asked people to assess a number of the key formal institutions of society. In the present chapter we shall examine the attitudes and perceptions respondents expressed concerning nine major social organizations.

We can compare the level of discontent between various groups by averaging the number of complaints toward each organization. Table 34 lists nine organizations in the order in which the highest number of criticisms appeared in the total sample of white interviewees. In every instance but one, MARs have a higher average number of criticisms than does any other population group.

Not only do the MARs exhibit a pattern of generalized discontent, the level of their criticism in some instances, such as that directed toward the federal government and welfare agencies, is especially high compared to other groups.

Unions, while receiving more criticism from MARs than from Low Income Americans, receive roughly comparable levels of criticism from Affluents and High Education Middles. Corporations, are criticized most by MARs and least by Low Income respondents. Local government seems to come in for particularly severe attack from MARs, compared to other popu-

TABLE 34

MEAN ALIENATION FROM ORGANIZATIONS
(AVERAGE NUMBER OF COMPLAINTS: RANGE 0–7)

	Low Income	MARs	Average Middles	High Education Middles	Affluents
National Government	3.1	4.7+	3.5	3.6	3.8
Welfare Agencies	2.4	4.0+	2.9	2.4	3.2
Unions	2.4	3.8+	3.0	3.3	3.5
Corporations	1.8	3.4+	2.7	2.7	2.7
Local Government	1.9	2.9+	2.0	1.9	1.6
Local Schools	1.7	2.1+	1.6	1.4	1.4
Own Workplace	1.1	1.8	1.3	1.6	1.2
Police	1.3	1.7	1.3	1.5	0.9
Churches	1.1	1.7	1.3	1.7	1.3

lation groups. The local police receive most criticism from MARs, and least from Affluents.

If we add the number of criticisms across all organizations listed and supply a summary index, we have a measure of the extensiveness of organizational alienation. Table 35 provides the fundamental data relative to such an analysis. Taking the upper range of the scale of total organizational alienation, we find that about 2 in 3 MARs have a "high" level of alienation. This is more than twice the level found for Low Income persons and a quarter more than for Average Middles, High Education Middles and Affluents. Looking at the opposite end of the scale, only about 1 in 9 MARs is in the bottom quartile of the organizational alienation score. This contrasts with better than 2 out of 5 Low Income Americans, a third of the Average Middles, a quarter of the High Education Middles, and a similar proportion

TABLE 35

ALIENATION FROM MAJOR INSTITUTIONS:
SCORE RANGE FOR ALL TYPES OF CRITICISMS

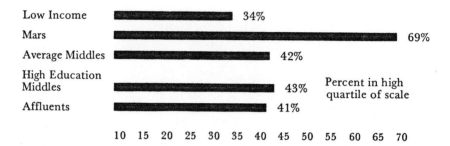

of Affluent Americans. Thus, our tabular findings dramatize the extent to which MARs are critical of the way social institutions function.

Let us pursue in detail our analysis of organizational alienation by selecting several kinds of structures which play important roles in both the community and the larger society. Table 36 presents an analysis of welfare agencies in terms of various criticisms. In 5 out of 8 instances, MARs are significantly more likely to be critical than are other population groups. In particular, lack of clear-cut policies, treating some people differently than others, not paying attention to needs, having too much power, and not showing respect are the dimensions especially subject to MAR wrath.

In examining attitudes toward unions, the pattern again reflects unique MAR alienation. Two areas of criticism which MARs stress are not emphasized by other groups. These are the views that unions do not have clear-cut policies and that people in charge are experiencing interference. These criticisms are significantly less frequent among Average Middles. We find, in contrast, the charge that unions have too much power—while shared by MARs—is more often emphasized by such groups as the Affluent and High Education Middles. In terms of unions being too big, MARs share a s...nilar perspective with Affluents. In regard to unions treating people differently, MARs share this

TABLE 36

DISSATISFACTIONS WITH WELFARE AGENCIES

	Low Income	MARs	Average Middles	High Education Middles	Affluents
Treat People Differently	49%	73%+	52%	42%	52%
No Clear-Cut Policies	44%	64%+	50%	48%	56%
Too Big	37%−	62%	48%	64%	64%
Don't Pay Attention	34%	57%+	41%	37%	39%
Too Much Power	33%	54%+	36%	25%	37%
Don't Show Respect	28%	49%+	32%	39%	36%
Interfered With	30%	39%	35%	36%	35%
Not Doing a Good Job	41%−	61%+	47%	57%	57%

view to a high degree with both the High Education Middles and Affluents. A similar pattern prevails in terms of unions "not paying attention to people like me."

Next we turn to group perceptions of corporations. MARs are significantly more likely to be critical of corporations on *all* dimensions in comparison to Average Middles. MAR criticism is unique in three instances: the charge that corporations are too big, that they lack clear-cut policies, and that they are experiencing interference. Although MARs lead the way in saying that corporations are not doing a good job, as we found in the case of unions, MARs are not distinctive in their criticism that corporations have too much power. In their evaluation of churches as organizations, MARs share the highest level of criticism with High Education Middles. It is interesting to note that despite their critical stance, MARs are only half as likely as High Education Middles to say that churches are not doing a good job.

We noted in the first tabular presentation of this chapter that

TABLE 37

DISSATISFACTIONS WITH UNIONS

	Low Income	MARs	Average Middles	High Education Middles	Affluent
Too Much Power	55%	69%	65%	75%	84%
Too Big	45%	60%+	51%	49%	59%
Treat People Differently	41%	60%+	46%	61%	62%
Don't Pay Attention to Me	38%	58%+	48%	55%	57%
No Clear-Cut Policies	36%	52%+	39%	28%	36%
Don't Show Respect	28%	47%+	35%	46%	44%
Interfered With	15%	32%	21%	16%	12%
Not Doing a Good Job	32%	50%+	41%	54%	58%

it is the federal government for whom the heaviest MAR criticism is reserved. Of the seven specific faults of social institutions, MARs on the average, listed nearly five for the government. What are the most prevalent complaints? Four out of five MARs believe the federal government does not treat everyone equitably. Roughly the same proportion feel the federal government does not "pay attention to what people like me want." Three out of four MARs say that the federal government does not follow clear-cut policies. In all three instances we have cited, MARs are significantly more critical than other groups.

There are two other unique concerns of the MAR: that the federal government does not treat people with respect, and that it is interfered with too much so that the people in charge cannot do their job. On an overall basis, MARs are the only group where a majority evaluate the federal government as "not doing a good job."

TABLE 38

DISSATISFACTIONS WITH CORPORATIONS

	Low Income	Average MARs	Middles	High Education Middles	Affluents
Too Much Power	40%	62%+	51%	58%	58%
Treat People Differently	33%	58%+	46%	55%	54%
Don't Pay Attention	36%	56%+	45%	51%	46%
Too Big	33%	52%+	40%	33%	37%
No Clear-Cut Policies	20%	41%+	28%	22%	26%
Don't Show Respect	18%	36%+	25%	35%	28%
Interfered With	16%	31%+	21%	15%	19%
Not Doing A Good Job	15%	35%+	23%	26%	24%

MARs also heavily criticize the federal government for being too big and too powerful. But these are not distinctive MAR concerns. Affluents and High Education Middles are equally concerned about these issues.

To illustrate our point further regarding the uniqueness of MARs' criticisms we have summarized the pattern across all nine institutions in order to show which dimensions met with a significantly higher level of criticism from MARs than from other groups.

Rules versus Flexibility

The institutional dimension most sharply separating MARs from other groups in terms of drawing criticism is "the lack of clear-cut policies". In 7 out of 9 instances, MARs are unique in their level of belief that this is true of organizations.

The MARs' view toward what has been called "normative flexibility" is such that, compared to lower status or higher

TABLE 39

DISSATISFACTIONS WITH CHURCHES

	Low Income	MARs	Average Middles	High Education Middles	Affluents
Treat People Differently	24%	35%+	27%	41%+	28%
No Clear-Cut Policies	17%	28%+	22%	32%	21%
Interfered With	18%	27%	20%	21%	14%
Don't Pay Attention	20%	24%+	17%	23%	24%
Too Big	15%	22%	16%	23%	25%
Too Much Power	17%	22%	17%	23%	14%
Don't Show Respect	8%	11%+	7%	8%	8%
Not Doing A Good Job	12%	17%	14%	36%	23%

status groups, they place great emphasis on the need for universal rules and clear, unambiguous standards of organizational and individual behavior. A prime instance of this attitude is reflected in the bitter West Virginia school textbook controversy. Alice Moore, a school board member who started the campaign during the summer of 1974, was quoted as follows:

> "I regret the things that have happened in the last few days [two men shot, one beaten, coal mines closed, businesses closed, Smith Transit damaged]," said Mrs. Moore, the wife of a fundamentalist Baptist preacher. "There is no justification for threats and violence. You can't lose everything you believe in in order to fight. You've got to hold on to the principles you believe in."
>
> "But how in the world could I not tell anybody what was wrong with those books," she asked. "How could I not tell parents the truth?"

Los Angeles Times, 9/15/74

TABLE 40

COMPLAINTS AGAINST THE NATIONAL GOVERNMENT
(PERCENT INDICATING EACH CRITICISM)

	Low Income	MARs	Average Middles	High Education Middles	Affluents
Treat People Differently	54%	81%	60%	60%	67%
Don't Pay Attention	62%	78%	60%	55%	53%
No Clear-Cut Policies	50%	75%	56%	60%	66%
Too Big	58%	74%+	61%	75%	78%
Too Much Power	40%	62%	51%	58%	58%
Interfered With	39%	53%	46%	38%	41%
Don't Show Respect	19%	38%	22%	20%	22%
Not Doing A Good Job	35%	58%	41%	42%	49%

As one journalist described the situation in West Virginia:

> *A considerable intellectual agility is required to maintain the proposition that community control of textbooks is fine for militant blacks in Manhattan, but altogether abhorrent for militant whites in Appalachia. The proposition is untenable. It might as well be abandoned.*

Los Angeles Times, *10/22/74*

One key figure in the textbook protest analyzed the situation in terms which pinpoint the general concern of MARs about universal rules:

> *Maybe it's the frustrations of the working class waging war against the professional class or the frustrations of parents who may be insecure about the control of their children. Sixty to seventy percent of this state is fundamentalist. . . . they take the Bible literally. With the swiftness of*

TABLE 41

COMPARISONS OF SEVEN DIMENSIONS OF ORGANIZATIONAL
CRITICISMS IN RELATION TO DISTINCTIVE CRITICISMS

	Number of times for the nine institutions listed Middle American Radicals are significantly above other segments of the white sample.
"They don't follow clear-cut policies."	7
"They don't treat people with respect."	6
"They don't pay attention to what people like me want."	5
"They are interfered with too much—the people in charge can't do their job right."	4
"They have too much power."	4
"They treat some people better than others."	4
"They are too big and complicated to be run well."	3

change maybe this kind of biblical literalism provides some symbol of stability that makes life make sense to them. To challenge that really creates an emotional issue, because you're challenging their last frontier of stability.

Washington Post, *10/24/74*

Organizational Disdain

The dimension of organizations "not treating people with respect" is the second most frequently defined distinctive MAR critique. Precisely this kind of perception has come to the fore in both the Boston busing and the West Virginia textbook battles:

One reason the textbook controversy became so bitter was that it was class warfare. The protesters implied in speeches and signs ("Even hillbillies have constitutional rights") that they had been ignored by the school board because it had contempt for them. . . . The protesters often said that they and their religious beliefs were being mocked by those who were educated or rich or powerful. They were right, of course. Their opponents called them "borned-again Christians" and "the Armies of Ignorance."

New Yorker, *9/30/74*

Organizational Neglect

Closely akin to the perceived lack of respect is the dimension dealing with organizations "not paying attention to what people like me want." This is the third most prevalent MAR criticism of social institutions.[28] Here is how one resident of Boston's "Southie" area puts it:

"Goddamit, I pay for this country out of my own pocket, but nobody gives a crud what I say."

One of the most militant of the West Virginia protesters shows the link between being ignored by government and a sense of disrespect for people:

"I drive a truck for a living, and I preach the gospel because the Lord called me." The people who found themselves negotiating with the school board on behalf of the protesters were poorly educated people and made no pretense of being anything else. What the boycotters were trying to do, one speaker said to the crowd that gathered outside the school administration offices during the negotiations, was "to get this government down to where they'll listen to us little old hillbillies."

New Yorker, *9/30/74*

The frustration felt by those unable to get the ear of government is voiced by a resident of the South Boston area:

"How far do you think we'd get if we wrote a letter to the editor?" grumps a man in a tam o'shanter at the South

Boston Information Center. "The highest up you get in this neighborhood is a cop. We got no open line to the mayor, you know. Sometimes you bust heads to get attention."

New York Times, *2/7/75*

The identical sense of being ignored is found in the West Virginia confrontation:

In a world where economic and political leaders often refer to them as "crazies," the protesters often found for the first time in their roving picket lines a way to make those leaders pay attention to what they have to say. ...

"They (politicians) never pay any attention to us," said a woman who declined to give her name. "The wealthy class parents, they don't care about their children. They have enough money to bail them out when they get in trouble. Working people like us, we don't have the money, so we have to care."

New Yorker, *9/30/74*

Diffuse Alienation: The Sense of Isolation

We have reviewed concerns dealing with work, the local environment, and major social institutions. In each case, there is evidence that MARs feel a unique sense of alienation. As we have seen, their three most prominent criticisms of organizations do not deal with the "greening-of-America" concerns about the size and overwhelming power of organizations. Not only do MARs share the criticisms frequently voiced by others, they also have their own set of special concerns as well. The failure of institutions to fulfill the expectations of MARs sometimes provides (as we see in Boston and West Virginia) a sense of militant protest. But for most MARs—at least from the vantage point of our core research—such failures may have other, more passive consequences.

It is quite clear from the sociological and social-psychological literature that a significant aspect of alienation involves social insularity: the estrangement that an individual feels from others whom he regards as significant persons. Afflicted with this sense of isolation, the individual confronts society and those around him in a framework of distrust and social disengagement.

In order to analyze the dimension of social isolation and "anomie" in our sample populations, several indicators were utilized. One of the most commonly employed measures in sociological literature is the Srole Anomie Scale. We chose one item from that scale: "These days a person doesn't know who he can count on," with the following results:

A majority, 51 percent, of MARs "strongly agree" with this statement. This is nearly twice the proportion of Average Middles, nearly three times the proportion of High Education Middles, and nearly five times the proportion of Affluent Americans who "strongly agree." Of special note is the fact that the Low Income Americans show a "strongly agree" response in only 37 percent of the cases.

The research literature measuring attitudes of anomie shows that higher social status is associated with low anomie and lower status with high anomie. A sense of generalized or diffuse alienation may be understood to be the same as anomie in the context in which we have discussed this outlook. MARs are high on such measures. Thus, we have a very useful index or indicator of the sort of "diffuse" alienation which is apparently felt by a number of individuals who are not at the bottom of the

TABLE 42

A MEASURE OF ANOMIE:
"THESE DAYS A PERSON DOESN'T REALLY KNOW
WHO HE CAN COUNT ON."

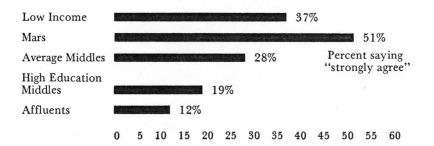

social scale, but who fit in the category of our MAR ideology group.

As a further indicator of MAR estrangement from society, we measured the extent to which major media are felt to be out of touch with one's group. The particular statement which we utilized is: "My views don't get fair treatment on television." The strength of MAR agreement with this statement is significant. Nearly three times as many MARs as Low Income Americans take such a view, while only 8.1 percent of Average Middles choose this alternative. Nearly 3 out of 5 MARs either strongly agree or agree that their views are not represented on television. This contrasts with only about a third of the Low Income group, 2 out of 5 of the Average Middles, and a similar proportion of High Education Middles and Affluents. This data again points up the diffuse alienation felt by the MARs.

Bitterness toward the local newspapers and electronic media has been sharply in evidence in both the Boston and West Virginia situations. On September 22, 1974, a thousand persons demonstrated against the *Boston Globe* with the slogan, "News Media Lie." At his trial for assaulting a cameraman, a major leader of the Boston anti-busing group—John Kerrigan—repeated his favorite epithet about the "Maggots of the Media."

TABLE 43

ATTITUDES TOWARD RESPONSIVENESS OF TV
TO RESPONDENTS' VALUES:
"MY VIEWS DON'T GET FAIR TREATMENT ON TELEVISION."

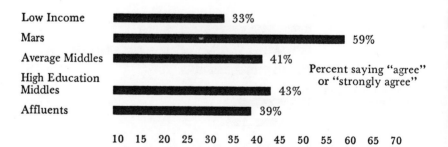

A *Washington Post* story described his "obscene gesture toward reporters sitting in the jury box."

In organizing his economic boycott against the *Globe,* Kerrigan boasted that:

> *I'm going full force on that [economic boycott]. I think you've done a lot to destroy the credibility of the* Globe. *It pleases me no end when the* Globe *had to put bullet-proof shields up and when the TPF [Tactical Patrol Force] had to stand guard at the* Globe *and not at the* Herald.

> New York Times, 7/24/74

In a *Ramparts* magazine analysis, the anti-media feelings are described:

> *The residents there were only made more furious by the lies of the Mayor's Office and the media, by being treated as children even in the throes of their worst tantrum in history. Fed up with the official "rumor control center," Southie parents moved to set up their own office with the telephone number BOY-COTT.*

> Ramparts, *December-January '75*

Distrust of Leaders:
A Key Element of MAR Alienation

In both the Boston busing controversy and earlier in the development of the National Action Group that grew out of the Pontiac, Michigan, busing tensions of 1970–71, the contact which many parents had with school officials led them to question how "authoritative" and truthful their public servants were. This same theme has come to the fore in the more recent West Virginia textbook fight:

> *"It's come to the point that we can't trust Superintendent Kenneth Underwood or the school board to do what's right,"* one protesting mother said today. *"After 30 days these filthy books can be right back in schools. We want them all out now."*

> Washington Post, *9/19/74*

If, as we have indicated, the sense of targeted alienation from a variety of social institutions characterizes the MAR, and further, if the sense of futility and isolation from society is one concomitant of such feelings, then we should find that not even cherished institutions escape MAR wrath. Let us take, for instance, the involvement in the Viet Nam war. At the time of our survey, the withdrawal process had been underway but was far from complete. On the war itself, a majority of MARs agreed that "our main problem in Viet Nam is the lack of patriotism in the United States." (See Appendix: Table 5.) The kind of "super patriotism" generally associated with "Middle Americans" would certainly seem evident in these responses. An example from the West Virginia setting catches this spirit as well:

> *The most outspoken (demonstrator) was Linda Hapney, a petite mother of an 11-year-old son, who said she wants a return to basic education without too much interpretive or depressing material. "These books say our flag is just a piece of cloth, just a rag and you can step on it and it doesn't matter. I say it stands for all our freedom and all the great things we have in America."*

Chicago Tribune, *10/30/74*

But does this sense of pride in America prevent the MAR from having a deep alienation from national leaders? Does it grant them a kind of immunity out of reverence for authority? Our study indicates that the answer is an emphatic "no." Here lies the paradox about MARs which has lead many observers to misinterpret the "silent majority." Data in Table 44 about the Viet Nam war points up the issue: A majority of MARs—nearly 3 out of 5—"strongly agree" that "you can't trust the leadership in Washington to tell you the truth about the Viet Nam war." Even the generally anti-war High Education Middles show only 32 percent strong agreement here. Bear in mind that these replies were made before Watergate, before the CIA investigations, and prior to the resignation of Spiro Agnew.[29]

In both the Boston and West Virginia protests, the theme of a radicalized distrust of community leaders—of schools, the church and local government—has emerged in sharp focus. This

TABLE 44

ALIENATION FROM THE NATIONAL GOVERNMENT:
"YOU CAN'T TRUST THE LEADERSHIP IN WASHINGTON TO
TELL YOU THE TRUTH ABOUT THE VIET NAM WAR."

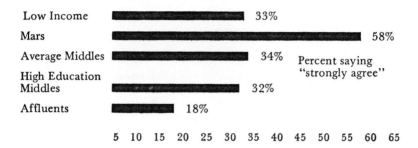

Low Income	33%
Mars	58%
Average Middles	34%
High Education Middles	32%
Affluents	18%

Percent saying "strongly agree"

5 10 15 20 25 30 35 40 45 50 55 60 65

description of alienation from the church in South Boston is a
case in point:

> The worst of the current impasse is that the community
> feels betrayed by its most trusted institutions. Southies have
> always loved their politicians, but now they hear only in-
> effectual slogans. The police, many of whom grew up in the
> community, were also local allies; now the popular local
> hangout, the Rabbit Inn, has been made a shambles by the
> Tactical Police Force—and the battered door still bears a
> sticker that says, "Support Your Local Police." Even the
> church has turned away: Catholic students boycotting the
> public schools have been refused admittance to the parochial
> system and not a single priest has agreed to lead an anti-
> busing prayer meeting. "Everyone left us really down in the
> dumps," said Pat Harvey. A mother named Mary Whittington
> added, "I've given up on my church."
>
> "Bad Times in Southie"
> Newsweek, 10/21/74

Even more pointed in its distrust of church, national and local
leaders is this description from Boston:

> Many Southie Irish Catholics feel betrayed by their own
> leaders: Humberto Cardinal Madeiros, who has given strong

*moral support to the busing plan and refuses to let parents
enroll their children in parochial schools just to avoid it;
Senator Edward Kennedy, whose pro-busing stand made him
a target for curses and raw eggs at a recent anti-busing rally;
and Mayor White, who is often referred to in Southie as
Mayor Black.*

"From the Schools to the Streets,"
Time, *10/21/74*

In the West Virginia textbook controversy we find the same
theme reiterated:

*It is a controversy that raised the questions of who has the
right to determine what children learn—their parents or professional educators.*

*On one side of the issue are the professionals, like School
Superintendent Kenneth Underwood, who believes in the
educator's responsibility to select a curriculum for the public
schools. It should be "multicultural and multiethnic and it
should reflect the world as it is."*

*On the other side are protesters like Phyllis Harmon of St.
Albans who has kept her two daughters out of school since
September. Mrs. Harmon believes it is her responsibility, not
Underwood's, to determine what her children will read.*

*"We're the ones who worked and raised our children and
suffered the pain of bearing them. When something like this
arises and you can't get the kind of education you want for
them it really riles you up."*

Washington Post, *10/24/74*

Perhaps the *New Yorker* article by Calvin Triller has the most
succinct grasp of the underlying issue:

*[Textbook protest] leaders claimed not that they were
more expert than the teachers who chose the books but that
experts were not to be trusted.*

New Yorker, *9/30/74*

The aftermath of this realization in South Boston is described
this way:

*Southie has had little but its myths and its heroes to
sustain it for the last few years, but those myths are being*

exposed and now the community is finding that its heroes
have feet of clay. The people of South Boston always
thought they could rely on the Catholic church and their
politicians to protect and care for them. . . .

Southie didn't know, doesn't know, where to turn for
help, or quite where to vent its fury.

                                    "Busing: A Symposium,"
                                    Ramparts, *12/74*

MAR Alienation: Summing Up the Contradictions

In this chapter we have reviewed evidence that a wide range
of discontents exists among a large segment of our society.
Whether or not this discontent will lead to widespread protest
actions is highly problematic. In subsequent chapters we shall
analyze the extent to which MARs and other groups have, in
the past, taken steps to respond to their problems.

Our findings point toward important dimensions of social
policy. The discontent about our major organizations and institutions must be met and so must the MAR attitude about what
organizations should do vis-à-vis other population groups. We
shall return to this theme and to the policy implications of
multiple views of desired organizational behavior. The challenge
to both the operating agency as well as to those designing
national and community programs for public institutions is a
substantial one.

MARs believe that formal organizations do not hold to clear-
cut policies (perhaps because of rule-bending minorities) and are
not responsive to MAR concerns (perhaps because the goals
have been confused by both government and minority influence). However, they do not want these organizations to become smaller or to be restructured. Instead, they want new
leaders who will institute and adhere to equitable rules directed
toward realistic goals. Out of this desire stems the MARs'
growing impulse to take some type of action.

The rise and sustenance of the MAR ideology derives in large
measure from the continuing clash of social principles in which
basic group interests are at stake. Nor are these interests abstrac-

tions. They are investments that represent the capital accumulation of years of work, home, savings and family educational aspirations. If the MAR views the major function of large scale institutions to be the upholding and promulgation of universal rules, then the adoption by such structures of other goals is at the heart of MAR alienation. In our core study, we did not devote specific attention to the special role which the court system plays in supporting or denying the rule-generating functions of unions, the government and related institutions. There is no doubt that the courts have played a crucial role, implicitly or explicitly, in generating MAR attitudes and reactions.

A clear instance of the kind of clash in social principles that has spawned the MAR perspective occurred in Detroit, early in 1975. A complex court battle developed around one of the most visible of local institutions: the police. The problem centered on the action by the mayor of Detroit—Coleman Young—to reduce both police and fire department services in the face of the declining revenues of the city. Early in April of 1975, the announcement was made that more than five hundred officers would have to be laid off. Serious protest was entered by the DPOA (Detroit Police Officers Association), stressing the harm to those who would suffer job loss. As the day for the department cuts approached, two separate court actions were entered. The first was on behalf of all the black officers who would be affected, and the second was on behalf of women police officers. The injunctions were filed in separate courts, with specific briefs charging that the "affirmative action" efforts which had brought substantial increases in the proportions of both female and minority personnel to the police department would be undermined. The argument was essentially that a higher proportion of non-white, male officers would be laid off due to the seniority principle on which the mayor's original order was based.

After the court actions were entered, Young—the first black mayor of Detroit—announced that the layoff instead of affecting 313 blacks and 210 women, would be confined to 550 white male officers. Young was quoted as saying that his rationale for the revised order was: "I'm not going to put myself in the position of being in contempt of a federal court order on a civil rights issue."[30] Thus, the issue was drawn in a uniquely sharp way: seniority versus overcoming social inequity. All of this action took place at a time when a majority of both black and white families in Detroit opposed busing to achieve integration, and yet a court action ordering busing was moving toward specific implementation.

One can only guess at the seething felt by MARs in this situation. The relative quiescence was due perhaps to the severe economic squeeze felt by Detroit residents. Many families with a MAR orientation were struggling for economic survival and that may have prevented massive action to protect their group interests.

Not all of the MAR discontent will boil over into visible and direct action social protest. At present we see only those which capture media attention. But the stormy and spasmodic character of such open battles gives a false perspective. MAR alienation is a truly endemic force in American society. It will be expressed in arenas and on issues far beyond those we have been able to draw upon in our study. Indeed, the very submergence of the MAR consciousness may be its most pervasive influence on our society. We shall return to this issue of the diffusive pattern of the MAR perspective when we discuss additional survey data collected in the early part of 1975.

6. SOCIAL PARTICIPATION
AND POLITICAL MOBILIZATION

If MARs do not find effective ways to express themselves within the system, how will their frustration manifest itself? What outlet will be found and what effects will be felt on the political scene? Can MARs become an effective force in changing our society? On what organizational bases can they build?

Before responding to any of these questions, we must recall that MARs have had two main organizations as their advocates, the labor movement on the one hand and the church on the other. Both the union movement and the church (and here I am speaking of the Roman Catholic Church particularly) are very large-scale, universal organizations. They tend to operate on the notion that there is a set of important principles with universal appeal. The MAR is particularly concerned about the need to have a very structured orientation to the world, and no doubt for some very good reasons. As a group MARs have only recently emerged from poverty. They have derived stability and representation by allegiance to union and church. However, as these institutions have undergone change, MARs no longer view them as their "own" advocates and they are looking for new organizations which can really serve their interests. The question becomes "What sort of organization would this be?" The answer may emerge from studying past patterns of MAR participation and mobilization.

Use of Organizational Resources

Let us turn to the more formal aspects of social involvement and participation, specifically membership in voluntary associations (see Appendix: Table 16). In Table 45 we have summarized the number of memberships reported by different segments of the population. Not surprisingly, the overwhelming majority of all population segments belong to at least one organization. However, the difference between the groups is extensive. Thus, 20 percent of Low Income Americans have no organizational memberships compared with only 1 percent of Affluent Americans. In terms of having a multiple membership pattern—that is, belonging to two or more organizations—we find that the Affluents are significantly higher than other groups. Thus, 63 percent of this group has four or more memberships. This is nearly twice the proportion for High Education Middles, three times the proportion for Average Middles and MARs and six times the proportion of Low Income Americans.

The MARs' pattern of formal group memberships more closely resembles that of the Low Income American than that of the Affluent American. About three out of five MARs have

TABLE 45

NUMBER OF ORGANIZATIONAL MEMBERSHIPS

	Low Income	MARs	Average Middles	High Education Middles	Affluents
Four +	10%	24%	21%	37%	63%
Three	11%	16%	18%	23%	17%
Two	24%	21%	25%	15%	11%
One	33%	27%	25%	14%	8%
None	21%	13%	11%	11%	1%
Not Ascertained	1%	0%	0%	0%	0%
Total	100%	100%	100%	100%	100%
Mean Number	1.6	2.4	2.3	2.9	3.9

two organizational memberships. This contrasts with about nine out of ten Affluent Americans and three out of four High Education Middles.

In terms of MARs versus Average Middles, their organizational membership differentials are quite small. Thus, both groups have a similar mean number of associational memberships, 2.4 versus 2.3. These are roughly in the middle between the Low Income person (1.6) and the Affluent American (3.9).

MARs have a high level of membership in labor unions and resemble Average Middles and Low Income Americans to some extent in their affiliations with fraternal lodges, veterans organizations and church groups. Although MARs are twice as likely as Low Income respondents to be members of social action groups, they are only one-fourth as involved in such groups as are High Education Middles and only one-fifth as active as Affluents in this area. A similar gap exists in political memberships.

If we view the process of effective political action as one which begins with an initial utilization of community institutions, we then need to examine the role of individual contact with such structures. The participants in the 1972 survey were asked the following question:

In the last few years have you or your family ever contacted any of the following . . . to get information or to get something done?

A total of 14 types of groups were mentioned. In several instances, MARs have significantly greater contact with organizations than do Low Income Americans. At the same time, both Affluent and High Education Middles have a significantly greater degree of contact with organizations than do MARs.

We find a pattern in which MARs more closely resemble Low Income Americans in terms of the following types of organizational contacts: with a U.S. government official, with state officials, contact with the media, neighborhood associations, civic groups, social action groups and ethnic organizations. In all of these instances, while MARs do show contact at approximately twice the level as that indicated by Low Income Americans, there is at least another doubling of the proportion of contact for High Education Middles and Affluents.

In examining differences between Middle Americans and Average Middles, the pattern we find is one of relatively slight variation with a significant difference occurring in only two instances. The first has to do with contacting friends "who have influence with important people." In this case, 23 percent of the MAR group mentioned such contacts, compared with only 14 percent of Average Middles. This level of contact by MARs begins to approach the level manifested for the same kind of contact by High Education Middles and Affluents.

By contrast, if we examine contact with a social action group, we find that MARs, while they do show greater contact than Average Middles (6 percent versus 4 percent), this same level is only one-fifth that manifested by High Education Middles. At the same time, MARs have contact with unions in 1 out of 5 cases compared with about 1 in 8 for High Education Middles. This is the only instance in which MARs exceed High Education Middles in the level of organizational or individual contact. (See Appendix: Table 17.)

In terms of highly specialized types of contact with organizations, MARs do approximate some of the higher status groups. In a wide variety of other contacts the pattern seems to be consistently lower than either High Education Middles or Affluent Americans. At the same time, we find that Middle Americans are significantly more likely to contact particular structures than are Low Income Americans. These include local school officials, the local police, religious groups, U.S. government as well as local government and state officials, influential people, the media, labor unions, neighborhood associations and city groups. In the case of social action groups and ethnic organizations, MARs show about the same level of use of such institutions as do Low Income respondents.

On the basis of multiple organizational contacts—that is, two or more—the difference between MARs and Average Middles becomes statistically significant. In the first instance, 61 percent took at least two actions compared to 54 percent of Average Middles. In the number of organizational contacts, MARs came closer to the pattern manifested by High Education Middles than to the pattern for Low Income Americans. (See Appendix: Table 18.)

Affluent Americans are markedly different from other groups in the extent and variety of organizational contacts. When compared to MARs, the Affluents are twice as likely to report contact with union officials, about twice as likely to say that they have contacted a United States government official or the mass media. In the case of neighborhood associations, Affluents report such contacts 37 percent of the time compared with only 11 percent for MARs. In the category of civic groups, the ratio is four to one in favor of Affluent Americans. In the case of social action groups and ethnic groups, both the Affluent and the High Education Middles show a dramatically greater level of contact than do MARs.

Thus, if we were to make an initial assessment of the potential for MARs to take effective political action, we would have to say that to date this seems to be limited to highly individual and informal modes of contact and not based upon experience in dealing with specific institutions and groups whose purposes are political in a direct sense. Yet MARs seem more willing to seek the help of organizations than to participate in associations.

Individual Political Actions

Organizational "savoir-faire" may be one step toward direct political activity. To gauge such efforts and contacts with political structures, we asked the following question:

Here are several different things people say they have done to call attention to a problem or to get something done. Have you ever done any of these things?

The list included a total of eight actions ranging from writing complaint letters to picketing or to engaging in a boycott effort. In Table 46 we have the pattern of responses in regard to each of the types of political actions. Differences between MARs and other groups emerge into two patterns: first, MARs tend to

TABLE 46

TYPES OF POLITICAL ACTIONS TAKEN INDIVIDUALLY

	Low Income	MARs	Average Middles	High Education Middles	Affluents
Signed a Petition About Some Issue	41%	53%	56%	74%	74%
Wrote a Complaint Letter or Letter to the Editor	10%	13%	15%	34%	36%
Contacted an Official About Some Action or Policy	20%	36%	26%	53%	59%
Helped Get Court Action to Change a Policy or Program	5%	7%	6%	13%	21%
Helped Pay for a Political Ad in the Newspaper	5%	5%	7%	21%	26%
Took Part in a Boycott Effort	5%	5%	7%	18%	14%
Picketed an Agency or Organization	2%	4%	5%	3%	3%
Went on an Action March	6%	3%	2%	13%	8%

resemble Low Income Americans more closely than Affluents in six of the eight specifically listed actions. In comparison with Average Middles, however, we find no significant differences on any of the specific types of political action with the exception of contacting an official about some action or policy.

Thus, in the list of more direct forms of political influence, and particularly in the case of collective actions, we find that MARs are slightly below the levels indicated for Average Middles. In the case of such collective action as boycotting, going on action marches, or other types of collective action, they are about a third as likely to have engaged in such activities as High Education Middles. In the case of action marches, the Low Income group reports a slightly higher percentage than do the MARs. Overall, Low Income respondents are significantly below MARs in only two instances: that of having signed a petition about an issue or in contacting an official about some action.

Probability of Collective Action

Given the level of past organizational contact and political activism, one might reasonably ask: "What mobilizing factors provide a good basis for predicting how people are likely to act in the future?" The evidence that we have presented thus far in our analysis suggests that MARs as a group—while having slightly more organizational contacts than Low Income Americans—are far less likely to be active politically than are the High Education Middles or Affluents. In this sense, both the Boston and West Virginia conflicts might be extremes—atypical of the MAR readiness to act collectively.

Our evidence suggests that the process of mobilization needs careful scrutiny. For example, Table 47 shows the responses that individuals made to the following statement: "Before joining a group it is important to find out if people with respectable social positions belong to it." In effect, this statement implies that one should be cautious in entering into group action or at least make sure that it is legitimate or certified by prestigious individuals.

We note that nearly one out of five MARs strongly agree that one should find out before joining if respected people belong to the organization. This is significantly more than either Average Middles, Low Income Americans or other groups. At the same time, we note that while 46 percent of MARs either strongly agree or agree with this statement, so do 41 percent of Low Income Americans.

TABLE 47

BARRIERS TO ORGANIZATIONAL ACTION:
"BEFORE JOINING A GROUP IT IS IMPORTANT TO FIND OUT
IF PEOPLE WITH RESPECTED SOCIAL POSITION BELONG TO IT."

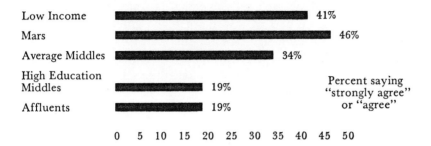

Low Income	41%
Mars	46%
Average Middles	34%
High Education Middles	19%
Affluents	19%

Percent saying
"strongly agree"
or "agree"

0 5 10 15 20 25 30 35 40 45 50

To a degree, MARs share with Low Income Americans a reluctance to join in groups without having some form of certification associated with prestigious members. The sort of diffuse alienation described in the earlier text is consistent with MARs' general lack of readiness to join in with regard to collective behavior.

We would argue that before people can or will respond to their discontent through a form of organized activity, they must first believe that collective effort can be *effective* in problem solving. We have seen that MARs are clearly not unwilling to join in such efforts, but in order to do so they feel there must be some authoritative or prestigious legitimation. A measure of the attitude of interest or recognition of the necessity of collective action is expressed in the following statement to which we asked respondents to react: "Nowadays in America to get anywhere you need to be part of a well organized group." This statement by itself may only measure the extent to which people perceive that others who have "gotten anywhere" have had to be organized in some collective way. It may not imply that one believes that about one's self. But, at the same time, if a person agrees with such a statement, it does suggest at least an initial recognition that individual problems require collective action.

Table 48 shows that MARs, in 1 out of 3 cases, strongly agree to the need to be part on an organized group. This is twice the proportion found among Low Income Americans and three times that among High Education Middles. It is more than four times the proportion found among Affluents. More than two-thirds of the MARs at least agree that in order to get anywhere a person must be part of a well-organized group. This is a view which is shared by a significantly smaller proportion of all but the Low Income group. Thus, we have some evidence that both Low Income and MARs tend to see themselves needing some form of collective organization.

Reference Groups as the Basis for Mobilization

In a complex and highly differentiated society such as the United States, group relationships emerge not only from family, neighbor, job and similar traditional roles, but from a wide variety of other settings as well. There are likely to be strong group identifications in the world of leisure, in sharing hobbies or special interests, and to some extent in common regional backgrounds. In order to probe this diversity of primary group ties, we listed a series of such identities and asked respondents the following question:

TABLE 48

NEED TO BE PART OF A GROUP:
"NOWADAYS IN AMERICA TO GET ANYWHERE
YOU NEED TO BE PART OF A WELL-ORGANIZED GROUP."

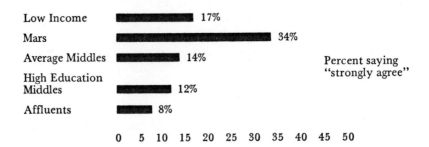

*Besides friends and relatives people sometimes feel a special
closeness because they have a lot in common with others of
the same nationality, religion, line of work, or those who are
living in the same neighborhood or community. Do you have
this feeling of special closeness to any of the following
groups?*

We listed a total of nine types of groups and then asked
respondents to indicate those for which they felt "a special
closeness." Table 49 summarizes the pattern of responses. Inter-
estingly, it was not neighborhood or social class grouping but a
sense of having similar interests or activities that emerged as the
most frequent source of closeness. High Education Middles and

TABLE 49

TYPES OF GROUPS RESPONDENT FEELS CLOSE TO

	Low Income	MARs	Average Middles	High Education Middles	Affluents
People with the Same Interests or Activities	75%	79%	80%	94%	88%
Race	56%	68%	61%	46%	46%
Your Neighbors	64%	56%	54%	44%	47%
People in the Same Line of Work	46%	48%	51%	71%	62%
People from the Same Section of Country	39%	48%+	37%	45%	39%
Religion	42%	46%	41%	47%	42%
People with the Same Income	42%	45%	41%	38%	35%
Same Education	41%	42%+	36%	57%	44%
Same Nationality	38%	42%+	31%	26%	28%

Affluents especially chose this kind of primary group identification while a significantly smaller proportion of Low Income,
MARs and Average Middles did so.

The second most frequently mentioned source of closeness
was that of race. MARs, even more than Average Middles, are to
a significant degree more likely than other groups to mention
this as a basis of closeness.

Neighbors were the third most frequent source of closeness
and it is notable that the Low Income group stands out as
particularly high in this regard. MARs, while significantly lower
than Low Income Americans in their feeling of closeness with
neighbors, are nevertheless more likely than the remaining
groups to build close ties with neighbors.

If we compare the five population groups we have employed
in a substantial part of our analysis we now come up with a
highly differentiated pattern. Table 50 contains the relevant
findings. For MARs there is a significantly greater identification
with a racial group than for Low Income Americans, High
Education Middles or Affluent Americans. In the category of
nationality, MARs are higher than other groups although the
differences are not statistically significant. For religious identification we find that High Education Middles show the greatest
such identification and the difference between themselves and
MARs is statistically significant. To a significant degree MARs
are the least likely not to have either a religious, nationality or
racial group as the one they feel closest to. Table 50, then, has
shown that for MARs there is a special role to "ascribed" social
groups—those identities which are not readily created, changed
or discarded.

The emphasis which MARs place on ethnic and racial ties has
implications for the way in which more traditional and "visible"
ethnic and racial minorities may compare. Therefore, one perspective on the MAR phenomenon is to view it as yet another
new group consciousness, albeit one formed out of the other
ethno-religious groupings. One might well ask: "As a social
group are MARs more similar to the white majority of the
society or to more conventional minorities?" Data from the
national survey permits some response to the query. The an-

TABLE 50

GROUP IDENTIFICATION FOR THE FIVE POPULATION SEGMENTS

	Low Income	MARs	Average Middles	High Education Middles	Affluents
Feel Closest to a Racial Group	25%	34%	30%	20%	23%
Nationality Group	9%	13%	10%	9%	8%
Religious Group	26%	22%	24%	31%	26%
None of These-Closest to Class, Region, Same Interests, Etc.	36%	25%	33%	36%	38%
Don't Know, Not Ascertained	4%	5%	3%	5%	4%
Total	100% (N=314)	100% (N=496)	100% (N=521)	100% (N=112)	100% (N=178)

swers which both black and chicano individuals gave to the question about "feeling closest" lead to a tentative conclusion that indeed MARs resemble such groups more than they do other whites. Table 51 provides the tabular results. MARs, in nearly 1 out of 2 instances, identify their closest group as either racial or nationality; for blacks the proportion is exactly half; for chicanos it is nearly 3 out of 5. By contrast, non-MAR whites say their closest group is a racial or nationality link 35 percent of the time.

Stages of Group Identification

What is the relationship between individual identity and social action? Andrew Greeley,[31] in his discussion of the various stages through which ethnic groups pass in their progression toward some form of assimilation or economic security, sug-

TABLE 51

PERCENT OF RESPONDENTS WHO FEEL CLOSEST TO A NATIONALITY
OR RACIAL GROUPS: MAR'S, BLACKS, CHICANOS, AND OTHERS

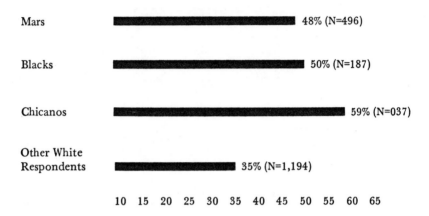

gests a line of fruitful inquiry. Greeley argues that there are distinct problems which ethnic groups focus on at different time periods and that the form of organization as well as the content of values may change from stage to stage.

In his formulation Greeley indicates six phases of ethnic group evolution: a) initial "cultural shock" based upon migration and disruption of previous life styles; b) "organization and emerging self-consciousness;" c) "assimilation of the elite" members of the group; d) militancy where direct protest actions are developed; e) "self-hatred and anti-militancy," and, finally, f) "emerging adjustment" where the ethnic group member neither seeks a separate group life from the larger society nor is restricted by the larger society in the pursuit of ethnic heritage and consciousness which may have been denied in earlier stages.

We are not able, given the nature of our sample, to completely test such a hypothesis, yet an approximation to the

Greeley ethnic group stages was developed. We asked all of our respondents who indicated that they felt close to a nationality, religious or racial group to respond to the following questions:

Let us consider a group you felt close to. Could you tell me which of the things on this card best fit where they stand today?"

We then listed a series of alternative stages which the individual could select. These included the following:

1. "We should organize to protect ourselves against unfair treatment."
2. "We are just beginning to get recognized and organized."
3. "We already have some power and recognition mostly because of a few people at the top."
4. "We have a lot of recognition and power. We are united and struggling for our rights."
5. "We don't have to struggle so much any more—we are confident and don't have to care what others are doing."

In addition, there were two alternatives which could be interpreted in the first instance as a sort of pre-ethnic consciousness—"we just enjoy spending time with ourselves instead of others." In addition, individuals could indicate that none of the six possible stages applied to their particular group.

We find several diverse patterns: a significantly larger proportion of MARs as compared with every other population group indicates that they are in an early stage of militancy; that is, they feel they should organize or they are beginning to organize and have some power. This represents 21 percent of the individuals in the MAR grouping in contrast to only 8 percent of Average Middles.

In terms of being in a "late" (in Greeley's sequence) stage of ethnic group organization, we find a steady increase from the Low Income group to the Affluent group. Thus, 19 percent of affluents compared to only 12 percent of Low Income respondents say that they are either united and struggling or they are confident and do not have to worry about what others think. Among Affluents, when we compare those regarding themselves in later group stages with those in early militant stages, the ratio

TABLE 52

STAGES OF GROUP CONSCIOUSNESS: WHERE RESPONDENT IS CLOSEST TO A NATIONALITY, RACE OR RELIGIOUS GROUP

	Low Income	MARs	Average Middles	High Education Middles	Affluents
Should Organize	6% } 11%	14% } [21%]	4% } 8%	3% } 12%	4% } 7%
Beginning or Already Have Some Power	5%	7%	4%	9%	3%
United and Struggling	6% } 12%	6% } 13%	9% } 16%	6% } 15%	9% } 19%
Confident, Don't Worry About Others	6%	7%	7%	9%	10%
Just Enjoy Being Together	16%	19%	18%	13%	10%
None of These Apply To Us	56%	44%–	55%	55%	59%
Don't Know, Not Ascertained	5%	4%	4%	5%	6%
Total	100% (N=187)	100% (N=347)	100% (N=330)	100% (N=067)	100% (N=103)

is approximately 3 to 1 in favor of "comfortable" perceptions. The ratio for Average Middles is about 2 to 1 and that for MARs tends to be reversed: 20 percent in the early militant stage and 12 percent in the later, more confident stages. For those designating racial identity as the basis of their closest group even fewer saw themselves in a "comfortable" stage of development.

In Table 53 we have taken the MARs, other white respondents, blacks and chicanos who picked a stage of group development and compared them in terms of perceived stage of their group. In terms of viewing themselves as being in an early militant stage, MARs are closer to chicanos and blacks than are other white Americans. The difference between MARs and chicanos is only 10 percent and that between blacks and MARs in only 3 percent.

TABLE 53

STAGES OF GROUP DEVELOPMENT FOR BLACKS, CHICANOS,
MARs, AND OTHER WHITE RESPONDENTS (WHERE RESPONDENT
FEELS CLOSEST TO A RACIAL OR NATIONALITY GROUP)

	Other Whites	MARs	Chicanos	Blacks
Should Organize	11%	25%	15%	28%
We're Beginning or Already Have Some Power	5%	5%	25%	34%
United Struggling	5%	8%	10%	9%
We are Confident and Don't Worry About Others	21%	11%	5%	10%
We Just Enjoy Being Together	40%	38%	25%	15%
None of these Apply To Us	18%	13%	20%	4%
Total	100% (N=296)	100% (N=191)	100% (N=20)	100% (N=128)

While many blacks feel that they do have some power, whites in general and MARs in particular are not likely to hold this view. If we combine "early" and "later" militant group stages, MARs resemble chicanos more than others: 38 percent say they should or are already organizing compared to 50 percent for chicanos, 71 percent for blacks, and only 21 percent for non-MAR whites.

Given the level of past organizational contact and political activism and a sense of militant ethnic group identity, one might reasonably ask, "Do these background factors provide a good basis for predicting how people are likely to act in the future?" The evidence that we have presented thus far in our analysis suggests that MARs as a group—while having slightly more organizational contacts than Low Income Americans—are far less likely to be active politically than are the High Education or Affluent. At the same time, the phenomenon of MAR alienation is one which has been extremely visible in the sense that this group is on the verge of or in the process of being highly mobilized. (See Appendix: Table 19.) One of the most visible expressions of this, of course, has been such actions as the NAG movement in Pontiac, Michigan, busing protests in Boston, and actions against textbooks in West Virginia.

In order to tap the extent to which individuals support various kinds of protest actions dealing with the problems of middle income people, we asked a series of questions and posed some hypothetical situations. The first set of measures having to do with likely support for political action included those dealing with a series of movements which have been reported in the press at various times. We introduced these situations with this statement:

> *The following are some instances which have occurred at one time or another. Can you tell me if you strongly approve, approve, disapprove or strongly disapprove of the various actions taken?*

The first of these situations involved workers on strike. Table 54 shows the different segments as they responded to this situation. We distinctly found that the middle income

TABLE 54

LEGITIMATION OF DIRECT ACTION BY VARIOUS GROUPS IN SOCIETY
"The following are some incidents which have occurred at one
time or another. Can you tell me whether you strongly approve or approve of the various actions taken?"

	Low Income	MARs	Average Middles	High Education Middles	Affluents
Workers on strike keep people from entering a plant	18%	27%	27%	15%	10%
Taxpayers in the middle income group, who feel they are paying more then their fair share of taxes, go to the state capitol and stop legislative sessions	20%	41%	22%	26%	14%
A group of women, who feel that a magazine is discriminating against hiring women, organizes a picket line and stops publication of the magazine	13%	19%	15%	19%	10%
Blacks, who feel they are being discriminated against by a local company, set up picket lines and keep people from entering the plant	7%	9%	11%	21%	10%
When police don't stop crime in a neighborhood people set up their own police patrol	36%	43%	39%	47%	47%

groups—as reflected by MARs and Average Middles—were
most likely to support the action of the strikers. Significantly
fewer Low Income, High Education Middles and, particularly, Affluents indicated approval of this same action. This
certainly reflects the self-interests of the different segments
of the population.

Yet another situation which seemed particularly to reflect
the mood of the MAR is the basis of the following statement:

> *Taxpayers in the middle income group, who feel they are
> paying more than their fair share of taxes, go to the state
> capitol and stop legislative sessions.*

This instance of a taxpayer revolt showed a very significantly
differential reaction among the national sample. Rather than
Average Middles and MARs taking a similar view, we find that
nearly twice as many MARs supported this action as Average
Middles—41 percent versus 22 percent.

Using three other situations we tapped the degree to which
various groups were willing to legitimate the actions of organized minorities. In the first of these the statement read:

> *A group of women, who feel a magazine is discriminating
> against hiring women, organizes a picket line and stops pub-
> lication of the magazine.*

Support for this action is about equal among the three
middle income groups. It is at the extremes of the social
structure that we find the lowest support for protest action by
women.

The most directly racial situation involved blacks setting up
picket lines as a protest against discrimination. A lower proportion of MARs—9 percent—support this compared to 19 percent
for women's protest action. But the same is also true for Low
Income Americans—7% versus 13%. Only High Education
Middles were equal in their support for direct action by blacks
and women to end discrimination—19% and 21% respectively.

One of the situations which has occurred in a number of
communities is the need to take some action outside of the
established police structure to deal with crime. A very large
proportion of all population groups support people setting up

their own police patrol when the police do not stop crime in their neighborhood. MARs are not unique in their approval of this action. In fact, both High Education Middles and Affluents surpass MARs in the degree of their support.

Thus, of all the situations which we listed to measure the legimitization people gave to direct action, it was the taxpayer revolt situation which produced the most distinctive MAR response. Nearly twice as many MARs as Average Middles approved this action, thus giving further credence to the image of MARs as feeling overburdened with taxes in proportion to direct benefits derived therefrom.

Taking an across-the-board look at legitimation of direct action, we can see more clearly the potential for MAR mobilization. Very few of the respondents in all categories legitimate all four situations. But the 29 percent of MARs who legitimate three out of the four is the highest score of any group and is significantly greater than the 19 percent for Average Middles. High Education Middles also show a high level of legitimation for several of the direct actions. The groups least likely to legitimate three or more such actions were Low Income and Affluent Americans.

Busing as a Focus
of MAR Legitimation of Direct Action

We find perhaps the most visible and stereotyped set of direct action concerns is in the area of school busing. This controversy, although somewhat ameliorated by the actions of Congress and the slowing down of pressures to integrate schools, remains a "hot issue." At the time of the present survey, problems of busing and the role of Federal court decisions represented one of the major concerns in the national, as well as state, politics around the country. In order to tap the likely reaction of people to cross-district or similar kinds of desegregational efforts involving busing, we asked respondents to react to the following statement:

Suppose a federal court order on school busing meant the children would have to go to inferior schools. Which of the

*following should parents do? Tell me if they definitely should,
probably should, probably should not or definitely should not.*

Five kinds of action were listed. MARs are much more likely
than other groups to say that people should definitely or
probably not accept busing. In terms of collective forms of
resistance to the hypothetical busing situation, MARs stand out
in their advocacy of keeping their children home and organizing
public marches.

For the other direct protest action alternatives, MARs are not
especially distinctive in their support. On an overall basis, however, MARs are the group most likely to resist busing programs.

TABLE 55

REACTIONS TO THE PROBLEM OF CHILDREN BEING BUSED TO INFERIOR SCHOOLS:
"Suppose a federal court order on school busing meant that children would have
to go to inferior schools. Which of the following should parents do?"

	Low Income	MARs	Average Middles	High Education Middles	Affluents
Definitely or probably not accept this	50%	75%	59%	55%	60%
Definitely or probably contact elected offi-cials	61%	80% +	71%	74%	83%
Definitely or probably keep children home	22%	37%	20%	13%	20%
Definitely or probably organize public marches	20%	35% +	23%	44% +	31%
Definitely or probably stop schools from operating by setting up picket lines	6%	13% +	8%	4%	5%

Political Activism: MARs at the Brink

We have found that the activism reflected by past types of associational ties as well as forms of organizational contact indicate a general tendency for MARs to prefer individualized, informal types of political or quasi-political problem solving. The trends indicated in a number of the analyses we have explored in this chapter do not follow the consistent pattern of MARs as a politically aroused and mobilized group in comparison with other segments of the population. Rather, we find that the High Education Middles are very likely to be supportive of direct action as well as to have engaged in such action to a very significant extent in the past.

What distinguishes the two relatively more mobilized groups, that is, MARs and High Education Middles, is that the former group is likely to support actions in hypothetical situations rather than to have engaged in such actions in the past. Whereas, in the case of the latter group, the High Education Middles, there is support for direct action which seems to be an outgrowth of past experience. Thus, one general conclusion to be drawn from our analysis is that MARs are distinctive in the relative support for direct action but on the basis of rather limited past experience with organizational contacts and, in particular, specific collective political action.

Throughout our discussion of the MAR phenomena we have alluded to a pair of major exceptions to the low mobilization profile of this group: the Boston and West Virginia school conflicts. Let us provide at this point a more complete picture of the sequence of protest events which have occurred in these controversies and rely on the actual histories to provide illustrations of what happens when the MAR group does become mobilized. What are the tactics? How does a grass-roots effort work following the MAR "style"?

We start with the Boston anti-busing action. The sequence of protest strategy and mobilization can be traced through the following events:

*"I've seen evidence of what can happen," Cadegan says.
"One day it was a quarter to 12 and they got word of*

*something going on at the high school. By five minutes of 12
there were a couple of hundred mothers in front of the
school" South Boston Information Center has become the
center for an after-school tutoring service at which eight
teachers meet four days a week with some of the boycotting
students.*

*Sound trucks and mimeograph machines operate out of
the Information Center, supplementing the block captains,
and volunteers man the telephones.*

*The women from ROAR run South Boston's resistance
like an election campaign. Almost everybody knows almost
everybody else in the tightly knit community, and over the
past five years a system of block captains has developed.*

*"When something happens, we call the block captains and
they, in turn, call ten people and those people tell their
friends," says Virginia Sheehy, a ROAR member. "Within a
couple of hours it's very easy to reach hundreds of people."*

"Mrs. Hicks Rallies Bus Foes,"
Detroit Free Press, *11/10/74*

*Mrs. Sheehy said the groups have chosen Sundays as the
day to meet in order to "stay clear of any accusations that
we are disrupting the schools." She said her group and her
anti-busing organization have been unfairly charged in the
past with seeking to promote violence and disruptions in the
school.*

"3,000 at Anti-Busing Rally in North End,"
Boston Globe, *11/18/74*

*Dorothy Ahern of South Boston sat in a room at her
daughter's school (the very one which educated former
House Speaker John McCormack) and told a visitor: "Every
parent I have talked to is preparing to go to jail." A poli-
tician, Joseph Timilty, tells strangers, "This is going to make
law-breakers out of law-abiding citizens."*

"Uptight in Boston,"
The Progressive, *June, 1974, p. 30*

*Question 7: "Shall the School Committee, which now
consists of five members, elected at large for terms of two
years, be replaced by neighborhood school councils elected*

by parents, teachers and residents, and by a decentralized school administration and by a superintendent of schools appointed by the mayor, with the approval of a city-wide advisory committee."

The major strategy of the anti-busing forces was to link the busing issue with school reform. That strategy apparently worked.

"Question 7 Opposed at Busing Rally," Boston Globe, *11/24/74*

"I think people look to the elected officials for encouragement and support, but as far as work goes people have taken the bit in their own mouth."

Mrs. Kopps, who works in the Tri-Neighborhood Information Center in Roxbury, said many people don't speak up, but they are very well informed on busing issues through a self-education process. They no longer depend on politicians.

"I used to read myself to sleep with books, but now I read legislation."

Many parents are now taking overt leadership roles away from elected officials. They are keeping the movement going and even giving it new impetus. They organize the meetings, staff the phones and quell rumors while most of the politicians, with the exception of those looking into legal measures, merely make appearances at motorcades, rallies and some anti-busing meetings.

Elected officials only come to the ROAR meetings as invited guests.

"White Parents Shape Anti-Busing Campaign," Boston Globe, *11/24/74*

The spawning of new and unique tactics by the Boston anti-busing protestors is indeed instructive. Nor are the approaches restricted simply to direct boycott and demonstration. One of the major consequences of MAR mobilization is that it can become the basis for institutional responses even if initially only on an ad hoc basis.

Mrs. Alice Tallent, member of ROAR: "We're also looking into the possibility of organizing our own (private) freedom schools," she said.

Other residents say they will send their youngsters to private schools or to already crowded parochial schools.

Los Angeles Times, 9/13/74

The school board of the Catholic Archdiocese of Boston has modified its year-old policy designed to keep Catholic schools from becoming a refuge for white students trying to avoid court-ordered desegregation.

"We're hoping to discourage transfers, but the schools are in such hard financial straits that we don't want to say they can't take them if vacancies permit," Brother Bartholomew Varden, Catholic School Superintendent, said yesterday.

Students are accepted on any one of three conditions:

1. *If the applicant would further integration in the school to which the applicant is applying.*
2. *If the applicant would fill a vacancy which has developed through normal patterns such as transfer and drop out.*
3. *If the acceptance is consistent with the fundamental principles of social justice as well as the administrative policies of the archdiocesan school board.*

"Boston Area Catholic Schools Modify Transfer-Student Policy."
Boston Globe, *1/31/75*

Now let us turn to the school textbook protest in Kanawha County, West Virginia. Initiation of the effort was a school boycott in Charleston, West Virginia, in the fall of 1974. The height of the controversy was reached in October 1974, when the Midway Elementary School was bombed after the school system adopted a series of textbooks and supplementary readings containing sections which the protestors said were un-American and un-Christian. The books include contemporary works of such authors as Malcolm X, Eldridge Cleaver and Allen Ginsberg.

The protestors began with a boycott of classes and then started to picket coal mines and other industries to dramatize their cause. Reverend Martin Horan organized a group calling itself "Concerned Citizens." Officers of the United Mine Workers District 17 called a mass rally at a city park in mid-September of 1974 in an effort to resolve the situation. At first

the UMW maintained that its members should not respect the
protestors picket lines. It is a prime example of the effort to
by-pass conventional union response and appeal to the members
themselves that the following sequence occurred:

*"There were roving bands of up to 1,000 pickets". . . . One
such band of roving pickets shut down a construction site by
threatening to rock the unfinished structure until they shook
the workers off . . .*

Washington Post, *9/13/74*

*More than 6,000 miners ignored orders from union leaders
and supported the protest by refusing to work. At one point
bus transportation for 11,000 commuters was halted by
pickets.*

Los Angeles Times, *9/14/74*

*Attendance by the county's 44,500 students was spotty
and almost non-existent in mining areas at the eastern end of
the county. School officials said the absenteeism ranged up
to 90 percent in that area.*

*Mr. Graley, Pastor of the Summit Ridge Church, gave the
education board officials a list of demands that was signed
"The People." It asked that:*

1. *The books be permanently removed and that any miner
   who lost his job because he joined the protest be rein-
   stated.*
2. *Court injunctions forbidding protest be withdrawn with
   no reprisal against any student who was absent from
   school and that County Superintendent Kenneth Underwood resign.*

Los Angeles Times, *9/18/74*

*The group which seemed to reflect the split in the protest
movement refuses to accept a compromise agreement worked
out last week that provides for the removal of about 90
percent of all new language arts texts and a review of the
books by a board appointed citizen review committee which
will make the final determination within thirty days.*

Washington Post, *9/18/74*

*. . . Kenneth Underwood, School Superintendent from
Fargo, S.D.: "These people don't just make threats. They*

*mean what they say. I was born on Chicago's South Side. I've
had confrontations all my life but when they talk about
physical violence they really mean it."*

*Underwood and family left town during the height of the
controversy. Since then a number of other persons including
board members and even some leaders of the protesting
miners have dropped out of sight.*

Los Angeles Times, *9/19/74*

*The arrests, coupled with the growing economic pinch felt
by the striking miners, led to the suspension of most mine
picketing and protest activities today.*

Washington Post, *9/21/74*

*The protesters were not good at ridicule themselves, but
they did have at their disposal the one weapon they have
always used in class warfare; their use of it transformed the
school boycott into an industrial strike. "The common man
don't know what to do except what he'd done, and that's to
go home and sit down," Marvin Horan told the school superintendent.*

New Yorker, *9/30/74*

*Around the gym, clusters of people were saying the same
thing. A few were saying that if violence is the only way to
keep the controversial books away from their children, then
that's the way it may turn out.*

Chicago Tribune, *10/20/74*

*"This is compounded by other hidden issues represented
by the textbooks: class conflict and a suppressed racial problem. People have to grasp something to release their frustrations. They're concerned about everything from inflation to
corruption in government, but the book issue is something
they can grab hold of and have an impact on," said G. Kemp
Melton, County Sheriff.*

Chicago Tribune, *10/21/74*

*"It appears that someone tossed an explosive into our
boiler room" at Kanawha County Board of Education Offices
after the board meeting with citizen committee reviewing
textbooks.*

Los Angeles Times, *10/31/74*

On April 18, 1974, Reverend Marvin Horan was convicted on conspiracy to bomb the Midway Elementary School. A coal miner on trial with Horan was found guilty of actually constructing the bombs. U.S. District Judge Hall did not revoke bond for the two defendants but did impose restrictions on their participating in further textbook protests. Reverend Avis Hill, another leader of the protest, commented, *"I was disappointed in the fact that he* [Horan] *was told to refrain from protesting, but I don't think it will cause any real problems in the movement because the people will continue to work to get these filthy books out. He has been made a martyr before the nation"* (*Ann Arbor News,* April 18, 1975).

In fact, of course, Reverend Horan's conviction failed to receive more than passing back-page notice by the press. The West Virginia protest was aptly summarized this way in one newspaper review:

> *Parents can't fight TV, books or movies which they think have dirty material but they can sure fight a teacher. You are going to see more protests. There's going to be a parental revolt.*
>
> Chicago Tribune, *12/15/74*

7. ACTIVISM OF MARs:
SOME PRINCIPLES
TO BEAR IN MIND

Our analysis has described an important ideological perspective in terms of an analysis of the current trends in society as seen by nearly 3 out of 10 white Americans. We found in both our preliminary community interviews and our national study that a significant portion of the MAR group does not seek to take action through a third party movement or to find support for structural changes in major institutions. As a result, we often find that the MAR is someone who is mobilized around local issues and whose institutional modes for expressing himself are likely to be local organizations such as schools, police, government officials or voluntary associations such as block clubs and other organizations that exist in the local community. Where people do not have institutional avenues through which to act they may indeed be frustrated but do nothing about it. We found this to be true of a significant portion of the MAR group.

The Formula for Mobilization: Some Key Patterns

In the past, MARs seem to have been active only in a "parapolitical" sense. Their level of contact with various institutions of government and other structures was higher than their level of direct political action. In effect, the kinds of contacts reported were expressions of a limited, indirect and usually individualized use of organizational resources.

The consideration of how individuals contact organizations

116

has an important bearing on the whole question of political mobilization. For example, the "conventional wisdom" about how individuals participate in the political process implies a sort of cumulative or additive process: first the individual belongs to organizations, next these structures are used by the individual as resources in problem solving, and finally direct political actions follow the sophistication obtained from earlier contact.

It is important to discover whether this model fits the manner of political mobilization demonstrated by the MAR group. We have identified a range of attitudes and perceptions which imply that MARs either feel isolated from others in society because their values or "real interests" are unique, or they join a temporary coalition formed around specific, short-term issues that tend to disguise the very basic differences which underlie a surface ideological unity. If, on the basis of models of political mobilization, MARs emerge as unique, there will be important conceptual and policy ramifications.

We shall confine ourselves to two main models of political mobilization. The first holds that as individuals become more involved in the institutions of their local community and larger society, they are more likely to diversify the means used to achieve their goals and to become more politically "sophisticated." This model presumes that the channels of political action are available and that all one has to do is learn how to use them. A corollary is that those who are more active are presumed to be more effective and thus to feel less "estranged," "alienated" or "discontented." A further assumption is that as individuals become better acquainted with the political and organizational resources of their environment they will develop greater allegiance to those structures.

A second model of political mobilization argues that the individual who becomes politically active does so because there are problems which cannot be resolved through conventional channels. The development of more direct means of social action is a result of frustration and disillusionment with the already "institutionalized" means of political influence. Consequently, the individual who has tried political action, instead of growing in "sophistication" and trust in the efficacy of "the system," may in fact become increasingly alienated and more willing to take non-institutionalized forms of action.

Our data from the national survey permits a general comparison of the two models we have outlined with regard to political mobilization. Among the indices of past political or para-political "sophistication" we have already described findings on the number of voluntary associations respondents belong to, the number of different organizations and representatives of groups they had contact with, and finally the number of specific political actions they had taken.

When the additional step is taken to intercorrelate these three indicators for both MARs and other white respondents and, in turn, to work out their correlations to direct protest, the appropriate "mobilization model" can be assessed. If, in fact, MARs follow the first model we outlined—where organizational ties reduce the need to use non-institutionalized procedures— then the correlations between organizational memberships, contacts and past political actions should be interrelated and not linked to support for militant protest. (See Appendix: Table 20.)

For MARs, conventional political action can arise either out of past organizational memberships or from contacts with organizations. Support for direct militant protest has a similar dual routing: it may spring as much from organizational contacts as from past political actions.

For non-MARs, conventional political action occurs in relation to membership in organizations. But support for militant direct action arises somewhat more from past political actions than from organizational contacts.

For non-MARs, organizational membership seems to provide an alternative to political mobilization. For MARs, however, political activism is highly linked to such membership and, in turn, such past political action is tied to support for direct action protest militancy. The findings support a unique model of mobilization for MARs—one derived from successive levels of political involvement leading to greater militancy and support for direct action and its legitimation as a problem solving approach. Although relatively few MARs are already politically active, the process of contact and "political savoir-faire" can quickly escalate to a greater sense of anger and alienation from the established political processes of the local community and the larger entity of the federal government.

Thus, we have the nature of MAR mobilization in a cyclical form. Once triggered, the pattern of ever greater militancy seems to prevail. But the barriers to collective action by MARs need to also be stressed—desire for individual autonomy and influence, tactics stressing informal structures and personalized contact, and a resistance to forming groups which do not already have some prestigious leadership.

The formula for MAR mobilization requires, moreover, a specification of the "catalytic" factors: localism and a linkage to "ascriptive" group identities—race, nationality or religious reference points. When such collectivities are seen to be weak and barely conscious of their identity and interests, the MAR individual sees direct action and non-traditional leaders and protest efforts to be the answer, to provide a way to "talk back" to any bureaucracy—union, church or governmental—to the mass media, to organized minorities, to federal courts, and to any other perceived source of oppressive policies.

MARs' strong roots in neighborhood and the local community are often neglected by all political parties. Moreover, MARs do not have to have an elaborate organizational structure to take effective action. They do not need constant participation. The MAR does not feel that he has to attend all the PTA meetings. Process is not as important as product. "What is that school turning out?" "What is the result?" These are the primary concerns of MARs.

System versus Personalized Problem Causes

If our analysis is correct, there are several possible leads that have to be followed up. People interested in social action must first decide whether the lack of action on their problem area is a result of a lack of information about the problem or a lack of organizational resources for action. We found that for MARs the tendency to view problems in personalized terms made it less likely that collective action would be taken. This points up the importance of understanding what people regard as the causes of social problems. For instance, we think MARs clearly differ from many blacks in that the latter group feels that racial problems are "system caused" and they are seeking institutional solutions such as equal opportunity or preferential recruitment to make up for past biases, etc. MARs, on the other hand, tend to see problems in terms of faulty leadership and improper functioning of the system, not in terms of the system itself.

MARs define problems as personal and look upon institutional efforts at change as often being unfair. In fact, it is precisely these institutional changes that seem to be one of the most significant levers for the creation of the MAR phenomenon. Our analysis suggests that the need not only to sensitize people to given problem areas but to alter the causal analysis that people bring to a problem must be considered.

What seems to characterize the MARs phenomenon is that issues such as cross-district busing seem to be the unifying factors and the broadening out of the MAR group is the direct result of the concerns about the way various institutions are functioning.

If we go outside the southern United States we find that the unification of diverse groups making up MARs is built upon the performance of various social institutions. In southern states this does not seem to be the case and we might well argue that the MAR ideology has a more traditional basis in this region of the country. Therefore, the more recent recruits to the perspective of multiple group threats result from the behavior of particular bureaucratic organizations. We argue that such institutions that exist in the local community play a pivotal role in terms of heightening or reducing this perception.

One of the crucial dimensions of our broader policy arguments is to suggest that the MAR phenomenon is a highly localized one. As a result the targets of change are not simply the national government, although MARs are extremely unhappy with the way that major institutions function. It is exactly the across-the-board sense of the way a number of organizations—all the way from welfare agencies to unions—are carrying out this nonmerit and preferential treatment orientation that seems to bring together groups who might otherwise be extremely diverse geographically, socially and politically.

Social Policies to Avoid

One general policy premise to be borne in mind is that the alienation of MARs seems to derive from the shift downward to the local community of social programs which formerly had resided at the national level.

The MAR seems to be responding to forces which formerly did not seem close at hand but which have now reached the local community. Therefore, alienation from the more distant social institutions is not the crucial generator of the MAR ideology. On the contrary, the behavior of organizations in the local arena is bringing home a series of value clashes and generating important criticisms that previously were directed at larger, more distant structures. In this sense we seem to have a crucial difference in vantage point between MARs and other groups who have a series of important complaints against various institutions.

Higher status groups in the population may well begin their critique of American society and its problems with a sense that the national structures need to be brought closer to local communities. By contrast, MARs would appear to be arguing the opposite: it is precisely this intrusion of national structures into the local arena which they most significantly object to. It may well be argued that the original form of that kind of equation was in a particular region of the country, mainly the southern states.

It was around the issue of school desegregation that we first heard arguments about states' rights and the need for local determination. We find that in many regions of the country the issue is not just school desegregation, although that is a unifying factor, but the kinds of policies and programs followed by the federal government, which have become more intrusive and visible in the local context. But one may well argue that this has been the case over a long period of time and that the New Deal itself was built upon the idea of the national government being able to reach down to local communities to make social change and respond to urgent problems. But perhaps what we have now is an important difference. The difference would seem to lie in the fact that under the New Deal and earlier social welfare programs the concept of universality was more widely practiced.

Whereas the upper middle class and intellectuals object to the uniformity of federal programs and the rigidity with which they are often developed, we may well find that the MARs see such universal rules and principles as compatible with their own value system. Thus, as unions pursued the notion of seniority, so the federal government developed concepts of categorical aid and the need for standardized programs that would aid whoever was located in a particular area and had experienced a given type of problem.

More recently, the tenor of many federal programs has been one of specialized compensatory efforts. The fact that minority groups have been the apparent beneficiaries of such an effort to single out given individuals so that their particular problems can be addressed by large scale government has, of course, been a major source of the development of the MAR ideology. In addition, many political scientists and analysts of the policies and programs of the federal government, as well as decision makers themselves, have been urging a greater flexibility in federal government programs and the need for allowing states and local communities to define their own programs free of Washington bureaucratic red tape.

Are we arguing that MARs feel that this kind of federal government red tape should be maintained and strengthened? This is true, I believe, in the case of the *product* of federal programs rather than the *process*. While there is among MARs a great deal of emphasis on the fact that organizations do not pay attention to them, at the same time there is an absence of the theme that organizations are too large. In contrast, Highly Educated and Affluent respondents tend to place as great an emphasis on the size and extensive power of organizations as they did on other factors. This important difference in the expectations and criticisms people have about organizations directly relates to the point we have been discussing. MARs appear to be more concerned that the product of the organization they deal with—whether union, corporation, local or state government—be a product which is uniform and predictable.

If the local schools, for example, are given the mandate to educate children, the concern is that no special compensatory efforts be made. The test of the effectiveness of the schools should be what they turn out rather than what racial balance exists among students and faculty. In other words, MARs are saying, "Let us not differentiate the input, let us just assume that the product is as universal and fair as possible."

In many areas of community functioning we find individuals who have come to view the performance of organizations as violating some basic premises of how such structures should be working. It is clear that the most visible dimensions of this criticism have to do with issues of race. But it is implicit in the MAR ideology that the same sort of concerns are voiced toward the privileges of the rich as well as toward organized welfare clients and other groups such as students and newly emerging "minorities" such as women, native Americans, chicanos and others. The basic issue becomes should the redress of grievances by these groups involve the restructuring of major social institutions, particularly those of the local community? The answer implicitly given by MARs is "no." It is in terms of these most immediate local structures that MARs see the erosion of the values they most highly prize.

Is the Meeting Ground Bureaucratic Accountability?

We then come to an important basis both of polarization by the MAR group and perhaps of coalition. A significant portion of the black community is arguing in favor of increased decentralization of institutions so as to be able to address the problems of small-scale, highly unique segments of the community. In addition, blacks have been placing a great emphasis on the performance of institutions in terms of the quality of their products.

Would MARs support this perspective? In one sense decentralization and the concept of neighborhood government might well be viewed as important potential bridges between MARs and racial minorities. In another sense, the issue is one of financing and efficiency and here potential gaps are possible.

There is no question but that having highly decentralized educational systems is an expensive procedure. The advantages of large-scale purchasing of materials and the standardization of the context of textbooks certainly represents an economic saving. Moreover, the emphasis on the product of organizations, while a basis of common perspectives, may well become viewed as a source of tension for MARs. We might well argue that the product is assumed by the nature of the institution itself. MARs, because they seem to place a high level of trust in existing structures, are willing to an extent to accept the dictates of the professionals who run such organizations. By contrast, blacks are demanding that organizations be accountable precisely *because they have in the past been biased and supporting the values of groups other than their own.* Consequently, the apparent unifying emphasis on the product of organizations may come out in reality to be one of the major sources of controversy, particularly in the local community context.

During a period of economic cutbacks we should anticipate that the movement toward decentralized forms of administration and the efforts to evaluate and to examine the goals and the product of given institutions may not be given any support at all. The cost factor must be recognized as a crucial one in terms of the functioning of all governmental institutions. During this period, even if it were possible to argue that the two trends we have identified are an important basis of coalition, the feasibility of responding and moving on these issues in the immediate future looks dim indeed.

Is Decentralization of Services
a Depolarizing Strategy?

We are left a situation in which governmental programs, although implicitly turned over to state and local control, are viewed as insignificant sources for generating services and as inequitable in the distribution of benefits. Since the urban riots of the mid-1960s, there is a widespread belief that it is impossible for the federal government and for local institutions to free themselves from the task of serving mainly the minorities. As long as this belief system is present, no matter how equitable the distribution of the governmental and local services might be, it may not be possible to undo MAR alienation.

It is important to recognize that we are describing not only individual experiences and observations but a constantly reinforced ideology about the state of American society as it has evolved over the last half decade. We can call this the issue of "credibility." Distrust and hostility which local government cials describe in many of our early community interviews reflect the level of cynicism which has been generated among MARs.

MARs' basic trust in institutions remains high, but their faith in specific "politicians" is extremely low. We might well argue that if the efforts of groups supporting greater decentralization of government remains at the level of focusing on process, MARs will probably not be attracted. They believe that the system works to the extent that it is run by responsible persons who are allowed to do their jobs without interference.

The MAR view that governmental organizations are unresponsive to their interests and that they pay too much attention to minority groups has two facets: the first suggests that officials of various agencies do not really know what goes on in a given local area; the second view argues that they do in fact know what is going on but their hands are tied to do anything about it. This latter perspective is mostly associated with the behavior of the police. For example, when the city of Detroit introduced a program involving plain-clothed officers going out into the community to deal with crime (the so-called STRESS program) the MAR view was that this program would be interfered with and thus would not be successful.

The view that officials of more distant institutions at the state and federal level really do not know what is occurring in neighborhoods is more likely to be addressed in terms of such programs as welfare and unemployment. Consequently, if decentralization implied that, in fact, officials would be present on the scene, MARs might feel that at least they would have a channel through which to express their grievances and a local official with whom to interact.

Since we have found that MARs tend to prefer informal individualized forms of political action, the existence of local representatives of federal and state programs, analogous to the agricultural extension worker, could well be a useful institutional response. Such officials could act as short-circuiters of the chain of command and be able to offer on-the-spot solutions under conditions which would be consistent with some of the value perspectives of MARs.

The concept of organizing neighborhoods in terms of formal structures to be the vehicles for expressing local concerns does not seem especially compatible with the values of MARs. The fact that a neighborhood is formally organized often indicates to white residents that the neighborhood is on the decline. The need to devise forms of informal mobilization must be an agenda item that policy makers focus on if they are to develop the maximum opportunity to involve MARs and to respond to their needs meaningfully.

While block clubs and some other structures may well be appropriate vehicles in black communities, they do not seem to be the kind of structures which MARs would utilize. In a black community these structures tend to be controlled by specialized cliques within the neighborhoods and often are composed of the upwardly mobile residents and those who are most likely to move out in case there is a change in the area.

Given the fact that MARs are often residents of all-white communities or of communities where their own social position is in a middle income group, the use of local institutions as formal linkages with the more distant institutions of the society does not seem to be an especially promising approach.

By "local control" MARs mean the opportunity, through informal channels, to obtain a response to their grievances and to know that officials are at least somewhat in touch with what is occurring and are willing to pursue solutions. The multiplication of new organizations and structures composed of elite white groups or elite black groups will not attract among MARs. Instead, this will only confirm their sense that their class and race interests are not being attended to by community organizations.

Access Is More Important Than Control

The church and the union have both come under severe criticism precisely because their leadership and their programs seem to be favoring groups which MARs feel already have powerful advocates of their own. This sense of disaffection and withdrawal from some of the more traditional organizations that MARs are intimately involved with is bound to maintain the current sense of polarization. Our survey data indicated that it was among the MAR and middle income groups that contact with governmental structures tended to be least likely to accelerate a sense of alienation. While MARs do tend to have somewhat higher levels of contact with a range of organizations, their linkage with governmental structures is more similar to that of low income groups than it is to the more affluent.

The relative isolation that MARs have from the workings of the local government and the national government serves as one of the main fulcrums for the maintenance of the MAR ideology. Contact as a goal of social planners and decision makers may certainly provide one of the important avenues for reducing the polarization that MARs feel. But this would not be carried out most effectively by generating new quasi-institutional or adjunct structures of existing agencies. Thus, establishing model cities' boards and similar voluntary organizations which are, in fact, forms of federal or state programs would, in our view, provide little in the way of incentive for MARs and, perhaps, only confirm them in viewing their effectiveness vis-à-vis the government as extremely limited. Rather, it is the need for government officials themselves to seek contacts with MARs and to have their presence felt in local neighborhoods that is most crucial.

The creation of new intervening and linking structures between MARs and governmental institutions may turn out to be simply more barriers to contact and thus sources of increased frustration. In some respects a number of governmental structures and other organizations such as unions and the churches have begun to take on a dynamic with MARs that resembles that between the police and the black community. On the one hand, police officials see blacks as uncooperative and unwilling to make use of their services. On the other hand, black citizens complain that when the police are contacted they fail to respond quickly or they respond in an indifferent manner. Thus, the agency sees its potential constituents as hostile or uncooperative, while the constituents feel that the services available to them are likely to be at best meager and then available only after other more powerful and effective groups have had their interests taken care of.

If we pursue this analogy of the police and the black community to a range of social institutions as perceived by MARs, we can appreciate the relatively low level of contact which occurs between MARs and local and national government officials. The fact that, as we noted in our findings, MARs did seem to contact a large range of other organizations gives further credence to this perspective.

The willingness of the MAR group to use a channel of individualized contact indicates that an entire range of institutional mechanisms might well be established so that an individual citizen could speak with and have his views and concerns heard by a representative of a governmental institution. The phone-in programs on radio and television are examples of how this works in a non-governmental setting. Any mechanism by which individual citizens are able to "get to" public officials represents, we would argue, one of the models of effective expression which may well be one heavily utilized by MARs. For example, it might be a useful bit of research to examine the callers in terms of social characteristics in a number of the phone-in programs. We would argue that they disproportionately would come from the kind of strata that we have been focusing on in our present study.

There is certainly a need for governmental agencies to explain and articulate their programs and policies more effectively to the MAR segment of the population. And this should be a two-way street. The very fact that MARs are distrustful and cynical with respect to the workings of large organizations indicates the need for such organizations to reach out more effectively to seek contact and communication with this segment of the population.

To summarize, our initial investigation shows that MARs do have a sense of discontent which may stress slightly different problem areas than non-MARs. Their discontent is broad-ranging yet it seems to come from a strong sense that the very poor and the very rich are in alliance with government officials at their expense. They are prepared to act in certain specific problem areas,—but only those for which institutional or personal alternatives have been worked out. We would hypothesize that they would in addition be inclined to act in other areas as well if they could find an institutional way to do so.

8. THE MULTI-GROUP BASE
OF MIDDLE AMERICAN RADICALISM:
SOME POLICY SPECULATIONS

Critical to our earlier analysis has been the identification of social components of the MAR segment of the population. Given the heterogeneity of this group, it becomes important to identify how individuals with different characteristics (but who share the same ideological perspective) respond to their "collective" situation.

Such an analysis raises several intriguing issues. For example, under this definition of MARs it is possible for a considerable part of the society to develop a MAR orientation, perhaps within a short time period. It depends to what extent they are all facing a common problem. Thus, during the Depression of the 1930s, the vast bulk of the nation was affected by a similar experience. Past loyalties of party and economic doctrine were abandoned.

During the present situation many people have been affected by the economic downturns and inflation, or by the rise of the economic and political power of minorities. In the present chapter we shall compare respondents who share a high score on the MAR ideology scale in terms of demographic, socioeconomic and nationality group variables. The divergences in these attributes have implications for the response of individuals who share the same multiple threat perception that is the crucial identifying attribute of MARs, but who have specialized response patterns.

The Age Factor

We find that the younger MARs (particularly the person under age thirty) is especially favorable to the idea of a third

130

national political party. By contrast, the senior citizen MAR favors this idea far less than the younger person and is less oriented toward Wallace identification. For the under-thirty MAR, there is a greater tendency to identify race as one's closest group, to be unconcerned about high status people being members of groups that one intends to join, and to feel no special need to be part of an organized group. There is a sense of being in an early stage of group militancy. Moreover, younger MARs are high in terms of the number of past organizational contacts they have had. They are not noteworthy for their support of a hypothetical taxpayer revolt.

There is a greater likelihood of MARs in this age group seeing a connection between their immediate problems and the possibility of a national social movement. Clearly, they and not their older counterparts would form the "advanced cadre" of such a movement.

It is important to note that the response direction for the younger MAR may well be centered on the national rather than the local government. This would be in part a consequence of the higher rate of geographical mobility of younger families. In addition, because the length of tenure in neighborhoods is likely to be shorter, local issues will tend to be less salient for the younger MARs than for the middle aged or senior aged Middle American.

The willingness of younger MARs to participate in collective action may well mean that vigorous efforts should be made on the part of community organizations to draw MARs of the younger age group into greater political activity. This should be especially true for national political parties. With the high level of past contact that younger MARs have had with organizations, it is clear that they are willing to make use of various structures and, at the same time, have a high level of distrust toward them. Consequently, the arguments that we have discussed earlier with regard to style of bureaucracy may well be particularly applicable to this group.

The older aged or senior aged MARs are individuals who are reluctant to join groups unless these have been certified by high status persons who are already members. The senior aged MARs have less distrust of institutions but feel a greater need to

become part of an organized group. Their low level of past
contacts with organizations, coupled with their distrust of the
use of direct protest measures, suggest that the important forms
of involvement for this group might well be through an established organization in which individuals in "visible" political
positions are already members. This could well be organized
through the local community. Moreover, increased contacts by
local and national bureaucratic structures should have a great
deal of impact with regard to this group of MARs. Thus, the
general strategy here is to increase contact with senior citizens
in the MAR group, as well as to develop offshoots of established
organizations as ancillary voluntary associations. In this way,
the participation of senior citizen MARs would be facilitated
and would be a form of organization that would be compatible
with the values of this group. The lack of interest in the idea of
the third party and the Wallace movement suggests that for
senior-citizen MARs the focal institutional participation areas
should be in the local arena.

Sex of Respondent

Our survey analysis shows that women MARs tend to be
strongly interested in the issue of tax reform. At the same time,
they seem to be characterized by a lower level of past contact
with organizations as well as political action. Thus, it is among
women in the MAR group that we have the most extreme form
of the contrast between low past political involvement and
legitimation of direct protest action.

In the area of busing as well as in tax reform women who are
in the MAR group are most militant in desiring some form of
redress of grievances. At the same time, women MARs tend to
be characterized by a high level of "diffuse" alienation—a sense
of anomie as well as a somewhat higher level of tension headaches. Compared to males they also have a somewhat lower
level of distrust of major institutions. They are less interested in
the idea of a third party than are male MARs.

Given these findings, the strategy of response to the women
MARs would involve specific efforts to develop avenues of

participation. They do not have as great a concern as men about high status people belonging to a group, and it is possible that new forms of ancillary voluntary associations could be established. In our community studies we found that female members of the MAR group seem to be more oriented toward the use of verbal skills and/or participations in organizations. It may well be that precisely through more voluntary association work or involvement in a range of community organizations women MARs can gain a thorough hearing and make their greatest contributions.

The general "anomic" sense which women in the MAR group manifest clearly acts as a barrier to any form of group action. Consequently, it might be argued that the willingness to use highly individualized forms of contact with agencies would be the most effective. Furthermore, the relative disinterest in national political movements suggests that it is in the local arena that female MARs would most readily become involved and where they would have the greatest focal concerns. Clearly, the issue of busing is a central one. The fact that women MARs have a special concern about tax protests suggests that greater efforts should be made to involve women in economic policy making as well as to keep this group informed about the various types of economic policies and tax reform efforts.

In contrast, organizations will need to reach out to male MARs in more elaborate ways. Their greater interest in the idea of a third party suggests that unions and other institutions in which male members predominate need to give more attention to the linkup between their structures and their membership.

Region of the Country

We found important differences within MARs in terms of regional patterns. Not surprisingly, Wallace had his greatest support in the Southern states. We also found that MARs living in Western states tended to show a higher degree of anomie and at the same time a greater willingness to join groups without regard for high status membership. The high level of past organizational contact of persons from Western states in the

MAR group, together with a high level of alienation from organizations in these states, is a clear indication of MAR distrust of politicians and organizations. The willingness, though, to join grass roots organizations indicates that these might well be more effective in California than in North Central and, particularly, Southern states.

In the Southern states we find that trust in organizations is less of a problem and that the identification with the personal leadership of George Wallace is the most crucial part of the MAR ideology. The fact that individuals will not join a group which does not have high status members further underscores the way in which Southerners in the MAR group define their organizing efforts: they support a visible national leader and are more interested in the idea of a third political party than are MARs in other locales. A rather limited degree of past political and organizational contact is coupled with the Southern MARs' lack of support for direct protest action.

The MAR phenomenon in the South is a personalized charismatic movement. Counteracting this force would require the emergence of other high status individuals in Southern states whose role could be very important in terms of shifting the allegiance of MARs in those regions. Leaders who could compete with George Wallace as spokesmen for the South, as well as persons from local communities who might well become identified with special problems of the white MAR Southerner, could play an extremely vital role in reducing the alienation and isolation of the Southern MAR.

In Northeastern states (and here we are talking about New England and New York State in particular) we find that the need to be part of an organized group is the highest of any region in terms of the MAR respondent. At the same time, this is also the center of nationality groups, and the feeling of closeness to such groups is the highest of any region. Many persons who have such identifications feel that their groups are in a more advanced stage of organization.

The rather low level of anomie which characterized Northeastern MARs suggests that it is not a group seeking to become part of some new overarching organization. Rather, the identification which already exists needs to be strengthened by visible results which prove that their particular group is, in fact, getting their share of the pie.

It will be extremely difficult for existing institutions to make adequate responses to this particular pattern of the MAR ideology because this region has the highest level of alienation from bureaucracy. Still, an effort on the part of these institutions to reach out to ethnically organized MARs is very necessary. By using this particular lever, difficult as it may be, an important inroad may be made in terms of the isolation of MARs in these states. Treating their alienation in terms of a group contact implies that such individuals will respond in terms of the perceived well-being of the group with which they identify.

Thus, strategies of coalition in which existing ethnic groups are maintained as visible components become important. Seeking to reach these MARs individually may not prove to be effective. The major political parties and other institutions of the local community give special attention to how organized bureaucracies can address the concerns of organized ethnic groups.

The North Central states represent a still different character of the MAR ideology. In these regions there is a greater willingness to support George Wallace than in either the West or the Northeastern part of the country. In contrast to the West, however, respondents in the North Central part of the country are less willing to join groups without certification from higher status groups, and they have a higher identification with race than in any other region of the country. However, MARs in this region have had only moderate contact with organizations in the past and have a fairly moderate level of past political actions.

Given the moderate level of institutional alienation it is possible to strengthen the channels of communication through existing local organizations and to develop new ones. The crucial policy here would be to increase bureaucratic contact with MARs in the North Central region as a basic means of reducing the level of alienation. The cynicism of this group does not result from disillusionment growing out of a high level of past contact. In fact, it is based on the MARs' relative lack of contact with governmental and community organizations.

Militancy in terms of group development is at an early stage among MARs in North Central states. At the same time, the issue of race is perhaps more salient here than in any other region in the country. Thus, the particular response to MARs in these states should be based on the capacity of existing institutions to recapture the allegiance of this group. This applies especially to unions and traditional political parties. Given less of the personalized identification with Wallace as a charismatic leader and more with the kinds of issues that he defines, it might well be that institutions (especially in the local community) could begin to address themselves effectively to the needs of MARs.

If we were to extrapolate the trends which we note regionally it might well be argued that in the Western states the MAR has had a great deal of organizational contact, is not oriented to George Wallace and is, therefore, in some sense shopping around for a charismatic leader who has yet to emerge. In the South such a leader has already been identified and a large portion of the MAR group is willing to follow that leader regardless of the direction in which he might lead.

In the Northeastern part of the country there is an emphasis upon group identification and, therefore, if ethnic groups begin to identify themselves visibly with George Wallace or a similar leader, we could expect that significant portions of the ethnic MARs in this part of the country would go along.

In the North Central region there is a willingness to follow the lead of George Wallace. In that sense, MARs are somewhat more mobilized than those in Western states. Thus, we might well see a circuit of maintenance of the MAR ideology in which the South becomes the fulcrum, followed by firm North Central support and potential Northeast strength, with the West finally falling in line with the overall movement. But as we have indicated, roots of a different kind appear in all regions of the country.

Family Income

The Middle American earning between $15,000 and $25,000 is unique in the willingness to join groups without having the certification of high status members and in feeling close to a nationality group in an early or later stage of militancy. Such individuals also have had extensive past contact with organizations and have taken political actions. They are in favor of strategies of direct action against busing but are not characterized by strong support for George Wallace. Thus, the high income group, while not especially oriented toward national action, is willing to become part of an organization whether or not it is already well established. Thus, it is among this group that there is the greatest potential for organizing new forms of ethnic consciousness. This group as an "advanced cadre" of the militantly defined "new ethnics" may well be a major force in determining what direction MARs will take in the immediate future. Clearly it is this group which will become part of the basic resources available to any movement which draws upon the Middle American ideology.

Like the younger MARs, those with high income will be shopping for forms of group identification. They do not have a particularly high level of anomie and are, therefore, ripe for being organized. Their high level of alienation from institutions suggests that it will be extremely difficult for such structures to find a ready response if they seek to reach out in the more conventional ways.

But it is clear that among the high income MARs it is precisely institutional alienation which can become the most significant basis for their mobilization. Moreover, this group of MARs is not focused on the taxpayer revolt issue and, as such, may well be threatened by efforts to organize around this particular issue. Their concern is largely in the area of busing and ethnic identity.

The major strategy here is to insure that this group is able to find organizations in the community which respond to their ethnic interests but without necessarily fostering the MAR ideology. This group has the resources to act upon its concerns. It can move quickly and can encourage other MARs to act politically either at the national or at the local community level. Therefore, this is an extremely important group for institutions and various groups in the local community to reach.

By contrast, the low income MARs, those earning under $6,000, are characterized by a very low level of past political involvement. Even when mobilized in support of direct protest actions, they do so to a more limited extent than other MARs. These MARs do not have a high level of institutional alienation and are not particularly oriented toward taking collective action, although they do feel the need to belong to some kind of group. They are less oriented toward racial identification than are some of the higher income MAR individuals.

This group is, to some extent, the most passive of all MARs. They have a sense of being beaten and downtrodden and are thus not particularly inclined to become part of any collective political movement. They represent a major portion of the MAR group and they come from what can only be called the classical low income, low power, low status "under class." The allegiance of this group may well be eventually mobilized or swayed by the more demagogic or more affluent members of the MAR strata. Clearly the major institutions of the community have an opportunity to be responsive to the needs of this group before this happens. Moreover, such action will find a fairly receptive climate given the low level of institutional alienation, at least in comparison to other MARs.

It would appear that the procedure of "grass-roots" organizing is called for as a way of linking this group with the major institutions of the local and national scene. As it stands, federal programs for these white Americans whose income position is that of the "working poor" have been limited and will be more so in the future. They are more easily aligned with the "welfare" poor in terms of their immediate problems and even in terms of "class" interest than are other MARs. The fact that they focus less on race as a problem also makes them more open to the possibility of coalition with black Americans. It is possible that forms of coalition will emerge in urban areas, starting with the lowest income white MAR and blacks. This racial coalition could perhaps then be linked up with the ethnically-oriented MARs who tend to be more affluent.

In this sense, the low income MAR may serve as an important bridge between the more affluent and the minority groups in the American society. Clearly they have much to gain from coalition with minorities and less resistance for status reasons to such coalition efforts.

Education

One out of five MARs has attended college. MARs at this educational level are least interested in tax protest and most interested in organizing public marches in a busing situation. They are least supportive of the candidacy of George Wallace and are not especially focused on the idea of a third party. They are low on anomie and do not feel that high status people need to belong before they will join a group. They are most likely to feel closeness to a nationality group, and they describe the groups to which they belong as being in an early or militant state of development.

All of these factors suggest that this segment of MARs has a great deal of political sophistication but has not as yet found any particular focus or outlet for its sense of alienation. The key concern appears to be the busing issue.

Given the relatively high level of formal education among those MARs, educational institutions can aid in coalition building and in reducing the sense of alienation. This might take the form of more extensive contacts and greater involvement in the programs and activities of public schools. Moreover, it may well be that the educational institutions of higher learning from which this MAR college-educated group has come from could be the basis of such bridging efforts. Included here would be alumni associations or other ancillary structures of universities and colleges which could serve as the vehicle for linking this group with both the higher educational structure itself as well as with programs and activities which are aimed at improving the level of education among major segments of the society.

Thus, universities have a particular role in trying to reach those individuals among their constitutents whose attitutes reflect the Middle America ideology. Universities should keep them imformed and invite input from them with regard to major social problems and, in particular, educational policies and programs.

We find that the MAR who is a high school graduate is distinctive in terms of support for a third party, feeling close to racial groups, and supporting the protest actions of women. Furthermore, direction of coalition building for this segment of MARs cannot be initially focused on racial alliances. It is the issue of busing as well as other ancillary concerns that makes this group the most willing to support direct action protests of various kinds. At the same time, the taxpayer revolt issue is not the most basic of all.

The potential of this group to be involved in a national movement is one which should clearly be recognized. Having had past contact with organizations and a fairly high level of political action, this group becomes pivotal in determining the direction and character of the MAR reaction over the next few years.

The rather high level of alienation from organizations is in part attributable to some of the experiences that these persons have had with organizations in the past. It is crucial to reverse the hostility or indifference which previous experiences produced, rather than to attempt to develop new forms of organizational contact.

The willingness of high school educated MARs to join groups irrespective of high status members belonging suggests that coalition efforts be directed at specific issue topics which can move the mobilization of this group out of the area of race and busing.

The person who has attended but not completed high school is the most open to forms of organized group activity and at the same time the most reluctant to join groups without having high status members certify it. Thus, it could well be that if the college educated MAR were to initiate a group this segment might well join. The consequence is that there could be fairly extensive mobilization of this group as one of the segments to follow the advance cadre of other groups.

The highest level of Wallace identification is found among respondents with this educational level in the MAR group. This may be related to their feeling that they cannot count on anyone to be really responsive to their concerns. We also find, though, that there is a low level of institutional alienation relative to other MARs. •

It would appear that this group is most likely to respond to any form of contact by large scale local or national bureaucracies. Efforts aimed at this segment of the MAR group might well find an initial success on the basis of increasing the level of contacts which occur. Since this group is extremely high in its willingness to support taxpayer revolt actions, it may well be that specific issues around which institutions might develop the basis of contact would have to do with economic policies or, in particular, with taxing programs at the local or national level.

MARs who have not attended high school represent a group which has, on virtually all indicators, not mobilized in the past and is not now active. The exception to this is the support for taxpayer revolt kinds of actions. Consequently, these MARs are not likely to become mobilized in terms of some form of collective action and yet they certainly appear to advocate it. Lacking extensive past political and organizational contacts, they would appear to rally around some form of *ad hoc* program which would address itself to the tax issue.

Occupational Level

The white collar segment constitutes about one-quarter of the MAR population. These particular MARs are characterized by a high level of concern and willingness to use collective action in opposition to school busing. They are less interested in a taxpayer revolt. With a strong record of past political action, they are often involved in nationality groups. They feel that the groups they are closest to are in early or later stages of militancy. The kind of suggestions we made with regard to the high income MARs seem to be appropriate for this group. They will respond on the basis of existing group identification and it is through these structures that efforts to depolarize should be employed.

There are important differences between the skilled blue collar worker and the semiskilled blue collar worker within the MAR group. The former group gives the strongest support among all MAR groups to the idea of a third party and has a high level of identification with George Wallace. They are less alienated from institutions than are semiskilled blue collar workers, less likely to have tension headaches and to reveal a sense of diffuse alienation through anomie. They are also less concerned about the need to have high status people belong to their organizations, but have a much stronger sense than semiskilled workers do that they need to belong to an organized group.

Among all MAR groups, the skilled blue collar segment is most willing to consider collective action in order to redress grievances and also to link mobilization to a national movement: moreover, this group has the highest level of identity on a racial basis among MAR occupational groups. These MARs also feel that the groups which they belong to are in an early militant stage. They have had extensive contact with organizations in the past, but only to a moderate degree have they taken political action.

Consequently, the skilled blue collar person represents one of the most volatile centers of MAR ideology. As a group they are more likely than most other MARs to take collective political action and to extend this action beyond the local community. The crucial institution in terms of defusing these MARs is the labor union. The union's response to the demands of skilled workers in terms of contract negotiation and other issues becomes paramount.

Skilled blue collar MARs are more militant than their white collar counterparts. At the same time, they are not noteworthy for their militancy on the busing protest. Thus, we find the opening wedge for some policy formulations. This group seems to support various kinds of direct action protests and could well be willing to link up with a number of other groups, possibly even blacks, with respect to economic problems or other concerns.

Therefore, the skilled blue collar worker is in some respects one of the most crucial groups in terms of reducing racial animosities. The policies of unions, employers and local community groups in terms of the issues uppermost in the minds of the skilled blue collar worker can become a lever for the defusing of race issues among other MAR groups.

If it is possible for major institutions to respond to the racial fears and concerns of skilled blue collar workers, these individuals may well become activist on behalf of movements at the local and national level, which can help to reduce polarization in American society. Such coalitions if they involve racial minorities represent special difficulties. But since this group is particularly high in terms of feeling close to a nationality group what is needed is not the strengthening of existing grassroots or other voluntary associations in which skilled blue collar workers may have been members, but rather the development of new forms of community organization around the interests of skilled blue collar people. We find that compared with semiskilled blue collar workers, skilled workers have a lower level of organizational alienation and a higher level of past organizational contact.

We suggest the formula of attempting to increase direct contact between bureaucratic structures and skilled blue collar workers. Such workers may well be more willing than others to participate in programs of the union and other institutions which they now feel are catering too much to the needs of minority groups. They have sufficiently high levels of commitment to such structures and a degree of political sophistication to make effective use of them. The skilled blue collar workers' need to be part of an organized group argues that the role of the union may well be one which either requires the development of specialized, more visible subgroupings which address the skilled blue collar worker, or that ancillary institutions in which skilled blue collar workers are uniquely active become the basic vehicles of social influence. We suggest ancillary rather than new organizations because the skilled blue collar worker does have a greater reluctance than the white collar worker to join a group without having high status members belong. The unskilled blue collar worker is characterized by a high level of institutional alienation, anomie and the need to be part of an organized group. At the same time there is little concern about needing high status members to certify group participation and a low level of involvement or identification with nationalities or racial groups. Thus, the unskilled blue collar workers form an important group in terms of bridging across racial barriers. Their lack of feeling a sense of militant group development coupled with no need to have a status certification suggests that if a group were initiated and had as its special target participants from this segment of the community it might well be quite effective. This initiative, if it came from existing bureaucratic structures, would have low initial "pay-offs," given the high level of alienation. But if these structures were to focus more on the local neighborhood or community level and would, in the best sense of the word, help provide "grass-roots" structures, they might be important sources of defusing the Middle America ideology among this segment of the population.

Protestant-Catholic Patterns

We find that for Catholic groups, Middle American ideology is synonymously associated with a high level of institutional alienation. They feel a closeness to nationality groups and the need to be part of an organized group. Such individuals feel that their group—whether religious, racial or nationality—is in an early or a later stage of militancy more often than do Protestants. Busing actions represent one of the important sources of mobilization of this group. At the same time we note that it is the support for taxpayer revolt which distinguishes the Catholic from the Protestant MAR. There is also among Catholics a greater willingness to support protest actions by women. This has implications for the importance of the abortion issue as a rallying point for MAR mobilization.

Thus, we find among Catholic MARs a willingness to support various kinds of direct actions linked to a broad set of issues which might form the basis of coalition efforts. But these are least likely to find early success when they include and are focused on the race issue. It would be important to de-emphasize race as a "visible" concern on the part of the church and related structures, and to address instead various economic issues confronting MARs. One such topic to draw upon initially is the interest that women have in developing a greater participation in the work force on an equal basis with men. A climate of support exists in the MAR group for this "bridging issue."

MARs Viewed as a Loosely Combined Coalition

The variability of MAR mobilization is matched by the diversity of individual characteristics of those sharing this ideology. Religion, income, education and age provide different problem foci around which the MAR individual rallies. However, background factors recede when a single problem merges or intersects with other problems and both the intensity and extensivity of MAR political mobilization reaches a new natural consciousness.

In general, MARs support direct action in order to keep organizations from changing their basic structure or deviating from more universal principles or "rules." We have noted the fact that some MAR groups are willing to legitimate direct action but have little actual political experience and feel that institutions need to change their programs and be reduced in size. In other words, some wish to take direct individual action, while others prefer collective action through organizations.

What should occur if the two clusters within the MAR group, one legitimating direct action and the other experienced in political action, should come together? They would indeed form a powerful political block. The potential basis for such a coalition within the MAR group seems to be in terms of the particular style of using informal contact. Thus, the MAR who has taken extensive political action in the past is someone who has relied upon informal influence somewhat more than social action. Clearly the match between those groups who favor direct collective action and those who tend to use individual action would be the emergence of new forms of either grass-roots structures or a national third party movement which would address itself to local community concerns. This certainly is the direction which George Wallace champions.

What distinguishes the MAR who is a political activist and the MAR who is not but who supports various kinds of direct action is the question of organizational policies and programs. The one group of MARs which has not taken much direct political action in the past tends to feel that organizations should not change what they are doing. Consequently, if local structures such as schools, police and local government are able to demonstrate the effectiveness of their programs, the need to change such programs (which changes are advocated by the MAR political activist) might well be reduced.

It is important to note at this point that we found in our factoring analysis that there were many persons outside the MAR group who were political activists and shared many of the same concerns as those holding the MAR ideology. Non-MARs who have been politically active tend to support women's and minority group protests as well as taxpayer revolts.

Thus, we might well see a three-fold coalition in America involving those who hold the MAR ideology and have taken political action, those who do not hold the ideology but have been politically active, and those who have not taken action but support the ideology. Were MARs to be drawn into large scale existing political structures, this coalition might well have a more progressive approach. A reasonable strategy would be for local and national political parties to draw representation more fully from individuals holding the MAR ideology and having extensive political experience, and then to draw into this group those MARs with less extensive political contacts and actions. The aim then would be to shift the base of MAR alienation over toward more specific programmatic bases of multiple group interests.

It is precisely the relative isolation of MAR activists and their singleminded dedication to the Wallace movement or other more conservative or "racist" movements which hinders the joining of the two kinds of political activists into one organization. The attempt to throw out Wallace delegates and other efforts to restrict and purify local Democratic party precincts is a strategy which should be avoided in the future. Politically active MARs will be a significant force irrespective of their inclusion as part of the established parties. In fact, it is precisely because they can not find a home in the established structures that they have become an important arm of the Wallace or similar third party and right wing movements. In addition, MARs who are not activists and who have engaged in collective political action rather than individual forms of political action may well be tutored to more effective means of political participation by being in touch with either a MAR or a non-MAR political activist. By broadening the spectrum of strategies of influence that activists are willing to employ, many more MARs may well be willing to become active. The extent to which this turns out to be a constructive program in terms of depolarizing American society depends, then, on the capacity of existing political institutions to incorporate the politically sophisticated MAR activist into their ranks.

The most concrete expression of the MAR group forming a coalition around diverse social action is ROAR. This group, initially formed as a result of anti-busing efforts in Boston, was linked early in 1975 to the West Virginia school textbook protest movement. The name—Restore Our Alienated Rights— aptly defines the core of values that characterize the MAR. Partly reactionary and partly an expression of the independent spirit of revolutionary protest that formed the nation two centuries ago, ROAR epitomizes where the MAR has come in the last few years. But it is not the only expression of this seemingly paradoxical force in present-day American society.

9. MARs ON THE NATIONAL POLITICAL SCENE

Recent surveys show a clear increase in the number of independent voters and a decline in the number of committed party voters. The MAR phenomenon is part of that pattern. It is generally true as well that people are demanding more from public officials in terms of policy accountability, and unless government delivers we can expect strong action. As we have seen, MARs are increasingly ready to take such action. There is a new growing recognition on the part of national leaders that the success of federal programs is dependent less on whether technical input is sought from experts in the field and more on whether people out in the grass-roots have some say in what programs are devised and how they are administered.

In this chapter we shall explore the emergence of the MAR on the national level of political action in light of both the 1972 basic study and the events focusing on the forthcoming presidential election of 1976. In both instances the focus of our inquiry is closely overlapping with the tactics and political fortunes of George Wallace.

The key to Wallace's appeal has been that he reaches his potential followers at the local level on issues that affect their daily lives. The MAR often has strong roots in neighborhood and community. In 1972 McGovern, with his following of the poor, affluent liberals, college students, blacks, chicanos and anti-war dissidents, was the epitome of what the MAR resents on the American political scene. Furthermore, the neighborhoods and local communities were being neglected by both political parties in their preoccupation with the Viet Nam war. Hence, the rise of the Wallace movement seems directly related to the MARs' new sense of political awareness and new appreciation of how to make government pay attention to the "silent majority."

The Wallace movement, like its predecessor in the 1930s (the Coughlin Social Justice Movement), has been facing the problem of how to move to the national level from the regional or local identities of its goals and leadership. The position of the Democratic party in dealing with Wallace is highly reminiscent of the problem former energy czar and now Secretary of the Treasury William Simon faced during the winter of 1973–74. In that period the "Truckers' Protest" emerged as a challenge to the centralized decision-making involved in energy conservation efforts.

The often violent protest of truckers fits very well into the type of action with which the MAR can identify. It occurred in an industry that was highly decentralized, it required very little local action to get underway, and only in the protest sense was it part of an "organizational effort." This was evident to the negotiators on the government side, who were not sure that they were dealing with real representatives of the truckers or whether the Independent Truckers Association was, in fact, a genuine organization.

The paradox of the MAR emergence in national politics rests in part with the inconsistency between a commitment to broad and universal structures which traditionally have served MARs—particularly church and union organizations—and the decision-making process in large scale organizations. Thus, with MARs the issue is whether *any* national entity can really represent their interests.

In the 1972 survey we sought to tap the special appeal that a third party had to MARs. We asked respondents in the study:

Do you think it is a good or bad idea to have a strong third party for the next presidential election?

Overall, almost half of the sample said it was a good idea. But MARs were not more likely than other groups to support the idea of a third party. (See Appendix, Table 21.) In general, all of the middle income groups support such a view more than either low income or high income groups.

The third party idea again arose in the Boston busing protest in 1974. The "American Party," whose gubernatorial candidate in Massachusetts said that busing was the primary issue, earned the 3 percent of the total vote necessary to establish party status. According to W. Norman Gleason, a former director of the Massachusetts Election Division, the American Party—an offshoot of the Wallace National Party of 1968—is the first organization to win major party status since the 1930s.

Candidate Preferences in the 1972 Survey

During the interviewing in January and February 1972, we asked respondents to react to a list of the probable candidates who had yet to be tested in the forthcoming presidential primaries of the spring of 1972. We asked people the following question:

Who comes closest to representing your point of view? A significant number of respondents mentioned candidates who subsequently did not appear in either of the national party conventions as viable candidates. In effect, then, the interviews in our national survey provide a view of how voters were reacting at a very early point in the presidential campaigns before the political parties had certified a choice, or where candidates within the same party had engaged in primary contests with one another. Voters who were early supporters of Richard Nixon tended to reflect a very low degree of alienation on the measures we have discussed in the previous chapters. The candidate patterns as shown in the survey reflect those individuals who had made a definite choice in a situation in which a number of voters were subsequently forced, because of the elimination of their particular candidate, to choose a second or even third or later preference.

In Table 56 we show the pattern of responses obtained for the major candidate as they appeared early in the 1972 campaign. We note that among MARS about 1 in 5 indicated that George Wallace came closest to representing their own point of view. This level of identification with Wallace is significantly higher than that displayed by any other population group in the

TABLE 56

PRESIDENTIAL CANDIDATE WHO MOST REPRESENTS RESPONDENTS
POINT OF VIEW
(EARLY 1972)

	Low Income	MARs	Average Middles	High Education Middles	Affluents
Wallace	9%	20%	6%	1%	2%
Nixon	31%	26%	30%	32%	42%
McGovern	2%	2%	4%	13%	7%
Kennedy	14%	13%	16%	8%	3%
Muskie	11%	11%	15%	19%	25%
Humphrey	8%	7%	6%	5%	6%
Agnew	3%	4%	4%	3%	5%
None of These	13%	10%	8%	5%	3%
Don't Know	9%	5%	7%	5%	2%
Other Candidates	1%	3%	5%	9%	5%
Total	101%	101%	101%	100%	100%

sample. It is more than three times the level displayed by Average Middles and more than twice as high as that shown for Low Income respondents. Thus, in the MAR group as we have operationalized it, we clearly have isolated the center of Wallace support.

As Table 56 indicates, the number of MARs identifying Nixon as representing their point of view was only slightly greater than the Wallace group. This relative neck-and-neck race within the MAR group is not replicated in any of the other population segments. Thus, among Affluents, Nixon supporters are significantly higher than they are among any other population group. Moreover, among Low Income individuals, Nixon has a higher proportion of support than among MARs. We also note from Table 56 that McGovern, who subsequently became the Democratic candidate, was half as likely to be supported by MARs as by Average Middles. The greatest support for George McGovern came in our sample from the High Education Middles with 13 percent at the early point in the campaign.

Other candidates who did well among MARs included Ted Kennedy and Edmund Muskie. However, both candidates did even better among Average Middles and Low Income respondents, although the differences are not statistically significant. It is interesting to note that Muskie did substantially better among High Education Middle and Affluents.

Humphrey support was concentrated among low income and MAR supporters, but again the differences across groups are not significant. A slightly larger group of respondents in the low income and MAR groups indicated that they did not prefer any of the 7 listed candidates in our question. A significantly larger proportion of High Education Middles preferred other candidates than the front-runners. These include most frequently Shirley Chisholm and John Lindsey.

In addition to having asked about candidates that individuals felt came closest to their own view, we asked respondents to recall their presidential preference in 1968. In Table 57 these preferences of past voting are indicated. We should note the response patterns are subject to a "bandwagon" distortion in favor of the winning candidate. This fact aside, MARs show the same high level of reported voting for George Wallace in 1968 as the proportion identifying with Wallace in 1972. In addition, what is of interest in Table 57 is the fact that the reported voting for the Democratic choice in 1968—Hubert Humphrey—reflects a relatively low voting percentage among MARs in comparison with other population groups and a similar proportion with regard to Average Middles. Thus, as indicated for 1968, MARs tend to say they voted for Wallace in a significantly greater number of cases than Average Middles. At the same time, Average Middles show a significantly larger reported preference for Richard Nixon in 1968.

TABLE 57

RESPONDENT REPORT OF 1968 PRESIDENTIAL VOTE
(FOR THOSE INDICATING THEY VOTED IN 1968)

	Low Income	MARs	Average Middles	High Education Middles	Affluents
Nixon	56%	51%	61%	59%	66%
Humphrey	35%	29%	29%	38%	31%
Wallace	8%	21%	8%	1%	3%
Others	0%	0%	0%	1%	0%
Don't Know	2%	0%	1%	0%	0%
Total	100% (N=196)	100% (N=331)	100% (N=343)	100% (N=081)	100% (N=162)

If we take the same trends in 1968 and project them forward in terms of actual voting behavior in the fall of 1972, we obtain the view that MARs who identified with Wallace may have followed the pattern of Average Middles in 1968: they voted for Richard Nixon. Thus, the percentages of Nixon support in the early part of the 1972 campaign shows a differential between MARs and other groups similar to the level of support for Hubert Humphrey in 1968. (See Appendix: Table 22.)

In general terms, our view is that voters who at the time of our survey had a Wallace identification later became, in many instances, Nixon voters. The relatively modest support for Humphrey in 1968 by MARs argues for de-emphasizing the importance of George McGovern's campaign strategy and its alleged errors.

MARs and Party Realignments: Recent Data

The widely perceived shift toward independent voting and the Wallace candidacy are continuing topics of discussion by both analysts of the political process and the public at large. In the Cambridge Report of March 1975 our analysis of MAR political attitudes provides a useful perspective on these issues, particularly since we have presented the MAR ideology as a unique combination of "right" and "left" attitudes. The allegiance of this group toward any given program or political candidate—and indeed the self-definition of MARs—must be viewed in the more "traditional" ways of defining political realities. One such "traditional" indicator is contained in the 1975 Cambridge Report. In that survey we analyzed responses to the question: "Would you describe yourself as more of a liberal or more of a conservative?" We note that MARs are more likely than other white respondents to see themselves as political conservatives. The fact is many MARs also call themselves "liberal"—3 out of every 10 do. The data suggests the subtlety of coalition which may arise when "true" rightists come to be in a common classification with MARs. Often political analysts have failed to make the distinction.

A second consideration of MAR links to the conventional political spectrum is party affiliation. Again the 1975 Cambridge Report is the basis of our empirical data. Here the question was: "Generally speaking do you usually think of yourself as a Republican, a Democrat, an Independent or

TABLE 58

"WOULD YOU DESCRIBE YOURSELF
AS MORE OF A LIBERAL OR MORE
OF A CONSERVATIVE?":
1975 CAMBRIDGE REPORT

	MARs	Others
Conservative	43% +	37% −
Moderate	23%	23%
Liberal	30%	33%
Don't Know	4%	7%
Total	100%	100%
	(N=418)	(N=944)

what?" Patterns of response (Table 59) show 48 percent of MARs with some linkage to the Democrats and 26 percent with a Republican affiliation; for other white respondents these percentages are 50 percent and 26 percent respectively. Thus MARs are about as broadly based in their political loyalties as others. Yet there are some trends to take note of. Table 59 shows, for example, that MARs are less likely to be "weak" Democrats or Republicans than independents who lean toward a major party. Moreover, MARs are proportionately found among those declaring strong party loyalties—27 percent compared to 25 percent for other white respondents. Overall, then, we find evidence that MARs are not the disgruntled independents alone. Nor are they those with easily loosened party affiliations. Their self-declared political persuasions are expressive of a distinctive brand of conventional party "conserva-

TABLE 59

POLITICAL PARTY AFFILIATION
"GENERALLY SPEAKING, DO YOU USUALLY THINK OF
YOURSELF AS A REPUBLICAN, A DEMOCRAT, AN
INDEPENDENT, OR WHAT?"
(March 1975)

	MARs	Others
Strong Democrat	19%	18%
Weak Democrat	15%	18%
Independent—Leans toward Democrat	14%	14%
Strong Republican	8%	7%
Weak Republican	9%	12%
Independent—Leans toward Republican	9%	7%
Independent—No Leaning	26%	24%
Total	100%	100%
	(N=418)	(N=944)

tism"—a very apotheosis of what makes the MAR so enigmatic to many traditional liberals and aspiring political hopefuls.

The Next Round:
MARs in the 1976 Presidential Election

From the analysis we have presented and the underlying issues we have stressed, both major political parties will be hard-pressed to garner the MAR vote. Yet it is equally important to point out how vital such support is for any candidate to emerge victorious in a national election in which votes are increasingly weighed outside of traditional party commitment.

In essence, we might well argue that it is not the "silent majority" that is to be wooed in 1976 or 1980 but rather the 1 in 4 Americans that we have indicated from our analysis who hold a distinct ideology and perspective about American society. It is from this group that we may anticipate a fundamental struggle in terms of allegiance in future elections. It is not only a question of whether this group identifies itself with the traditional right or the traditional left, but rather whether candidates come to the fore who seem to represent a rejection of both of these traditional political alternatives or extremes.

Initial assessment of the MAR on the 1976 presidential election is to be found in the Cambridge Report of March 1975. Here we obtained comparisons between MARs and others in terms of favorable and unfavorable "images" of a variety of leading political figures—not all of whom are announced or likely candidates. In Table 60 we have rank ordered nine such persons in terms of MAR preferences. President Ford heads this list closely followed by George Wallace. Ronald Reagan is the next most positively viewed political figure. He appears to be viewed equally by MARs and other respondents in the early 1975 survey.[32] George McGovern is far at the bottom with a 10 percent greater unfavorable than favorable reaction from MARs.

Table 60 also shows that Ted Kennedy ranks sixth on the nine-person list of public political figures—for both MARs and other whites in the 1975 survey. In fact for MARs there is a

TABLE 60

CANDIDATE IMAGES:
GENERALLY FAVORABLE OR GENERALLY UNFAVORABLE OPINION

	MARs			Others		
	Favorable	Unfavorable	Difference	Favorable	Unfavorable	Difference
Gerald Ford	55% −	35% =	+20%	66% −	28% =	+38%
George Wallace	51% −	35% =	+16%	46% −	44% =	+ 2%
Ronald Reagan	49% −	35% =	+14%	50% −	35% =	+15%
Edwin Muskie	45% −	34% =	+11%	51% −	25% =	+26%
Henry Jackson	31% −	22% =	+ 9%	32% −	19% =	+13%
Ted Kennedy	48% −	40% =	+ 8%	51% −	40% =	+11%
Hubert Humphrey	49% −	42% =	+ 7%	50% −	38% =	+12%
Nelson Rockefeller	45% −	42% =	+ 3%	49% −	40% =	+ 9%
George McGovern	39% −	49% =	−10%	41% −	45% =	− 4%

slightly smaller positive over negative margin in the MAR group than for other respondents—+ 8 percent versus + 11 percent. This rather unimpressive reaction by MARs is significant in light of a number of surveys since the 1972 presidential campaign which have provided speculation about a Kennedy-Wallace ticket. Particularly in the period prior to Wallace's near assassination and even more recently, chances for a blue collar coalition of rural and Southern state Protestants with urban white ethnics of Catholic identity seemed high. Events surrounding the Boston busing conflict in Ted Kennedy's own state seemed to lessen the possibility of MAR support for a Kennedy-Wallace ticket. In 1972 33 percent of MARs supported one of these two candidates (refer to Table 56). This compares with 23 percent of Low Income respondents, 22 percent of Average Middles, 9 percent of High Education middles and just 5 percent of Affluents.

Rita Graul, citywide president of ROAR in Boston and a symbolic leader of MAR interests, was present when Kennedy sought to address a crowd in East Boston during the fall of 1974. In refusing to try to silence the loud booing and denunciations of Kennedy she declared:

> *"He's never acknowledged a letter from any of the parents who have written him about school desegregation. What makes him think they'll listen to him today? The people of Boston turned their backs on Kennedy today. That is the true feeling of the people."*
>
> Quoted in the *Washington Post*, 9/10/74

Growing attacks upon Kennedy as representing the kind of political figure who is a significant enemy of MAR interests climaxed eight months later when Elvira Palladino, executive board member of ROAR, stated:

> *"We'd like to destroy him politically, and we will. . . . He's voting his conscience instead of the will of the people. If you read that then it is no longer a representative government . . .*
>
> Quoted in the *Ann Arbor News*, 4/8/75

The demonstration in Quincy, Massachusetts, involved severe jostling and heavy abuse aimed toward Kennedy. Rita Graul said she approved of such efforts against Kennedy "at any time possible."

At the time of the 1975 survey no word clearly indicating a Kennedy candidacy had occurred. The interviews that took place offered several hypothetical election run-offs for 1976. Table 61 contains three of these. We find that in the situation of Gerald Ford as the Republican and Henry Jackson as the Democratic candidate, independent Wallace prevails in the MAR group; Ford comes out the winner for other whites. A second race involving Ford, McGovern and Wallace results in a sharp victory for Wallace among MARs and a large margin of victory for Ford among other whites.

In the situation of a Ford-Kennedy-Wallace race, the strength of Kennedy among MARs is still evident. Wallace falls 5 percent behind there and 17 percent behind for other white respondents. Ford is a weak third among MARs, but a close second to Kennedy among other respondents. Moreover, among Democrat respondents the responses to the question, "Who would you like to see the Democrats nominate for President" yields a virtual tie between Kennedy and Wallace among MARs but a clear Kennedy victory among other white Democrats. (See Appendix: Table 23.)

The MAR Wallace Supporter: A Special Breed?

MARs who were Wallace supporters in 1972 do not have a personalized orientation to change that we found characteristic of MARs in general. Instead they supported the idea of a third party and of organizations being changed in fundamental ways, particularly regarding the programs they pursue. Paradoxically, those non-MARs who support Wallace tend to have the more "personalized" orientation toward change. In other words, for non-MARs Wallace identification is associated with characteristics found in the MAR group. But those MARs who *do* support Wallace seem to be of a special breed of MAR, individuals who are more oriented toward system change. The implication here

TABLE 61

HYPOTHETICAL PRESIDENTIAL
RACES: MARCH 1975 SURVEY

	MARs	Others
Ford - Jackson - Wallace (Independent)		
Wallace	32% +	20%
Jackson	26%	26%
Ford	26%	35%+
Undecided	16%	19%
Total	100%	100%
Ford - McGovern - Wallace (Independent)		
Wallace	36% +	23%
Ford	28%	37% +
McGovern	21%	22%
Undecided	15%	18%
Total	100%	100%
Ford - Kennedy - Wallace (Independent)		
Kennedy	35% +	35%
Wallace	30%	18%
Ford	23%	32%
Undecided	12%	15%
Total	100%	100%

is that what is typical of MARs in general, their legitimation of various kinds of direct protest, is particularly true of the MAR Wallace supporter.

There is a "value added" where this particular kind of MAR has a system view of change and that is to support the idea of a third party and to identify with George Wallace. In contrast, non-MARs who take a system orientation are not Wallacites. Where there is Wallace support outside of the MAR umbrella it is for reasons that we have associated earlier with some of the general value orientations of MARs. Thus, support for Wallace tends to include a substantial portion of the MAR population and also acts as a kind of bridge to others who, while not being MARs, accept certain values and attitudes common to MARs and advocated by Wallace. In this sense we may argue that support for Wallace has the potential to come from individuals who share some elements of commonality with MARs. At the same time, it reflects a new, highly sophisticated, and developed sense of political mobilization among the MAR group. Thus, the less politically mobilized among non-MARs may come to link up with the highly mobilized and system-oriented MARs.

On April 26, 1975, George Wallace officially announced his entrance into the 1976 Presidential campaign. A Gallup poll conducted at that time showed him with 22 percent of the vote. Wallace set the tone of his candidacy by indicating that:

> *The big social issue is the preservation of the middle class. The average citizen had defended the system and gotten no thanks. He's turned off and he's fed up. I don't just say that I have to run, but I say that these people should be represented.*

> Quoted in Newsweek, *4/21/75*

In sounding a theme that has great appeal for the MAR, Wallace went on to assert that:

> *The hierarchy and the leadership of the [Democratic] party wish I would go away. They have dealt with conventional politicians for so long that when all of a sudden the average man begins to express himself they don't want to hear it.*

> Quoted in Newsweek, *4/21/75*

Newsweek stated "like his politics, his tactics are improvisational." They further stressed that Wallace's chief issues are "a constellation of little-guy discontents with everything from lawlessness in the streets to busing between schools to sex in textbooks, TV shows and movies. . . . But grievance has always been the name of the Wallace game."[33] The evidence by mid-1975 was certainly on the side of viewing George Wallace as an even more formidable figure in the national

political scene than he was in the early 1972 presidential primaries. A flurry over statements regarding foreign policy prior
to World War II served to further link Wallace to the Coughlin
movement of the 1930s.[34] Despite the attempt by much of the
media to treat Wallace as the "spoiler" rather than a serious
possibility as the winner of a nomination, his more effectively
organized presidential effort for 1976 was widely acknowledged.

An Overview

The evidence from a number of political studies detailing the
erosion of traditional party loyalties adds further credence to
the argument that it is no longer a question of whether the
radical middle is a force in American national politics. The
question has become, "What are the counterforces?"

We have seen that MARs are distinctive in their alienation
from the national government and in their support for George
Wallace. They were not distinctive in their favoring of a third
party as the 1972 election approached, but they certainly
appeared to be a group with early firm convictions about their
personal identifications with particular candidates. Within the
MAR group there is a majority element represented by the
Wallace supporter. At the same time, it should be emphasized
that while a significantly larger proportion of MARs than non-
MARs identify with Wallace, a large portion of the group we
have defined as MARs do not. At the same time the appeal of
Wallace has been apparent among many groups not previously
loyal to him. To measure this the Cambridge study of March
1975 included a question which scaled how complete was the
opposition or support for Wallace. Table 62 summarizes the
patterns obtained. In the case of MARs about 1 in 3 are strong
supporters, another 3 out of 10 are moderate, with 1 in 5
indicating total opposition to Wallace. For other white respondents 1 in 4 are generally supportive and only 23 percent are
always in opposition to Wallace. These patterns show MARs to
be significantly favorable to Wallace but the differences from

TABLE 62

ATTITUDES TOWARD GEORGE WALLACE AS A PRESIDENTIAL
CANDIDATE IN 1976
(WHITE RESPONDENTS ONLY)

	MARs	Others
Always support	13% ⎱ 34% +	9% ⎱ 25%
Somewhere in between—leaning toward support	21% ⎰	16% ⎰
Mid-way between always support and always oppose	29%	32%
Somewhere in between—leaning toward oppose	15% ⎱ 37%	19% ⎱ 42% +
Always oppose	22% ⎰	23% ⎰
Total	100% (N=419)	100% (N=928)

other population segments are far from startling. In fact, compared to the results of the 1972 pre-presidential interest in Wallace, the appeal he manifests appears to have generalized and is not in the exclusive province of the MAR.

In previous chapters we have examined how the large majority of the MAR group expresses its alienation and discontent in ways other than support for George Wallace or the idea of a third party. It is in this context that we must view alienation and the MAR "syndrome" in terms of a range of responses. Some of these may be based on the kinds of direct actions we have noted in earlier chapters with regard to local community and school matters. In other instances the response may be one of personal sense of anomie. In still other cases, individuals may severely criticize the institutions of the society, but not become active in terms of either supporting protest, taking specific political actions or even addressing themselves to the political arena at all.

Let us now summarize specific points about MARs and the presidential candidates made from the 1972 and 1975 data:

1. MARs did not support the idea of a third party in the 1972 presidential election to a greater extent than did other population groups. Affluent and Low Income individuals tended to support the third party less significantly than did any of the three Middle Income groupings in the survey.

2. In terms of identification with presidential candidates, George Wallace draws support from 1 in 5 MARs.

3. Prior to the nominating conventions in 1972, Richard Nixon drew less support from the MAR group than from other population groups.

4. The extent to which President Nixon held the allegiance of Middle Americans appears to represent a second choice. Thus, at the early point of our present survey, a significantly smaller proportion of MARs were Nixon supporters and the support for George Wallace appeared to be a firm base from the 1968 to the 1972 interval.

5. While MARs appear to reflect a highly independent stance on many issues, in fact their party loyalty—while weak—still remains intact. As a group they are not distinctly Democrat in allegiance.

6. The Wallace candidacy provides a bridge between those in the MAR group who take a "system" view of their alienation and those who are not MARs but who also feel their concerns require collective action.

7. Wallace support in 1975 compared to 1972 is higher among MARs but is noteworthy for its increase among other whites interviewed; at the same time attitudes toward Ted Kennedy between 1972 and 1975 had increased in the same manner.

8. If we conclude that Richard Nixon was able to capture the total Wallace vote in his 1972 victory margin, then it becomes clear that without a shift in the preferences of MARs away from Wallace there is likely to be no election of a front-running Democratic candidate in 1976 without MAR support. At the time of this analysis the person most able to create this shift was Ted Kennedy.

10. REDUCING MAR ALIENATION

The Wallace movement, ROAR, and other collective expressions of MAR discontent converge in the belief that bureaucracies of all kinds have lost contact with the opinions and needs of ordinary people. Government agencies are perhaps the prime example of this, but it is also true of unions and the church—traditionally considered as "advocate agencies," whose primary function has been (at least ostensibly) to further the interests of these very people.

Areas of High Leverage in Reducing Alienation

The issue of organizations being "out of touch" of course suggests the related issue of "access" to organizations. A very common opinion is that all types of bureaucracies (but especially governmental) are responsive only to large organized groups which make their demands in an aggressive, perhaps even illegal manner. An individual person is unable to get anything from these bureaucracies. Thus, the individual is faced with a choice between joining in some type of political pressure group or becoming apathetic toward the functioning of these bureaucracies—having as little to do with them as possible—and "rolling with the punches" where contact is unavoidable.

A second factor which proved to be a major independent source of alienation and political mobilization was that of the stage of group "consciousness." Those who felt that their closest group is just starting to become recognized or should seek to become recognized also expressed a strong sense of multiple threat from blacks which extended beyond economic considerations to status, power, and cultural concerns. Individuals who were more prosperous and highly educated than other respondents in the national survey were more likely to feel the need for group mobilization. In contrast to concepts of economic "squeeze," we found that rising group consciousness as a basis for alienation and discontent grew out of improved conditions, not decline. This distinct source of polarization is therefore by itself a significant explanatory hypothesis apart from other considerations.

The question arises as to the policy implications of such results. Some might read these findings as indicating that if we want peace in our society we should move towards neighborhoods which have ethnic, racial and status homogeneity. But many of our basic beliefs about equality would be violated in the process. The history of opportunity structure in America clearly indicates that such homogeneous grouping of neighborhoods would end up discriminating against the poor.

Without any doubt, bringing people together who have different socioeconomic and cultural backgrounds is very likely to lead to friction. Nevertheless, such mixtures should be encouraged under conditions where conflict is recognized as a consequence of such mixtures and where some conflict resolution procedures are built into the neighborhood structure. In the absence of such conflict resolution procedures, the smallest differences are immediately blown up into large conflicts and one group or the other is inclined to leave.

At present, it is not entirely clear what such conflict resolution procedures would look like. On a city-wide level there have been various institutional procedures, such as the human relations commission, set up to mediate disputes between ethnic groups. However, the more appropriate analogy would be the adjudication procedures between management and unions in large corporations.

When unions were first recognized, the smallest conflicts between employee and supervisor ran the danger of being blown up into a full-scale strike. However, as the relationship between unions and management matured, there developed a whole series of adjudication procedures which start out at a personal level, moving to the convening of an officially sponsored local panel in the department, then to plant-wide mediation boards, and ultimately towards national impartial arbitrators hired by the company and union to settle disputes.

In the past we have looked at neighborhoods as, by and large, homogeneous enclaves where the higher status group wielded unchallenged power and had the economic ability to leave if conditions worsened. Thus we have never had to develop adjudication procedures at the local neighborhood level. However, the supreme court decision on schooling has almost made mixed neighborhoods, or the use of neighborhood facilities, the rule rather than the exception. For the first time it has become important to think about adjudication procedures if we are to hold to our ideas of equality.

Areas of Moderate Leverage for Reducing Alienation

Four of the ten hypotheses we investigated in order to pinpoint sources of alienation proved to have predictive value by themselves in only a limited sphere. These included absolute economic deprivation; the reduced quality of the local environment; inconsistency of organizational policies, and group status conflict.

Our speculations about the implications of the economic position can further be directed at two issues: (1) the extent to which various types of social participation are reduced once economic squeeze is felt, and (2) the type of motivations for participation. On the first issue, our findings suggest that those with an absolute economic squeeze were the ones who felt powerless and were less likely to participate. People who felt relatively deprived economically had no such problem. People with absolute economic squeeze cannot therefore be expected to form the core or catalyst for new community action efforts and in fact may be the first to drop out of such efforts.

Consequently, it is important in seeking to reach people who suffer an absolute economic decline to rely on existing channels and structures such as local PTAs or already built-in forms of minimal social participation. Moreover, the organizations in these categories of "established" structures may have to devote more effort toward initiating contact with the "absolute economic squeeze" family and may therefore have to shift their particular forms of communication participation style.

The motivation for sustained involvement in such collective efforts must be based less on the sense of outrage about the position of other groups and more on the meeting of essential services and the possible exchange of bartered resources—for example, cooperation in specific daily concerns such as child care, mobility for shopping, minor home repairs, etc. These are examples of types of programs which individuals with absolute economic squeeze would most respond to. In addition, such persons might well provide the final push in an effort for mobilizing a community or supporting a given candidate or "drive." Reducing social alienation for this group means essentially encouraging such persons to have a say in the final product but not relying on a continuous involvement where economic resources are limited and work time cannot be sacrificed.

In contrast to those individuals who feel absolute economic squeeze, those with relative economic squeeze tend to use abstract yardsticks derived from perceptions about how other groups are doing or the extent to which they have progressed in their individual career and standard of living achievements. Consequently, the role of specific information about the position of other groups especially as this is focused on the patterns within the local community may reduce polarization—and at the same time provide the basis for coalition with others once common barriers to achievement are delineated. That persons feeling relative economic deprivation tend to focus on "system" explanations suggests that this group can provide a key basis for organized efforts at change and would participate at a high level in collective actions. A mass media approach to this group coupled with a locality-oriented content can serve to stimulate interest and involvement in given neighborhoods for programs which subsequently require a community or state base for action.

Alterations in the standard of local services as such may not change the sense of concern many persons feel in regard to the proximity of racial minorities with different cultural, organizational and "status" styles. Providing more consistent policies in the treatment of different groups and making certain that clearer policies are enunciated and followed by organizations may prove less valuable than insuring that individuals are able to "reach organizations."

Responding to the militant feelings and group interests of white ethnics and racially identified persons may provide only greater awareness of the need to protect newly conscious group interests and parochial goals.

Consequently rather than proceeding to treat any of the four hypothesis conditions with specialized impact as areas of primary policy making, might be better to treat these as sub-headings under the major agenda of reducing status threats from blacks, providing greater access to major institutions, and developing methods of relating to average citizens in ways which generate a sense of worth and dignity—ways which assure them that they have "representatives."

Areas of Low Leverage
for Reducing Society Polarization

Among the explanations of the MAR discontent in our multivariate analysis, three conditions proved to be only slightly correlated: 1) the sense that bureaucracy was taking over society; 2) ethnic identification itself; and finally, 3) work dissatisfaction alone. These findings have important policy implication for the strategy and targets of interventions to reduce social tensions. In the case of alienation from bureaucracy, we have what may be a very basic disagreement between some of the very high status together with minority members of society who stress the need to "break up" or decentralize major institutions, and those who do not see size or centralization as particularly important aspects of the problem.

The failure of any program to seek direct coalitions between groups around such concerns is largely predictable, given our findings. Given their basically diverse views of the way organizations have gone wrong, to expect college students, blue collar workers, and blacks to join forces is to ignore the realities of differences in the types of complaints. The same goals which concern the "Greening of America" issues may not "turn on" many alienated MARs. Instead it is important to recognize that the common base is the concern over some aspect of the way local schools, government and other organizations are working. Decentralization is clearly not an area in which to begin to build support across diverse social groups in view of the important differences in what is perceived to be the nature of the "alienation."

It appears to the observer that the link between white ethnicity and racism or group consciousness and the need to have consensus in order to meet common problems is one which is a danger to American society at this historic moment. Our data suggest that such concerns are only partially justified. Ethnic ties *per se* are not important sources of alienation and political reaction. As we have indicated it is not ethnicity itself, but the perceived state of one's group that is critical to the MAR perspective. However, we have some evidence from our national survey that individuals with a firmly defined and organizationally secure ethnic identification may be less alienated and more supportive of non-institutional social action than persons lacking any form of group closeness.

Our multivariate analysis indicated that the hypothesis dealing with work alienation was the best predictor of direct political action in only one instance—the support for picketing in a busing situation. Otherwise we must conclude from our analysis that work alienation alone contributes very little to our understanding either of the Middle American ideology or of attitudes of social discontent and political activism. The fact that it may well be correlated with other economic and social tensions must of course be emphasized. The critical issue whether efforts to focus on the nature of work and the problems of the work organization should be a primary strategy for reducing polarization must therefore be answered in the negative. If our data are a valid basis for policy formulation, we would argue in favor of increasing the community role rather than the work role of people. Moreover, the focus on individual malaise in the workplace must be seen—given our findings—to represent a displacement from the concerns people feel about the functioning of non-work institutions. This "spillover" effect is a crucial basis for defining the direction of social interventions. In our view, the direction of influence is largely from non-work to work spheres.

Multiple Sources of Discontent

It is obvious by now that a number of factors play a role in MAR alienation and mobilization. Yet in terms of the social policy questions we find that some hypotheses were more important for predicting political mobilization as such, while others indicated the presence of "diffuse" alienation which greatly resists direct action or at least collective action. It would follow that if for a given individual more than one of the hypotheses were true, then the likelihood is that his actions would be oriented toward a fuller range of responses. It is important for us to identify consequences in a policy sense; for example, when individuals may be hit simultaneously by absolute as well as relative economic deprivation. Thus, absolute economic deprivation was the best predictor of identification with Wallace. Relative economic deprivation, on the other hand, was associated with both tension headaches and the attitude of needing to be part of an organized group. It might be argued for example that where the individual feels *both* concerns, a powerful basis of political mobilization is present.

The Catalytic and Unique Role
of the Middle American Radical Ideology

One of the major conclusions on the multivariate phase of our data analysis is that a "critical mass" of social discontent and beliefs maximizes alienation and political mobilization. We believe the existence of such combinations as, for example, relative alienation from bureaucracy and the major tenets of the MAR ideology is sufficient to produce major new directions in social action by individuals, as well as to break away from traditional party allegiances and forms of political participation.

At the same time, we would argue that in many instances the existence of either certain background factors or specific types of economic deprivation, ethnic consciousness, or various criticisms of organizations *without* the MAR ideological dimension is insufficient to bring about or account for political mobilization.

In terms of social background factors which predict the MAR ideology we found only two which were significant: first, the educational level of the respondent, and, second, the region of the country in which the person is living.

The policy implications of the major role played by education in predicting the MAR ideology suggests that what is required is not only the upgrading of formal education for all members of American society, but also the reduction in certification discrepancies between those who have completed high school and those who have attended college. It is this set of barriers which blacks and many Americans, including MARs, have perceived as inappropriate and unnecessary in terms of holding important jobs in both the private and public spheres.

The difference between MARs and other Americans is not a matter of socioeconomic position alone, but of important perceptions and attitudes about where American society has been and where it is going. At several points in our study we have found that MARs as a group are less concerned about the economy and what we might call material issues than are other members of the society.

National Policy Implications

Let us indicate several types of programs which seem to be more appropriate "bets" given the nature of the MAR phenomenon as we have described it.

1. *The significant role played by formal education of respondents indicates that in order to alleviate the alienation and types of beliefs associated with Middle American Radicalism it is important not only to encourage individuals to attain a great level of formal education, but to increase the accessibility of educational experiences for individuals living in local com-*

munities and neighborhoods where such resources are not available. This would include such notions as mobile classrooms and the equivalent of traveling university classrooms in which there might well be programs set up on a temporary basis in housing projects, local neighborhood centers or other locations where significant members of the MAR group could have access to the specific training and general information presently available only to students enrolled in a program of higher education. Included in this program would be incentives offered to both employers and employees to encourage adult education and other efforts and to provide appropriate incentives for pursuing such individual improvement and occupationally useful efforts.

2. *Increase in available economic resources is not a major source for reducing the Middle American Radical alienation.* This does not mean that we should not seek to improve the actual dollar earnings of MARs vis-á-vis other groups. But it is clear that the absolute level of earning differences between MARs, blacks, and other groups is not the most fundamental issue. It is, rather, in the context of particular status concerns that the MAR ideology flourishes most. Consequently we must be particularly attuned to the perceived status rankings of various kinds of federal, state and local programs. For example, U-235 housing becomes an important way by which Low Income and minority groups are able to move into better housing. But efforts must be made to allow for the kinds of status differentiations which avoid having persons with identical homes living next to each other, or in the same neighborhood, when one of those individuals is paying half the rent of the other. MARs are not against blacks having good housing, but they are concerned that in terms of some of the external trappings of status there was no basis for identifying those who had gone the conventional route and those who were being subsidized.

This, of course, does not mean that national programs in housing or elsewhere should enshrine rather trivial forms of invidious status distinctions. But it is extremely important to take into account the status value which individuals invest in what otherwise might be seen as the "frills" or fringe benefits of particular occupational positions or other social roles. This does not mean that we must deprive individuals who receive assistance from the dignity and equal treatment which they deserve as members of our society. At the same time we must recognize that our society differentiates among those who have worked long hours and who have a special investment in the appearance of housing, neighborhoods and forms of consumption. To wipe away these symbols of achievement and security is to undermine significantly the self-interest and psychic well-being of a major portion of the American middle class. Insensitivity to status issues must be avoided and greater care taken that the investments which individuals have in their statuses be left as undisturbed as possible when we begin to move in response to the real needs and the status needs of minorities and other groups.

3. *Forms of coalition between MARs and other groups must often take an indirect form.* We have seen that in many instances the capacity of MARs to form coalitions and to perceive common interests with other groups has been blunted by the sense of the effective organizing power of a number of racial and other minorities in society. Therefore, in order to describe bases of national, state or local coalitions there must be an addressing of the specific real interests of MARs as a crucial first step in efforts to reduce community dissention, polarization and conflict. Thus, in the very labeling of programs which imply that their primary purpose is to "bridge the gap" between groups, there may very well be a self-defeating mechanism. It is more valuable to begin the effort at bridging conflict by addressing concerns which arise our of the problems facing MARs and others in their immediate neighborhood context.

It is more important, for instance, that programs which are aimed at crime, racial conflict or deterioration demonstrate effectiveness in a small-scale area rather than being spread over a large metropolitan community all at once. Given the declining resources likely to be available from federal and state governments it is important to design programs which are scaled to the level of significant visible accomplishment rather than toward advertising the possibility of significant gains across a large community.

It is through the demonstration of capacity to change conditions that some of the more important value and ideological positions which have become enshrined in the MAR ideology may be altered. A successful pilot project may do more than an unsuccessful massive program in the effort to reduce alienation. In any event, it is crucial that the multiple character of problems be recognized and resources which are available be utilized in such a way that a level of success is assured even if the scope of the program may be limited.

4. *Programs for community change should include mechanisms for conflict resolution.* A major deficiency in the development of anti-poverty and other social programs of the 1950s and 1960s is that they do not have built-in mechanisms for dealing with the heterogeneity of a given neighborhood or part of a community. It is not possible to make alterations in one area of the community without effects radiating throughout a large segment of the entire community. It is this closed-system nature of urban society that presents us with some of our most difficult problems.

If we recognize that the improvements in one group will necessarily lead to visible or perceived reduction of attention to the concerns of other groups, we must seek to develop mechanisms for a redress of perceived grievances as well as for dealing with actual deprivations. Thus, various forms of ombudsman rules, citizen review boards, class action suits brought by a neighborhood legal service and various techniques of mediation, arbitration and fact finding to aid in dispute settlements at the neighborhood and local community level must be important parts of any form of public policy implementation. The absence of such mechanisms and, in particular, the failure of existing institutions to serve in this capacity represents a major source of the increased alienation of MARs.

11. MARs AND INSTITUTIONAL CHANGES

A substantial portion of our national survey was designed to discover what kind of society the people want and how our major institutions should be altered. In the present chapter we shall review the findings and explore the types of implied "directions for change" that MARs and other population segments support.

Included in the portion of the interview that dealt with organizations were a series of questions which asked:

People have different ideas of how various organizations can be changed when things aren't going right. For each organization please tell me which change it needs most?

Respondents were given a set of alternatives in which they could select the most needed change or could indicate that no change in an organization was desirable. Table 63 shows the results for the five major population groups involved in our study. We listed nine social institutions and asked individuals to indicate the type and character of change that they were most interested in. Important differences occurred in the level of need for change shown by different population groups.

We note that MARs, while showing a slightly higher percentage than Affluents and High Education Middles, were not significantly above these groups in terms of their interest in change. However, in comparison with Average Middles, as well as with respect to Low Income persons, there is a statistically significant difference.

Welfare agencies came in for a high degree of interest in change. We find that MARs as well as Affluents have significantly higher levels of interest in changing these agencies than do other population groups. Individuals least concerned with

176

TABLE 63

EXTENT TO WHICH CHANGE IN SPECIFIC TYPES OF
ORGANIZATIONS IS INDICATED
(IN ORDER OF MIDDLE AMERICAN PERCENTAGES ADVOCATING CHANGE)

	Low Income	MARs	Average Middles	High Education Middles	Affluents
National Government	62%	84%	71%	80%	82%
Welfare Agencies	50%	77%	68%	66%	76%
Unions	47%	66%	61%	69%	78%+
Local Schools	33%	56%+	46%	53%	53%
Corporations	34%	55%+	46%	59%	50%
Local Government	35%	55%	41%	44%	42%
Own Workplace	29%	39%	38%	46%	42%
Churches	24%	35%+	25%	53%	44%
Local Police	20%	32%+	25%	32%	19%

changing welfare agencies were Low Income Americans. Average and High Education Middles represent groups which lie intermediate between the Low Income group and the MAR and Affluent groups.

For Affluents there is greater interest in changing unions than welfare agencies; and this group is significantly more likely than Average Middles, Low Income respondents or MARs to advocate change in union organizations. MARs are not significantly more likely than Average Middles to advocate that unions change and they are not different from High Education Middles in this respect, either. Once again, Low Income respondents were significantly less likely to advocate change.

Fourth on the list of organizations which MARs feel ought to be changed are the local schools. Again, Average Middles and

Low Income respondents are significantly less likely to advocate change in such structures. We find that once again the differences between MARs, High Education Middles and Affluents is virtually insignificant.

Turning to attitudes about change in corporations, we again find that MARs are not uniquely high in their interest in change. This honor goes to the High Education Middles. However, we also note that MARs are significantly more likely than Average Middles or Low Income respondents to advocate that corporations have some change in their organization.

In the case of the local government we find that MARs are as interested in change here as they are in regard to corporations. Low Income individuals once again have the lowest level of interest in change. We find that Average Middles, High Education Middles and Affluents are similar in having a significantly lower interest in change in organization in comparison with MARs. Moreover, in Table 63 for the first time we find a pattern which was prevalent with regard to critical attitudes about organizations: namely, MARs are not seeking structural changes in major social institutions any more vigorously than are certain other population groups.

On the issue of change in the workplace we find that MARs are not unique in their outlook. High Education Middles and Affluents are somewhat higher in advocating change in the workplace. Low Income respondents are significantly less likely than other groups—including MARs—to advocate some sort of change in the organization in which they work.

With respect to the churches we find that it is the High Education Middles who are significantly above MARs in advocating change. At the same time, we find that MARs are significantly more likely than Average Middles and Low Income individuals to want to have churches change in some respect. Affluents stand midway. They are more likely than MARs and Average Middles to advocate change but not on the same level as High Education Middles.

Finally, we note that there is the least interest in change with regard to the local police. However, MARs are significantly more likely than Average Middles and Low Income respondents to advocate such change. In general, the Middle Income groups are more critical of the local police than either the Low Income or Affluent respondents.

The patterns shown in Table 63 confirm that on the issue of advocating change in organizations MARs emerge with only one uniquely high categorization: local government. In three instances MARs were the highest in terms of the other four population groups, but not to a statistically significant degree.

While being highly inclined to take direct political action, MARs, though very critical of organizations in a number of respects, do not desire to bring about changes in these structures to the same extent as one would expect, given the level of dissatisfaction with the performance and behavior of such structures. Overall, MARs are not significantly higher than other groups in desiring change either in specific kinds of organizations nor in terms of a large number of institutions of the society.

If Change—What Kind? Given the relatively moderate degree of interest in change which MARs advocate, it is important now to zero in on the character of the changes advocated by MARs and other groups. In the original survey respondents were asked to choose from the following possible alternatives in terms of change: 1) need to get rid of people at the top; 2) need to change many of the staff; 3) the organization is too big, make it smaller; and 4) organization is doing the wrong thing, it should switch what it is doing. Patterns of the most preferred type of change are shown in Table 64.

With regard to several organizations, respondents tend to mention one type of change most frequently. In the case of welfare agencies and churches, respondents advocate change in what the organization is doing. With regard to corporations all groups emphasized most the need to reduce the size of such structures. However, in 6 out of 9 structures, the most frequently made type of change varies with organizational type. Thus, with regard to the national government, MARs and High Education Middles both feel that it is important to get rid of people at the top. Affluents, on the other hand, most often recommend reduction in size of the national government.

TABLE 64

MOST FREQUENTLY MENTIONED TYPE OF CHANGE
FOR SPECIFIC INSTITUTIONS

	Low Income	MARs	Average Middles	High Education Middles	Affluents
National Government	Staff	People at top	Staff	People at top	Reduce size
Welfare Agencies	Programs	Programs	Programs	Programs	Programs
Unions	People at top	People at top	People at top, Reduce size	People at top	People at top
Local Schools	Staff	Staff	Staff	Programs	Programs
Corporations	Reduce size	Reduce size	Reduce size	Reduce size	Reduce size
Local Government	Staff	Staff	Staff	People at top	Staff
Own Workplace	Programs	Staff	Staff	Programs	Staff
Churches	Programs	Programs	Programs	Programs	Programs
Local Police	Staff	Programs	Programs	Staff	Programs

With respect to unions, we find that all groups advocate a change in people at the top. Average Middles also tend to emphasize reducing the size of the union.

In terms of the local schools, High Education Middles and Affluents advocate changing the goals of the schools, whereas other population groups stress the need to get rid of many of the staff. On the issue of local government all population groups have the same preference for changing staff except High Education Middles who more often advocate getting rid of people at the top.

With regard to the workplace, both Low Income individuals and High Education Middles advocate change in goals, whereas other groups stress the need to change many on the staff. With regard to the local police, MARs, Average Middles and Affluents have a similar emphasis on switching what local police are doing, whereas Low Income persons and High Education Middles both say get rid of many of the staff.

The patterns shown in Table 64 are significant for two reasons: first, they suggest bases of coalition among different population groups in terms of the type of change advocated in a specific type of organization. At the same time, they also illuminate the fact that while people may share an interest in change in the same kind of structure, they may differ in what they want altered. Thus, Table 64 provides a useful approach on how to build coalitions around specific change issues and, at the same time, indicates why there are barriers to broad support for change.

Across the Board or Variable Institutional Change?

For nine institutions as a whole, Table 64 shows that certain kinds of themes consistently occur among the different population groups. Thus, Low Income respondents tend to emphasize either changing the staff of organizations or changing the program. There are four mentions of staff change out of nine and three mentions of program change. In only one instance do Low Income individuals say that people at the top should be gotten rid of. We find that for Average Middles there is an equal concern with the idea of changing the staff and programs of the organization. Low Income and Average Middles have a rather similar profile in terms of the kinds of changes they advocate across the various organizations. For High Education Middles there is a particular stress on changing the goals, i.e., the activities of organizations. This occurs in 4 out of 9 instances with only one case where desire for a change in staff is most often advocated. Moreover, in 3 out of 9 cases, High Education Middles say "get rid of people at the top." Among Affluents, we find most emphasis on "program" change less (1 out of 9) on advocating the reduction in the size of the organization; and altering major portions of the staff in only two cases. In only 1 out of 9 instances do Affluents suggest getting "rid of people at the top."

Among MARs we find that there is an emphasis on changing the staff in 3 out of 9 cases, change in programs in another three cases, and getting rid of people at the top in 2 of the 9 organizational contacts. Thus, MARs seem to have a very diversified set of change goals for different kinds of organizations.

While Table 64 has indicated the variety of organizational change advocated across population groups as well as within different organizations for the same group, we have a special concern with the kind of change advocated for governmental structures. Table 65 provides such data.

Concerning the need to change what organizations are doing, we find that no significant difference occurs across the various population groups. All groups tend somewhat more frequently to advocate this form of change for the national government compared to the local government. Two groups focus on the need to reduce the size of the national and local government: High Education Middles and Affluents.

In terms of changing many of the staff members of organizations we find that there is a somewhat greater interest in this kind of change for the national government. At the same time, for local government MARs are significantly more likely than either Average Middles or Low Income individuals to advocate this form of changing the staff of the local government.

When we move to the type of change which involves "getting rid of the people at the top" we find that MARs are distinctive with respect to both national and local government: they advocate this form of change significantly more than do Low Income respondents, Average Middles and Affluents. At the same time, High Education Middles resemble MARs in advocating such changes. However, there is a difference between High Education Middles and MARs: the latter group, however, tends to focus on *both* change in many of the staff *and* getting rid of people at the top—a total of 56 percent. High Education Middles tend to advocate each of those changes less—a total of 43 percent—and 21 percent stress the need to reduce the size of the national government.

TABLE 65

TYPES OF CHANGES IN GOVERNMENTAL INSTITUTIONS:
NATIONAL AND LOCAL

	Low Income	MARs	Average Middles	High Education Middles	Affluents
Change what they are doing:					
National	17%	18%	17%	16%	16%
Local	11%	12%	12%	11%	13%
Reduce size:					
National	8%	10%	10%	21%	29%
Local	3%	2%	3%	1%	5%
Change many of the staff:					
National	20%	27%	27%	19%	26%
Local	13%	22%	17%	15%	17%
Get rid of the people at the top:					
National	18%	29%	17%	24%	10%
Local	9%	19%	10%	17%	7%

MARs stress the personalized versus the "structural" types of alterations of government institutions. Low Income respondents, where they do advocate change, tend also to emphasize personalized dimensions of the organization—38 percent—and not the reduction in size of such structures—8 percent. Average Middles place major emphasis on staff change, not on change in top leadership. Affluents stress the need for reducing the size or changing the staff of the federal government rather than getting rid of people at the top or changing what the national government is doing. High Education Middles have a high level of advocated changes in the national government divided evenly between structural and personal.

An Overview of Desired Institutional Change

We have argued that in the realm of governmental structures MARs tend to be stressing those dimensions of the organization which are not "system." In our exploratory community interviews we found that the kinds of respondents who fitted into the MAR types of communities in which we worked had a similar view when thinking about a range of racial, economic and other problems with which they were dealing. They tended not to think in terms of structural issues, but in terms of the personalized relationships between individuals in different groups or in different positions. This same tendency has been shown to emerge from the national survey.

It might well be argued that in order for a group to become the basis for a significant political movement there must be a shift from the personalized view of problems toward the "system" view of problems. Without perceiving that structural alterations in institutions can bring about desired goals, it is difficult for individuals to use collective structures and political actions as a basis when, in fact, they view problems at a personal level in terms of the individuals who hold office or work for institutions such as government, church or union. While they do focus on the need to get rid of people at the top of structures, MARs are really suggesting that they do not desire a fundamental alteration of either local or national governmental institutions. The position of High Education Middles is somewhat more ambivalent. While no structural changes of local government seem to be stressed, there is certainly an emphasis on reducing the size of the national government.

Table 66 follows up this analysis of types of change advocated in terms of "service institutions" such as schools, welfare agencies and the police.

TABLE 66

TYPES OF CHANGES ADVOCATED FOR SCHOOLS,
POLICE, AND WELFARE AGENCIES

	Low Income	MARs	Average Middles	High Education Middles	Affluents
Change what they are doing:					
Local Schools	11%	16%	14%	22%	17%
Local Police	7%	13%	10%	8%	10%
Welfare Agencies	28%	37%	37%	41%	40%
Reduce size:					
Local Schools	4%	10%	9%	12%	13%
Local Police	0%	1%	1%	1%	2%
Welfare Agencies	6%	7%	7%	11%	14%
Change many of the staff:					
Local Schools	13%	17%	15%	12%	13%
Local Police	9%	10%	9%	16%	5%
Welfare Agencies	9%	14%	11%	7%	13%
Get rid of people at the top:					
Local Schools	5%	14%	8%	7%	10%
Local Police	3%	8%	5%	6%	3%
Welfare Agencies	7%	19%	13%	6%	9%

Changing the goals of "service" organizations is something which is advocated most often for welfare agencies. MARs are not unique in this emphasis. Goal change in local schools is stressed more than for local police. In the former case, it is High Education Middles who have the highest emphasis on this change direction. MARs rank highest for desire to change police programs. Size reduction is generally mentioned by Affluents, although group differences are not marked.

On the issue of changing the staff of organizations, MARs are highest in supporting such change for the local schools and the welfare agencies but, in fact, they share views which are very similar to other groups. With regard to the local police it is interesting to note the comparison between High Education Middles and Affluents: four times as many of the former advocate changing the staff of the police.

On the desire to get rid of people at the top, we find that MARs are highest in regard to advocating such change for welfare agencies, local police and the local schools.

In Table 67 we summarize these differential patterns of desired change.

It is clear that advocacy for particular types of change tend to be highly differentiated by population groups. The favorite form of change for Affluents is to change the goals and in particular to reduce the size of organizations. High Education Middles are significant for their interest in changing the goals of organizations. Low Income individuals, where they do advocate a change, tend to place the emphasis upon either changing what organizations are doing or getting rid of many of the staff. Average Middles tend to stress changing what organizations are doing and changing many of the staff. MARs tend to emphasize both changing what organizations are doing, getting rid of people at the top and changing many of the staff: there is much greater emphasis on personalized forms of change rather than structural alterations.

Directions for Internal Organizational Change: MAR Priorities

In contrast to some other groups, MARs feel strongly that organizations are not doing a good job. Organizations which

TABLE 67

EXTENT TO WHICH FOUR DIFFERENT TYPES OF CHANGE
ARE ADVOCATED FOR ORGANIZATIONS
(PERCENT TWO OR MORE ORGANIZATIONS)

	Low Income	MARs	Average Middles	High Education Middles	Affluents
Doing the wrong things, should switch what they are doing	27%	42%	34%	48%	44%
Too big, make it smaller	15%	21%	20%	26%	34%
Need to change many of the staff	23%	36%	31%	29%	31%
Need to get rid of people at the top	15%	37%	20%	27%	17%

should be serving all the people are allowing themselves to be interfered with, are not treating people in an even-handed way, and are not following consistent rules. But rather than advocate change in the fundamental structure or system, MARs show a strong preference for changing the people who actually run the various bureaucracies.

As part of our examination of the important connection found between the functioning of bureaucracies and the MAR ideology, let us explore some implications for the internal functioning of various organizations.

We find that MARs as a group tend to be especially supportive of the idea of getting rid of people at the top in leadership of organizations. But MARs are by no means completely alienated from bureaucracies.

A rather sharp distinction is often made between low level bureaucrats and administrators and high level policy makers. Attitudes toward the former are often—but by no means always—rather favorable. Teachers, union stewards and local union people in general, parish priests and even welfare case workers ("they're just doing their job, it's the administrators who are to blame") generally get good or at least less negative evaluations than top leaders.

The respondents seem to identify with these low level bureaucrats since they themselves are often forced to work in a system such as factories where they must follow rules established by higher-ups. It is the upper level bureaucrats who sit in their plush offices and lose contact with the "common man" with whom the MARs find fault. MARs want to alter those who make policy in the organization, not necessarily those with whom they deal on a daily basis. We have here one of the most important hints as to the direction in which organizations, especially those which are focused on the local community, need to address themselves.

When MARs speak about organizational change they are referring to the need to change the leadership of a number of major institutions. It is this special target that sets MARs apart from other persons of middle income range or the more affluent who stress the need for altering staff to the exclusion of those in leadership positions.

In seeing organizational change in personalized terms, MARs do not appear to seek radical change. But it is quite obvious that in attacking the leadership of many institutions they are not likely to find a sympathetic ear from the very policy makers, administrators and professionals whom they criticize. The only recourse seems to be to develop mechanisms of influence and power outside of the white collar unions or other organizations to which they presently belong.

The devising of advocate pressure organizations for change in bureaucracies (or at least for an opportunity for the views of MARs to be more effectively felt) must, therefore, represent a major agenda item both for these institutions—especially those in the local community—and for organizers who seek to build coalitions between MARs and other groups.

MARs do not wish to replace the professional and bureau-cratic authority which is found among many existing institutions, but they certainly do challenge the performance and competency, as well as the integrity, of many of the specific individuals who occupy important leadership roles in these structures. Therefore, if coalition issues involving organizational change are framed in broad structural terms they will fail to strike a responsive chord among MARs.

MARs are not interested in challenging the authority of the school teacher to teach. However, they may well challenge the specific ability of one teacher or the competence of an administrator who seems to be unresponsive to the needs of parents and the local community.

MAR concern with local accountibility may be a potential bridge across racial lines. Black Americans too are challenging teachers and school administrators to be accountable for their curricula and methods. Thus, if white administrators are unresponsive to the needs of black students, this may well strike a responsive chord among those MARs who also feel that it is the top administration of schools that seems indifferent to the interests of parents. If, however, blacks stress the racist behavior of particular teachers without stressing the need for teachers to be under the authority of effective administrators, then the basis of perceiving common interests across race lines may be undermined. A community organizer attuned to the issues of both blacks and MARs could well seek to disentangle the two kinds of problems: in the one case, the blacks dealing with personal as well as institutional racism; in the second instance, the MARs who, while satisfied with the way in which teachers behave, find that school administrators are not accessible or are not doing the kind of job that they should be.

A similar kind of argument may well be made with regard to other institutional spheres, and in particular the workplace. Thus, black groups often do not distinguish between the authority structure of the organization and the personal racism of particular supervisors and co-workers. MARs may have less difficulty in terms of their relationship with co-workers and immediate supervisors, but a much greater problem with higher level supervisory personnel. If in shop factories and various work organizations, issues could be framed in such a way that particular interests were clarified and broadened, particular bridging and coalition issues might well be built which could benefit both blacks and MARs in a specific organizational milieu.

These indications of tactic and policy in the area of internal organization have been more suggestive than definitive. This is clearly an area where further research and new programs of social intervention are necessary if we are to deal successfully with the polarization which presently afflicts us.

Minorities have been particularly successful in pursuing their interests by bending organizational rules, changing policies and using organizations to reach their goals. The MAR, who has spent many years following the rules, is deeply concerned about this. MARs are not so opposed to welfare because it is large and comprehensive. They may be opposed to it if it is inequitable and gives certain people priority over others. But large organizations, as such, are not a problem for MARs. That is the first point.

Another governing factor: MARs do not want to tinker with the institutional structures, however large or small these may be. Whereas the conventional radical is apt to see a need to reduce the scale of schools and government to make them more accessible, the MAR is concerned with the way such institutions are run and complains that individuals in high positions are not powerful enough to do their jobs properly. As he sees it, the failure of welfare agencies to diminish poverty, of police to decrease crime and of government to increase services, despite the ever-larger amounts to the MARs tax dollar that are spent on them, prove his point.

Will MARs Mobilize to Seek Change or to Block it? The policy implications that emerge from this present chapter focus on the concept of coalition formation as well as on the question of MAR political action. On the first point we have noted that while individuals from differing perspectives may come to feel that a particular organization needs to be changed, they may view this in different ways. They may advocate change as a regular and necessary part of the adaptability and flexibility of the structures. Thus, we find people who support the idea of change without being fundamentally alienated from the structure. They see the need for change as normative. Or, individuals may desire a change in an organization, but view it in highly personalized terms.

We have found that MARs as a group tend to be in the second category of advocating change because they feel alienated from organizations, yet view change as requiring a focus upon the personal dimensions of the organization rather than its overall structure. In contrast, High Education Middles, who show a high degree of alienation and criticism for organizations, tend to emphasize the need to change the structure of such institutions. Thus, MARs represent a singularly paradoxical group in terms of political mobilization vis-à-vis basic organizational change.

In order to form a sociopolitical movement centered on change, it is necessary first of all to have a system orientation. This would provide a base for political mobilization to deal with their concerns about the performance of organizations.

MARs, while deeply troubled by the behavior of many of the most important institutions in the local community and the larger society, still seem to support those structures in their basic form. The MARs' emphasis is upon changing the personnel of such structures, either those who are in the leadership roles or those who carry out policy.

Affluents share with High Education Middles the structural emphasis, but tend to be relatively content with most organizations. Should this group come to feel that the performance of structures is not adequate, they are more likely to become mobilized and join with High Education Middles. Evidence for this kind of mobilization can be seen with respect to the issue of welfare agencies and unions.

MARs, like Low Income respondents, may not become significantly involved in programs of social change even when these may be in line with bringing organizations around to their point of view and acting in their interests. These perspectives help explain why MARs, as angry as they appear to be, have not formed themselves into a significant political force to change the major institutions which are the target of so much of their criticism.

The MAR's non-structural view of change is coupled with some of the resistances we have noted toward collective action (for example, Chapter 5 showed the MARs need to make sure that high status people belong to a group before they would join it). These factors add up to a kind of conservatism in that MARs want to restore the power of organizations, but they are unwilling to extend a great deal of trust to those who run organizations.

The mobilization of MARs must be developed out of some additional stages of experience and not simply from their sense that organizations are failing to do a good job or that their administrators should be replaced. Whether for good or ill, the fact that MARs will not readily join in collective action in order to redress their grievances suggests that in the future MARs may only rarely manifest anger in some form of collective action or participation in a political movement. Nor will they do so in terms of the issues of mobilization that have characterized the actions of the "new left" in the 1960s. These values are more often those of the High Education Middles or Affluents in our sample.

MARs, in their individuated and informal style of responding to problems, will need to construct forms of political expression which tend to be different from some of the models used by students, blacks, the organized poor as well as the typical bureaucratic professional. Such styles of political organization, once evolved, can become the vehicles for a more visible and cumulative expression of MAR power and discontent.

12. PROGRAMMATIC DIRECTIONS: SOME GUIDE LINES FROM MARs THEMSELVES

We have pursued our analysis to the point of specifying sources of discontent and the variety of responses MARs have to major institutions in American society. Our findings have provided a distinctive, paradoxical pattern: on one hand exists a high level of anger and alienation and on the other a desire for only limited forms of social change. It is this very dilemma and paradox of the MAR phenomenon that requires us to explore what sources of change can provide the basis for coalition between MARs and other groups. In addition, we must attempt to discover constructive mechanisms with which to address MAR grievances and allay their discontent.

In the present chapter we shall focus explicitly on the kinds of services, the quality of life and the individual well-being which MARs and other groups in society desire. In our national survey we introduced this topic with the following question:

Now let's talk about some services and community programs. How much are the following things needed in your community?

The list includes seven kinds of services and programs. In Table 68 we have presented the distribution of responses among our five population groups. For each of these groups we then computed the percentage of people who felt that the particular service was needed "a great deal."

In several instances MARs are significantly higher than others in terms of interest in a particular kind of needed social program or service. Thus, in regard to improved parks and play-

193

TABLE 68

INTEREST IN COMMUNITY-BASED SERVICES
(PERCENT INDICATING NEEDED "A GREAT DEAL")

	Low Income	MARs	Average Middles	High Education Middles	Affluents
Low Cost Medical Services	58%	63%	50%	47%	35%
Improved Parks and Playgrounds	24%	39%	24%	23%	24%
Improved Public Transportation	33%	33%	29%	40%	36%
Low-Cost Legal Counseling	22%	31%+	23%	30%	21%
Low-Cost Family Counseling Services	18%	24%	19%	27%	20%
Improved Garbage and Trash Collection	13%	23%	12%	10%	10%
Adult Education Programs	17%	22%	15%	20%	10%
Child Care or Day Care Centers	11%	16%	13%	29%	17%

grounds, MARs are significantly more likely to feel that this is needed "a great deal." At the same time, we find that low-cost legal counseling is felt to be needed a great deal significantly more by MARs and High Education Middles, than by Low Income respondents, Average Middles or Affluents.

Both MARs and Low Income persons are significantly more likely than other population groups to feel that low-cost medical services are needed "a great deal." In the 1975 Cambridge Report attitudes were measured toward a national health service. One in 5 MARs favored a totally government-run program and a majority favored a more limited national program. This was similar to the attitudes held by other respondents. (See Appendix: Table 24.)

In regard to family counseling services, improved trash collection and adult education, MARs in the 1972 survey were significantly more likely than Low Income respondents to desire such new services or improvements in present ones. Moreover, MARs—to a significant degree more than Average Middles—feel that such services as trash collection are needed "a great deal."

Table 68 also shows the important differences in terms of the ranking and significance given to particular kinds of new social services. In addition, it indicates some of the priorities among different population groups and provides a basis for possible coalitions around specific common concerns for new services. For instance, in regard to low-cost medical services, Low Income and MARs share a similarly high level of concern.

Improving public transportation has the most widely held need among all 1972 survey groups. MARs share with both Low Income and Affluent groups a high level of support for such services. In regard to low-cost legal counseling, family counseling services and adult education, MARs and High Education Middles show a fairly similar degree of concern. Moreover, the same two groups are somewhat more interested in such services compared to other population groups.

There are some distinctive group priorities. With regard to day care centers, High Education Middles are unique in their special interest. At the same time we note on two accounts that MARs also have unique interests: improved parks and playgrounds and improved garbage and trash collection. It should be noted that both of these are focused on the local community and represent kinds of services which already exist but where expansion or improvement in quality is needed.

Level of Service Needs

In Table 69 the total number of services needed "a great deal" have been added for each of the population groups so that

TABLE 69

EXTENT OF NEED FOR EIGHT PROPOSED COMMUNITY SERVICES
(EXTENSIVITY)

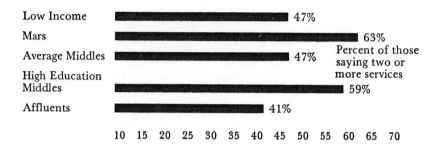

we may obtain a sense of the extensive character of interest in new services for the five population groups. MARs are significantly more likely than Low Income or Average Middles to have a need for five or more of the eight services listed in the study. At the same time, MARs are significantly less likely than any other population group to lack a strong interest in at least one of the suggested services or programs.

An additional area of public services and social policy has to do with the work arena. One of the questions that we asked respondents as part of the discussion of the workplace was the following:

If you had a chance to take a job training course and not lose pay, how interested would you be in this idea?

We find from Table 70 that significantly more MARs than Average Middles or Low Income individuals say they would be very interested in such a program. At the same time, we also note that an even larger proportion of the High Education Middles favor such an idea. While the kind of work alienation itself may not be similar (see Chapter 4), it is clearly one of the "bridging issues" between MARs and High Education Middles and is important in job mobility and additional training opportunities.

TABLE 70

ATTITUDE ABOUT FUTURE JOB TRAINING:
"IF YOU HAD A CHANCE TO TAKE A JOB TRAINING COURSE AND
NOT LOSE PAY, HOW INTERESTED WOULD YOU BE IN THIS IDEA?"

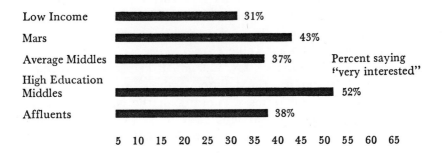

A Neglected Concern of MARs: The Justice System

In describing the kinds of policy directions that have emerged from our analysis we must now point out several areas in which there is a hiatus in terms of both the data we gathered and the issues that subsequently emerged. In our initial community interviews and in the national survey we failed to address in detail one of the most important aspects of public policy which had disturbed MARs: the functioning of the judicial system. We did find that dissatisfaction with the courts and the entire legal system was widespread and intense. The idea of preventing the police from doing their job was, of course, a frequently mentioned complaint. The perception that blacks get favorable treatment and that "slick lawyers can get anybody off if they have the money" was a pervasive MAR opinion. Another prevalent complaint was the sense that the correctional system does not rehabilitate criminals but returns them to society in worse condition. More recently, others have joined in this MAR criticism.

In the 1975 survey we found no difference between MARs

and other whites in terms of their own view that the crime problem was worsening or that they themselves had greater direct experience as a victim of crime. Nevertheless one question did elicit a different view from MARs than from others who were interviewed: how to deal with criminals. A majority (53 percent) said they felt stiff penalties and severe punishments were needed; a majority of other respondents felt that attacking social and economic conditions was the best approach. (See Appendix: Table 25).

In the 1972 interviews few individuals had any specific ideas about the reason for the failure of the courts. It was often expressed in vague terms of politics or the NAACP or some other pressure group. But it is clear that MARs are intensely unhappy that the courts are not in the forefront of protecting their values. We feel that in order to focus on the problems of the MAR and to reduce the alienation felt toward the national, state and local government it is important for the courts themselves and, in particular, members of the judicial structure to come to grips with the dilemma posed by improving the justice system in terms of its widespread racism and class bias and, at the same time, by providing more effective sanctions and rehabilitation programs.

Responses to the MAR Indictment

The "court watching" strategy employed by student and civil rights groups has been somewhat effective in making the courts more accountable in terms of their treatment of minorities. Certainly a similar effort could be developed with regard to the issues that are of the most interest to MARs. Greater contact with the judicial system and its problems as well as seeking solutions and assistance from the MAR strata might well be an important way to reduce alienation.

Restructing of the court system and the correctional institutions of the society represents one of the major challenges in the latter part of the twentieth century. With the rising crime rate this relationship between courts, the police and the basic protection of individual safety becomes one of the most important equations in the political arena at this time.

How to balance the increasing awareness of humanistic values which calls for the ending of capital punishment and the reform of criminal punishment systems with the rising tide of drug-related crimes is certainly the major task of urban governments today. It is precisely in this area of the handling of crime and criminal justice that the persistence of the MAR ideology is liable to find its most fertile soil. For with the decline of student activism and the relative quiescence of black-organized protests, the intensity and fundamental drive of the MAR backlash of the 1960s is likely to continue unabated. Thus, it is very possible that a continuation or "rolling" form of the MAR ideology—picking up new recruits and retaining old ones—will occur so long as individuals find they are threatened in terms of personal safety, the safety of their families and their sense of security in terms of the local community.

Unless the intellectual community as well as the decision makers in the arena of public services offer alternatives to the more reactionary concept of punitive justice and incarceration, it is likely that there will be no change in the fundamental conditions that foster the MAR ideology. There must be alternative concepts of police effectiveness and criminal justice systems devised in federal, state and local jurisdictions. This might well be one of the most important agenda items if we are to make headway with regard to the polarization between MARs and other segments of this country, between younger and older age groups, blacks and whites, and between the poor and the relatively affluent. This task is an enormous one, particularly since it involves much more than reducing just the statistical incidents of crime.

Our analysis implies that the fulcrum of MAR social tension has shifted from the campus to the courts and neighborhoods. Can our public institutions respond to the conditions of urban life in a way which is both specifically effective in the short run and which generates a sense of credibility and trust in the long run? This is, perhaps, the greatest challenge of the 1970s. We do not anticipate that, because there has been some shift in the focus of the MAR alienation syndrome, we will see the disappearance of the real concerns and fears of this significant portion of American society.

MARs as a Mirror of America

It is important to recognize that the perceived decline in social order in urban centers is yet another expression of the broader awareness of social disintegration which MARs have experienced. Further erosion of ties to union, church, class and traditional community can only make this group more vulnerable to the dire threats and fears which are founded in the reality of urban life. It is the loss of an anchor point in the broadest moral sense and the perception and visibility of such a loss in terms of the specific patterns of urban life that make MAR alienation an ever present and growing dimension of America itself.

A clear conclusion drawn from the early MARs interviews (and one supported in the attitudes of distrust found in the national study) is that a wave of bewilderment has swept over individuals who formerly had a sense of identity in what they believed, and who knew who their allies and opponents were. They do not see this shift in a conspiratorial fashion but, rather, in terms of the apparent united indifference to their concerns on the part of those who have power and make policy decisions. This sense of bewilderment helps make MAR converts.

It would indeed be misleading to argue that the MAR has lost faith in experts and totally rejected the capacity of the more highly educated person in society to be responsible and effective in dealing with major leadership tasks. But the sense of bewilderment is easily translated into a view that all public officials, as well as those charged with any kind of major responsibility for decision making, have become totally unable to act except in response to the most visible political pressures.

Some Directions for Reducing MAR Discontent

We have outlined some directions that might be taken to meet, on a rational and effective basis, the major grievances of the MAR population. We found that there were several areas in which new social services were needed and that the pattern held true for both MARs and High Education Middles in the number of services desired and in the response to job training. In terms of what would make an improvement in people's lives, we found that MARs tended to focus on quality-of-life issues as well as on the security of their job and its future benefits, and on areas of individual self-improvement.

The implications of the findings elucidated in this chapter are of two kinds: 1) those defining specific issues around which coalitions might be built; and 2) those defining the general stance that particular population groups—especially MARs—have toward their life situation. On this latter point, the stereotype of MARs as wedded to the status quo and not interested in new programs and services is not valid. Rather, there is a marked interest in a range of new social services, many of which are in areas that one might have thought MARs would resist, for example, family counseling and adult education programs.

In terms of coalition bases, we have found that there are some specific commonalities, especially between MARs and High Education Middles. The link between interests of Low Income Americans and MARs is also of note. The fact that MARs do not place a great emphasis on mobility striving suggests that some of the value issues that various groups—such as students and intellectuals—have promoted may well find support among MARs. This is a group whose focus on self--improvement and the need for job security may tend to obscure a value system in which the notion of raw economic striving is devalued.

We are suggesting that MARs have a willingness to pursue humanistic values and, in fact, may place those side-by-side with the kind of issues that focus on job security. At least this area of values should be explored to see whether new social programs and more areas of shared interest may emerge.

MARs, in their concern about the quality of their local environment, may well be seen as obsessed with problems of safety and crime. This should not obscure the fact that these are valid concerns about the quality of the environment even though they are not focused on problems of natural resources, water and air pollution. There is no qualitative difference between the desire to have adequate city services and the interest in reducing air pollution. The question is one of priority and what confronts one first in the immediate local environment. MARs tend to be somewhat parochialized and focus on the more immediate geographical context. It is important for other groups in terms of social policy planning to recognize this fact.

The emphasis for MARs is not exclusively on the local community to the exclusion of recognizing that what goes on in the larger society in terms of economic policy and taxation may well affect their livelihood in significant ways. What characterizes MARs is a dual set of concerns and interests in change and new programs at both the local and the federal level. The highly educated tend to focus their concern on broader, world wide and national issues such as foreign policy, the philosophy of a particular administration and congress, and the thrust of overall programs. MARs are more affected by the local consequences of national policies.

It is precisely in the apparent disinterest of many major social institutions in the local community that we find one of the greatest sources of anger and frustration among MARs. It is when social welfare agencies, the national government, unions and corporations seem to adopt policies which do not take into account what is occurring in the local neighborhoods and communities that MARs feel most left out. The composition of the Democratic National Convention in 1972 is but one visible indicator of the sense that major institutions do not look to the local community in terms of advice, participation or feedback.

Moreover, while we found that job discontent itself is not a major source of generating the MAR ideology, there is no doubt that the concerns centering on the job are as important, if not more important, to MARs than to other population groups. In contrast to the prevailing literature, it may not be the "soft" factors of the job that are most crucial to MARs, however. Safety on the job—as we found in our earlier discussion of work—as well as the pattern noted in this present chapter on retirement and fringe benefits along with steady work opportunities and security constitute the basis for their job discontent. The argument that working MARs are most interested in having a voice in decision making is not altogether accurate.

There are a number of objective conditions about the work setting that MARs feel are even more important.

The fundamental policy question becomes not "Is it going to be possible to avoid what MARs perceive as the one-sidedness of social change?" The question really is "How can we reverse the process and convince the MAR that 'losses' of the past will, in fact, be made up to some extent?"

The optimistic sense of reversing fundamental social conditions such as poverty, racism, sexism or other social ills seems to be distinctly absent from the world view of the MAR. The MAR does not anticipate the grandiose possibilities of structural change in society. Working from the context of potential job insecurity, MARs are likely to view with great caution the possibility of reversing what has already occurred.

It is with this kind of political realism that MARs have entered the 1970s. Rhetoric will not change such attitudes and perceived realities.

No formal organization whatever its coalition goals, is likely to be embraced by a wide variety of the MAR spectrum. Rather, the way to erode the threatened perceptions of MARs is through interventions that directly pin-point practical problems as experienced by the MAR in the local community, job and neighborhood.

13. MIDDLE AMERICAN RADICALS
ASSESS THEIR FUTURE

Finally, we now turn to a set of considerations which can serve as guideposts in terms of sensitizing American society to MAR attitudes and needs. These derive largely from our 1972 national survey. A series of questions in that interview focus on what expectations people had for their future. Among such inquiries is the following: "What will happen to the national economy during the following year?"

In Table 71 we show the responses to this question for the five major population groupings. A large portion of MARs expected things would be worse for them in the following year—1973. Indeed, they were right. This was not significantly more than the proportion of Low Income respondents who felt

TABLE 71

WHAT WILL HAPPEN TO THE NATIONAL ECONOMY
DURING THE COMING YEAR?

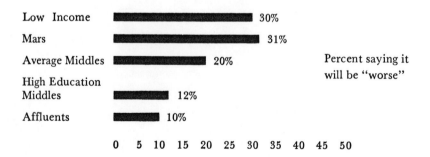

Low Income 30%
Mars 31%
Average Middles 20%
High Education Middles 12%
Affluents 10%

Percent saying it will be "worse"

0 5 10 15 20 25 30 35 40 45 50

this way, but it was significantly higher than the percentage of persons within the High Education Middle or Affluents. Moreover, if we look at the proportion of respondents who felt that things would be worse in the following year, we find that MARs and Low Income individuals share a significantly higher proportion of respondents with this attitude than do such groups as Average Middles, High Education Middles and Affluent responses.

Within the MAR group there is a kind of bifurcation: Nearly as many respondents feel that things are going to get worse in the following year as feel things will get better. In contrast, Average Middles are twice as likely to feel that things are going to get better than worse. Thus, overall we find within the MAR group a range from optimism to significant pessimism.

An additional question which seeks to capture the perspective of respondents as they perceive their future had to do with family income over the next five year period. Table 72 contains the relevant responses. Among MARs, a larger portion of respondents said "things would get a lot better" in comparison with Low Income individuals. However, only about half as many MARs indicated this view as High Education Middles. If we add together the proportion of MARs who feel things will

TABLE 72

HOW FAMILY INCOME WILL CHANGE: THE NEXT FIVE YEARS
Percent saying it will change for the better

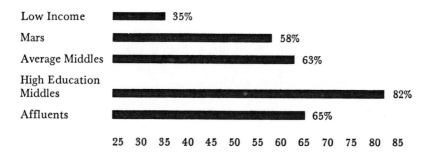

Low Income	35%
Mars	58%
Average Middles	63%
High Education Middles	82%
Affluents	65%

25 30 35 40 45 50 55 60 65 70 75 80 85

get a lot or a little better, this includes some 58 percent of the total group. This is significantly higher than the Low Income group and is only slightly below of Average Middles. MAR optimism is significantly lower than the 82 percent of High Education Middles who feel their family's economic situation will be at least a little better in the next five years. Sixty-five percent of Affluents feel this way.

Overall, we find that few of our respondents felt in 1972 that things were going to get worse in the next five years. However, the proportion of MARs who feel this way is slightly above that of Low Income individuals and significantly more than Average Middles or High Education Middles. Table 72 indicates that, despite a range of important differences found between MARs and Average Middles, the two groups are generally alike in terms of optimism in viewing their family income over the next five years.

Relative Deprivation: Its Implications for MARs

The 1972 survey suggests several ways of analyzing the hypothesis that MAR discontent emerges from the decline in their perceived economic well being as compared to the country as a whole. This can be accomplished first by comparing the way people described their own family economic situation in the period prior to the 1972 interview versus how they assessed the way things were going in the nation (see Chapter 3, Tables 11 and 12). The difference between self and society is a measure that may reflect either "relative deprivation" or "relative benefit." In effect, both situations show the individual out of line with the rest of the society. There might also be other combinations including consistency of one's self doing as well or as badly as the society.

We do not find that most MARs experienced "relative deprivation" vis-à-vis the society as a whole in the five years prior to the 1972 survey. In fact, MARs as a group have the highest of the opposite inconsistency: 45 percent report their own family's economic situation as *better* than in the country as a whole.

When we ask the same types of questions about self and the society in terms of the immediate future—the year ahead and five years beyond—the trends in discrepancy shift markedly. Thus only 13 percent of the MARs expect to be better off than the society. If we then compare this difference for all groups in our analysis, MARs have the steepest decline in the proportion of its members who expect to be better off than the rest of society. (See Appendix: Table 26.)

It is interesting to note that relatively few respondents feel that both they and the country are going to do worse in the next five years. At the same time, twice as many MARs feel this way as Average Middles. Only half as many MARs take this view as Low Income respondents.

In terms of some discrepancy between their own position and that of the country we find that all five population groups show very similar patterns: about one in two persons out of each group feel that there is going to be some discrepancy either favoring themselves or favoring the progress of the country. This contrasts with the pattern that we noted in terms of earlier discussions about the previous five years. For MARs, a significantly larger proportion of respondents felt some sort of discrepancy.

Turning to some data from the 1975 survey, further evidence of the relationship between the MAR group and perceived discrepancy between self and society is provided. When asked if the country's financial situation would improve during the coming year a plurality of MARs said it would be "bad." At the same time, the modal response of other whites interviewed is an attitude of uncertainty about the national economy. Moreover when asked about their own financial situation only 25 percent said it would get better—half said it would stay the same; for other respondents significantly more—34 percent—said they expected a better financial condition in another year, with 45 percent saying their situation would remain unchanged. These patterns are contained in Table 73. Thus MARs as a group are more pessimistic about both their own immediate financial state and that of the country as a whole compared to other respon-

TABLE 73

NEAR FUTURE ECONOMIC EXPECTATIONS: SELF AND SOCIETY
1975 SURVEY

Country's Financial Situation			Own Financial Situation		
	MARs	Others		MARs	Others
Bad	36% +	29% −	Worse	15%	12%
Uncertain	31% −	40% +	Same	50%+	45% −
Good	26%	24%	Better	25%−	34% +
Don't Know	7%	7%	Don't Know	10%	9%
Total	100%	100%	Total	100%	100%

dents. Thus earlier discrepancy between self and society appears to be lessened and to resolve into a more consistently negative situation.

The existence of a discontinuity between the situation of the individual and the perceived state of the society has some significant implications. The trends we have noted suggest that, in some respects, MARs may be falling into line with some of the concerns and economic patterns of other groups and that the cutting edge of distinct criticism which seem to characterize MARs in the recent past may be reduced. While not as pessimistic as Low Income respondents, MARs appear to anticipate that they may well be falling behind the economic gains of the country—reducing their previous built-up edge.

We may interpret this in two ways: first we might predict this relative economic deprivation will lead MARs to a "pulling in of their horns." MARs may become more interested in protecting the gains that they have had and this will result in a lowered political participation and visibility on the American political scene. Alternatively, it is perfectly possible to argue that the increasing relative deprivation which appears to be on the horizon for many MARs will lead them into a situation of feeling more interested in supporting taxpayer revolts or at least to be concerned about reforming economic policies at the local and national levels.

In the 1972 survey we already have a test for the effects of relative deprivation on activism. We know the kinds and numbers of economic cut-backs that some families had already experienced at the time of the core survey. We also know the role played by "status" threats as a key concept in defining the MAR. If we put these two "explanations" for social protest together we can obtain some idea of what may happen to MARs as they experience more frequent and prolonged economic deprivations—both absolute and relative.

To evaluate the "status" versus "economic" deprivation hypotheses about political activism we have taken third party support, Wallace voting, alienation from the national government, a sense of anomie, feelings about the need "to be part of an organized group," support for anti-busing and taxpayer revolt actions, and compared them to measures of perceived threat from blacks and the rich and the number of economic cutbacks people were experiencing. All of this information is summarized in Table 74. The correlation tells us whether a given type of attitude is related to economic or status threat variables. The first two columns on the left deal with the "status" threats, the two on the right with "economic deprivation" threats.

Table 74 generally shows a pattern in which the report of either blacks or the rich "showing off and thinking they are better than other people"—the status threat measure—is more often associated with alienation and political mobilization indicators than are the economic threat questions—property decline when blacks move in and number of spending cut-backs. In only three instances does any economic threat variable attain a value of +.20. By contrast, this is true for nine correlations of status threat variables.

Further evidence that the slowdown of the economy and the weakened economic position of MARs retards political mobilization is seen in Table 75. Here we have taken the five hypothetical situations of direct action first discussed in Chapter 6

TABLE 74

CORRELATION COEFFICIENTS BETWEEN INDICATORS OF STATUS
THREATS AND SELECTED DEPENDENT VARIABLES OF ALIENATION,
DISCONTENT, AND POLITICAL MOBILIZATION

	Status Threat of Blacks	Status Threat of Rich	Blacks Cause Property Values to Drop	Economic Cut-Backs
Support for a third party	−.01	+.05	−.01	+.07
Wallace identification in 1972	+.27	+.22	+.18	+.08
Legitimation of direct protest actions	+.22	+.20	+.21	+.06
Alienation from the national government	+.17	+.10	+.08	+.10
Alienation from the local government	+.19	+.19	+.11	+.15
Anomie	+.32	+.29	+.19	+.32
Need to be part of an organized group	+.27	+.20	+.10	+.16
Keep children home in busing situation	+.23	+.06	+.23	+.04
Organize public marches in a busing situation	+.06	+.01	−.03	+.03
Support taxpayers stopping a legislative session	+.13	+.18	+.07	+.11

TABLE 75

CHANGES IN LEGITIMATION OF DIRECT SOCIAL ACTION:
1972–1975
(PERCENT APPROVE OF ACTION)

	MARs			Others		
	1972	1975	Shift	1972	1975	Shift
"When police don't stop crime in a neighborhood people set up their own police patrol."	43%	47%	+ 4%	39%	39%	0
"Taxpayers in the middle income group who feel they are paying more than their fair share of taxes go to the State Capitol and stop legislative sessions."	41%	46%	+ 5%	20%	36%	+16%
"Workers on strike keep people from entering the plant."	27%	33%	+ 6%	20%	30%	+10%
"A group of women who feel that a magazine is discriminating against hiring women organize a picket line and stop the publication of magazine."	19%	26%	+ 7%	14%	23%	+ 9%
"Blacks who feel they are being discriminated against by a local company set up picket lines and keep people from entering the plant."	9%	12%	+ 3%	10%	20%	+10%

and compared the patterns of response obtained in 1972 and 1975. The trends are consistent with a relatively small gain in support for militant direct action. Instead what is noted is relatively large gain in support for such actions by other white respondents. Particularly is this true with respect to a "taxpayer revolt" situation where MARs show only a 5 percent gain compared to 16 percent shift for others.

The trend regarding protest by women is worthy of further elaboration. In this issue area MARs show a proportionally high increase in support—from 19 percent to 26 percent. The level of support is still quite low. Yet the rate of change is quite high—although this is also true for respondents who are not MARs. When asked if there was no need for an Equal Rights Amendment, 39 percent of MARs disagreed—nearly the same proportion—42 percent—as other whites. Given the major role that women thus far have played in the political mobilization of MARs the fact of economic problems and job layoffs may affect a smaller shift in the passivity of the female compared to the male MAR.

Careful analysis of the 1972 study suggests that very short term economic declines—lasting one or two years—may not be sufficient for MAR discontent to emerge. However, as our data suggests, a longer period of suffering economic loss has characterized the position both of the Low Income and MAR groups in our survey. Should such declines continue long enough, social protest from such economically squeezed groups may, in fact, reach a peak and then decline, given the limited resources that such groups can mobilize.

We are positing a kind of cyclical model of MAR activism: very short term economic decline does not generate alienation, while rather long-term decline debilitates and undermines collective action and ideological distinctiveness. In effect, the MAR "syndrome" cannot emerge with very short term declines. Yet, with prolonged economic squeeze, the MAR perspective merges with the problems confronting many other groups, even groups which MARs had previously seen as gaining at their expense. The result may be to enhance opportunities for pursuing com-

mon goals and the formation of implicit coalition efforts between Low Income, MAR, and such groups as retirees or white
collar workers displaced from jobs in the recent period of
economic downturn.

Quo Vadis MARs: An Overview

The patterns that emerge in the national surveys as well as in
our earlier in-depth analyses strongly point toward MARs as
being most active and constituting a growing political force
under economic conditions of high relative prosperity, coupled
with a strong feeling that their society is not in tune with their
own goals. In this situation they feel that their economic gains
cannot really be "cashed in."

"Leakage" from the larger society to the individual thus
becomes a measure of "inflationary" devaluing of the gains for
the family unit. If the society has multiple problems despite the
economic gains of its members, then such a discrepancy may be
a more powerful source of discontent than the more traditional
theory of "relative deprivation" of economic position. Since
such attitudes arise when alienated MARs have the economic
resources to act upon their discontent, job insecurity and general family retrenchment in spending, may dissipate such activism. The discontent may remain, but political mobilization is
not as likely.

By comparing themselves with others in terms of relative
deprivation in the future, MARs seem to be no different than
other groups. What is important is that in comparison with their
own past situation MARs seem to be moving more rapidly than
other groups toward a change from being ahead of the country
to a position of falling behind. This may reduce rather than
enhance their political activism.

We cannot derive as elaborate a picture of the future of
MARs as we have painted about their recent past, but we can
sketch in a few of the possible trends. MARs do not readily
move toward major structural change in organizations. Nor have
they become a consistently mobilized political group. As a

result, economic conditions may play a key role in the way MARs respond to their continuing discontents, but such economic deprivation will not itself be the cause of their anger.

The degree of affluence which MARs had experienced by 1972, their sense of making significant strides and of their ability to continue to do so, might well feed a sense of rising capacity to act and be efficacious in the political arena. Recent economic changes, however, may well have altered that perspective drastically. Opportunities to engage in political action and the affluence required for such efforts are important ingredients in the viability and potential of any political movement. Therefore, the MARs who retain their economic gains can act as a cadre for maintaining the sense of urgency and crisis in the MAR group. The strength of such a core within provides the continuity of MAR mobilization. Beyond such member resources are the institutional mechanisms—such factors as the extent to which various organizations in Boston or West Virginia such as ROAR (Restore Our Alienated Rights) or the Wallace candidacy become vehicles by which MARs can sustain a consistent sense of participation. The evidence strongly suggests that for the next few years MARs will continue to feel a growing sense of their own unique destiny.

Test Conditions for MAR Survival: A Final Note

The data we have collected indicate that there are a wide range of motivations for making MARs more conscious of the need to organize either around their ethnicity or around their economic interests. The behavioral manifestations of such mobilization remain to be tested. We must look to situations which, in miniature, seem to carry on the trends of the last few years, trends that have helped to generate the MAR ideology.

It is misleading to argue that the conditions of the past need to be duplicated exactly in the future in order for the MAR phenomenon to move from a very early stage of total mobilization to one in which a significant base of a mass social movement emerges. We have found that the MAR is not someone who wants only to cling to the status quo. Rather, MARs believe that their quality of life has eroded and they are very concerned that new social services be provided to reverse this trend.

There is no evidence that the malaise that we have identified with the MAR group is receding. Rather, there seems to be evidence that a number of other groups who might otherwise strongly dissociate themselves from the kinds of attitudes and perceptions of the "hard hat" find that their own life situations are leading them to agree with various aspects of the MAR ideology.

As the MAR views the future it may be that he or she is more sensitive to the fact that things appear to be quiet in terms of student activism, foreign interventions, urban riots and the militancy of various special interest groups. Thus, MARs may perceive more realistically than even a number of political leaders do how institutionalized gains of various groups which grew out of protest actions persist in undermining values held by many other groups in American society, Whether or not new kinds of protests by non-MAR groups gain visible attention, the pattern of enshrined and conservative bureaucracy is such that is not possible to easily undo reforms any more than it is to achieve them. This intuitive sense of the inherent conservatism of established structures may well mean to the MAR (as to other individuals) that the gains of other groups will not be wiped out even by support of a presidential candidate who implies that he has little sympathy for and would not support the interests of minority groups.

The fact remains that the dynamics of the situation have already been set in motion for the MAR to retain an identity. There is no reason to anticipate that one must have a renewed cycle of conditions that originally led to the emergence of the MAR for this perspective to remain a significant part of the American political and social reality.

For it is the ultimate triumph or, perhaps, tragedy of the MAR perspective that some dismiss it as a journalistic fiction of the late 1960s. It may well have already become incorporated in the fabric of political and social consciousness. It is this very process spurred on by the continued inability of social analysts, community decision makers and government officials to be sensitive to the direction of American society that may soon lead us to a situation where we will have to swallow the MAR ideology uncritically or where we will find ourselves unable to counter its basic reality.

The Nixon years reduced sharply the dialogue about social policy critical to the survival of democracy. For many in our society—including the MAR—there is no longer a willingness to debate or discuss and confront alternative solutions to pressing social problems. We are rapidly approaching the point where debate about social policy will increasingly take place within coteries of polarized groups whose internal dialogues will have no meaning outside of their closed social networks.

Such withdrawal of students, members of the academic community, disheartened liberals, exclusive defenders of ethnic consciousness, embattled union and business executives will only lend credence to the social frustrations expressed in the MAR ideology.

The most difficult task for our society's leaders is to address the concrete problems of MARs without succumbing to its restrictive denial of the promise of American society for all its members. MARs can aid in this process by helping us to examine where we are going by glancing at but not being focused on the rear view mirror. But acquiescence to their ideology in the political arena would be an atrophying and ironic confirmation that the MAR expresses the true spirit of American society.

14. MARs REVISITED:
A FOLLOW-UP ANALYSIS

We have noted at several points in our discussion the findings from a second national survey in which a basic set of questions to measure the MAR perspective were included. As a final note to our basic findings we shall present several trends which suggest where the MAR is at this writing—three years after the first study.

One question which has permeated much of our earlier discussion is this: "How contagious is the MAR perspective?" This query really involves two issues: conditions that can facilitate the rise and diffusion of the MAR ideology or simply the "cultural dispersion" of the ideology via the many channels of social influence found in our society—including the writing of this book.

The Cambridge Report data from March 1975 provides rather consistent evidence that the MAR perspective has begun to filter both upward and downward in American society. As a total of the white sample it has gone from 29 percent to 31 percent. In terms of family income levels (see Appendix: Table 27) the most important trends are the increase in MARs among those families in the over $25,000 range—and those over $15,000. Part of this may in fact reflect the inflationary conditions over the last several years, but more importantly it suggests that sustaining conditions for the MAR ideology is a financial level which permits people to pay a great deal of attention to status differences and the position of groups which threaten such gains. We can indeed anticipate a loss of the MAR perspective among those whose family incomes—apart from those on fixed pensions or retirement plans—have slipped into absolute economic deprivation.

Data from 1975 shows widening of the MAR perspective in terms of the age gradation. Those 25 or younger show signifi· cant increases—although the largest increase is to be found among the age group 46 to 55. (See Appendix: Table 28.) In regard to the individual's formal education level the shift in MAR ideology appears to go in one direction: upward. Despite the earlier argument that college education might act as an insulator against this perspective of multiplying threatening groups in fact the 1975 findings disabuse one of such an analysis. Among those with graduate training a sharp increase in the proportion of MARs occurs. (See Appendix: Table 29.) Those with a B.A. or equivalent degree also show a significant gain in MAR ideology.

In terms of religious groups we find a relatively unchanged pattern from 1972. However, the trend toward fewer MARs among Catholics and more among Protestants results in a virtual wiping out of religious differentials in the holding of the MAR perspective. At the same time we also note (see Appendix: Table 30) that persons without a religious preference show a marked gain in the probability of holding the MAR perspective.

What evidence is there of the impact of MAR ideology on various social policies in 1975? Table 76 presents data on several suggested ways that the government could address social problems. The trends show that MARs generally are more guarded in the role they see for the federal government. Yet in such policy areas as price and wage controls MARs are some- what more willing to see government intervention than other whites interviewed. In the case of a guaranteed annual income MARs sharply dissent from others—and while they generally support government guaranteeing of employment it is with far less unanimity than for other groups.

A strong case has been made throughout our analysis of MAR concern over the local community and issues that touch upon that immediate environment. We have discussed two con- troversies which have occurred in particular areas of the country that appear to resonate with the concerns of MARs: busing and textbook policies. On the first of these issues MARs are in close company with other whites interviewed in 1975: a large ma-

TABLE 76

ATTITUDES TOWARD GOVERNMENT ROLE
IN MAJOR POLICY AREAS

	MARs			Others		
	Favor	Oppose	Diff.	Favor	Oppose	Diff.
Guarantee jobs to everyone	68%	26%	+ 42%	74%	19%	+ 55%
Government interference in the economy is OK if it works	62%	27%	+ 35%	67%	23%	+ 44%
Federal aid to local schools	59%	24%	+ 35%	62%	21%	+ 41%
Price controls	55%	37%	+ 18%	54%	32%	+ 22%
Wage Controls	38%	51%	− 13%	34%	54%	− 20%
Guaranteed income	29%	53%	− 24%	36%	43%	− 7%

jority reject the use of busing to achieve racial integration. Not surprisingly MARs are even more emphatic in that attitude: 90 percent reject the idea; only 7 percent favor it. Of interest as well is the response obtained to a question about whether a busing program has been instituted in the local community where the respondent lives. A significantly larger percentage of MARs—49 percent to 38 percent—indicate this is the case. If the MAR perspective has increased, part of the explanation may be traceable to such efforts.

As part of the Cambridge Report respondents were asked about the right of parents to keep an undesirable textbook out of their local schools—"even if teachers supported that book." Fifty-four percent of MARs and 45 percent of other white respondents feel parents have the right—even if they are only 10 percent of the total community—to prevent such books from being used. (See Appendix: Table 31.)

TABLE 77

SCHOOL BUSING ISSUES: 1975 SURVEY
(WHITE RESPONDENTS ONLY)

	MARs	Others
"Do you support or oppose busing of children from one school to another in order to achieve racial integration?"		
Support	7%	13%
Oppose	90% +	80%
Don't Know	3%	7%
Total	100%	100%
"Is such a busing program presently conducted in this county?"		
Yes	49% +	38%
No	48%	60%
Don't Know	3%	2%
Total	100%	100%

Given the end of Viet Nam war and the re-evaluation of American foreign policy the role of MAR perspectives will play a major part in the public acceptance or rejection of such changes. One such area is the defense budget. When asked in early 1975 if defense spending should be cut, MARs were less willing to go along with that idea than other white respondents. Table 78 contains the relevant data. The trends are suggestive of what may occur as future foreign policy questions emerge.

The imponderables of human action are often brought under some rational understanding by resort to theories of "balance" or "equilibrium" or simply the swing of a pendulum. So it is with the issues of isolation and what used to be termed "internationalism." As our society seeks to restore social harmony which the Viet Nam war so weakened we must ask if this might occur around the issues which MARs have articulated. For the

TABLE 78

ATTITUDES TOWARD NATIONAL DEFENSE:
1975 SURVEY
"Which of these statements is closest to your opinion?"

	MARs	Other Whites
We need to expand our national defense and strengthen our military.	26% +	20%
Our defense is just right now and should neither be increased or decreased.	35%	32%
Too much is spent on defense; we would be safe spending much less.	31%	40% +
Don't Know	8%	8%
	100%	100%

TABLE 79

TAKING ACTION:
"The true American way of
life is disappearing so fast
that we need to use force
to save it."
1975 SURVEY

	MARs	Others
Agree	43%+	26%
Don't Know	11%	9%
Disagree	46%	65%+
Total	100%	100%

liberal who sees the resolution of inequality and the end to racist and other forms of discrimination such a view may indeed be repugnant. Yet we must confront the legacy of social conflict that is still so potentially dangerous in our present society. The outlets for such stresses may be inadequate to the challenge. To the MAR the preservation of a sense of traditional rules and fair play is hard to square with a loss of status to newly emerging minorities. In the 1975 Cambridge survey there is a summary expression of this attitude. People interviewed

TABLE 80

WHO FORCE SHOULD BE USED AGAINST TO PRESERVE
THE AMERICAN WAY OF LIFE*
1975 SURVEY

	MARs	Others
"Leaders"	22% } 36%	15% } 23%
"American government"	14%	8%
"Politicians"	4%	2%
"The President"	2%	2%
"Communists"	9%	6%
"To deal with crime"	8%	10%
"Radicals	3%	3%
"The Rich"	1%	1%
Big Business	2%	5%
Oil Companies	1%	1%
"Hippies"	1%	3%
Unions	0%	1%
"Outsiders"	4%	4%
Foreign Countries	2%	3%
Everyone, Whoever	10%	8%
Don't know	10%	16%
Others	7%	12%
Total	100%	100%
	(N=181)	(N=247)

*Percentages are based on "Agree" responses to the statement: "the true American way of life is disappearing so fast that we need to use force to save it."

were given the following statement to respond to: "The true American way of life is disappearing so fast that we need to use force to save it." To this rather desperate expression 43 percent of MARs said they agreed; 26 percent of other whites did also. (See Table 79.) Respondents were then asked to name who such force—if they agreed it was needed—should be used against. Table 80 shows the response patterns. Forty-two percent of the MARs who believe that force is necessary to save "the American way of life" believe such action must be directed at the officials in positions of public responsibility. For non-MARs 27 percent indicated similar targets for forceful action.

Clearly it is now fashionable to recognize that many Americans are distrustful and out of touch with their elected officials. And yet the most recent findings about the outlook of the MAR provides a sharp outline of just how endemic such a perspective has become. No democracy can tolerate that kind of dissatisfaction and not stumble into great danger. For a while MARs may indeed be subdued and less able to carry out via a party, a program or a leader what is implied in their anger and dismay with the course they see American society following. But unless bridges are formed and policy adjustments are made, the MAR perspective may grow to the point where it begins to pervade society and to affect the political and social fabric with possibly drastic consequences.

APPENDIX A

TABLE 1

DISTRIBUTION OF TYPES OF RESPONDENTS IN THE 1972 NATIONAL
SURVEY RELATIVE TO A SOCIOECONOMIC STATUS (SES) DEFINITION
OF "MIDDLE AMERICAN"
(WHITE RESPONDENTS ONLY)

	Men	*Women*	*Total*
Below on one or more SES criteria	21%	33%	28%
Meets SES criteria of "Middle American"	51%	43%	46%
Above on one SES Criteria	8%	8%	8%
Above on all SES criteria	16%	11%	13%
Incomplete SES Data	4%	6%	5%
Total	100% (N=714)	101% (N=976)	100% (N=1690)

TABLE 2

EMPLOYMENT STATUS OF RESPONDENTS GROUPED BY FIVE
MAJOR SEGMENTS OF THE SAMPLE

	Low Income	MARs	Average Middles	High Education Middles	Affluents
Currently working	35%	58%	64% +	63%	73%
Housewife	34%	26%	29%	19%	23%
Retired	19%	10% +	4%	5%	3%
Student	5%	2%	1%	12%	1%
Unemployed	4%	2%	2%	1%	1%
Disabled	3%	2%	1%	0%	0%
Not Ascertained	0%	0%	0%	0%	0%
Total	100% (N=314)	100% (N=496)	100% (N=521)	100% (N=112)	100% (N=178)

TABLE 3

RELIGIOUS GROUPS IN RELATION TO
MIDDLE AMERICAN RADICAL IDEOLOGY
(PERCENT QUALIFYING AS MARs)

	1972 survey	1975 survey
Protestant	28% (N=1139)	31% (N=693)
Catholic	35% (N=397)	31% (N=415)
Jewish	34% (N=056)	33% (N=073)
Other	13% (N=016)	25% (N=075)
No preference	19% (N=072)	33% (N=090)

TABLE 4

RANKING OF RELIGIOUS GROUPS WITH RELATION TO MIDDLE AMERICAN IDEOLOGY SCORE

	Percent High	
Free Will Baptist	43% +	(N=30)
Mormons	39% +	(N=28)
Church of Christ	39% +	(N=41)
Baptists	38% +	(N=246)
Catholic	35% +	(N=397)
Jewish	34% +	(N=56)
Episcopalian	27%	(N=45)
"Christian"	26%	(N=42)
Missouri Synod Lutheran	24%	(N=21)
Lutheran	24%	(N=162)
Protestant—General	22%	(N=49)
Methodist	22%	(N=234)
Presbyterian	21%	(N=78)
No Religious Preference	19%	(N=72)
Congregational	19%	(N=23)

TABLE 5

NATIONALITY AND MIDDLE AMERICAN IDEOLOGY (GROUPS LARGER THAN 10)

Italian	39%	(N=67)
Dutch	38%	(N=24)
French	38%	(N=43)
Polish	36%	(N=39)
Irish	36%	(N=179)
Scotch-Irish	34%	(N=35)
Dispersed Nationality	30%	(N=43)
English, British	30%	(N=208)
British Isles	28%	(N=54)
European (Not further specified)	28%	(N=29)
Norwegian	27%	(N=22)
Western Europe Combination	27%	(N=179)

TABLE 5 — *Continued*

AMERICAN	26%	(N=189)
Swedish	25%	(N=28)
German	24%	(N=307)
Scottish	20%	(N=30)

TABLE 6

FAMILY INCOME 1971

	MARs	Others
Under $3,000	9%	9%
$3,000–$4,999	13%	11%
$5,000–$6,999	14%	12%
$7,000–$9,999	21%	18%
$10,000–$12,999	18%	17%
$13,000–$14,999	6%	8%
$15,000–$19,999	9%	10%
$20,000–$24,999	3%	4%
$25,000 or More	5%	5%
Family Income Not Ascertained	2%	6%
	100%	100%
	(N=496)	(N=1194)

TABLE 7

NUMBER OF PROBLEMS MENTIONED AND PERSONAL
INVOLVEMENT IN PROBLEMS

	Low Income	MARs	Average Middles	High Education Middles	Affluents
Mean number of problems	2.4	2.8	2.6	3.2	3.0
Percent three or more problems	41%	53%	48%	65%	57%
Personal Involvement: Percent one or more problems	6%	9%	7%	8%	5%
Corrected for one or more Problems: Ratio of personal involvement to problems	14.9:1	11.0:1	14.2:1	12.5:1	22.2:1

TABLE 8

ATTITUDES ABOUT WIFE WORKING:
"IN A SITUATION SUCH AS YOURS, IS IT A GOOD OR
BAD IDEA FOR A WIFE TO WORK FOR PAY?"

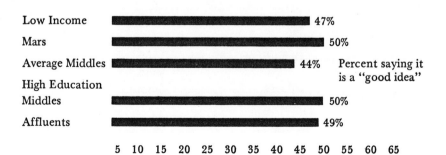

Low Income — 47%
Mars — 50%
Average Middles — 44%   Percent saying it
                          is a "good idea"
High Education Middles — 50%
Affluents — 49%

5 10 15 20 25 30 35 40 45 50 55 60 65

TABLE 9

HOW SERIOUS IS THE GENERATION GAP?

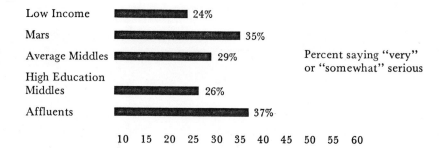

Low Income	24%
Mars	35%
Average Middles	29%
High Education Middles	26%
Affluents	37%

Percent saying "very" or "somewhat" serious

10 15 20 25 30 35 40 45 50 55 60

TABLE 10

"DO YOU FAVOR OR OPPOSE
TEACHERS BEING ALLOWED TO
USE PHYSICAL FORCE—SUCH AS
SPANKING—TO DISCIPLINE
CHILDREN?"

	MARs	Others
Favor	62%	54%
Don't Know	3%	6%
Oppose	35%	40%
Total	100%	100%

TABLE 11

AMOUNT OF CONTACT WITH NEIGHBORS

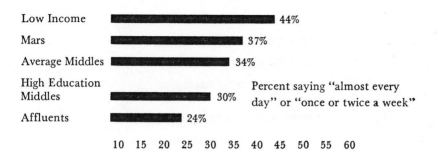

Low Income   44%

Mars   37%

Average Middles   34%

High Education   Percent saying "almost every
Middles   30%   day" or "once or twice a week"

Affluents   24%

10 15 20 25 30 35 40 45 50 55 60

TABLE 12

STATUS CONSISTENCY:
LIVING STANDARD COMPARED TO NEIGHBORS

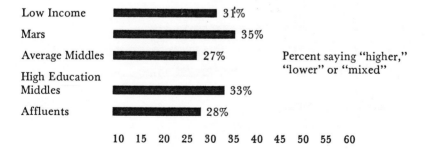

Low Income   31%

Mars   35%

Average Middles   27%   Percent saying "higher,"
                                        "lower" or "mixed"
High Education
Middles   33%

Affluents   28%

10 15 20 25 30 35 40 45 50 55 60

TABLE 13

SELF REPORT OF COMPOSITION OF NEIGHBORHOOD
WHERE RESPONDENT LIVES

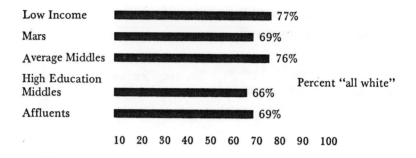

Low Income	77%
Mars	69%
Average Middles	76%
High Education Middles	66%
Affluents	69%

Percent "all white"

10 20 30 40 50 60 70 80 90 100

TABLE 14

ATTITUDES ABOUT URBAN PROBLEMS:
"RIOTS IN CITIES ARE CAUSED BY AGITATORS."

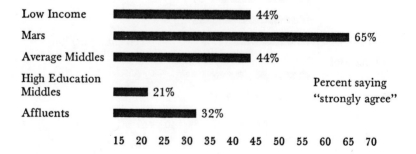

Low Income	44%
Mars	65%
Average Middles	44%
High Education Middles	21%
Affluents	32%

Percent saying
"strongly agree"

15 20 25 30 35 40 45 50 55 60 65 70

TABLE 15

ATTITUDES ABOUT THE WAR:
"OUR MAIN PROBLEM IN VIET NAM IS THE LACK OF
PATRIOTISM IN THE UNITED STATES."

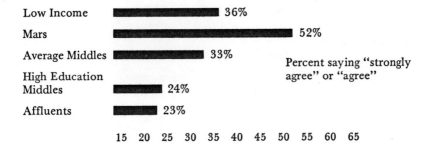

Low Income ▰▰▰▰▰▰ 36%

Mars ▰▰▰▰▰▰▰▰▰ 52%

Average Middles ▰▰▰▰▰ 33%

High Education
Middles ▰▰▰ 24%

Affluents ▰▰▰ 23%

Percent saying "strongly
agree" or "agree"

15   20   25   30   35   40   45   50   55   60   65

TABLE 16

TYPES OF GROUPS RESPONDENTS BELONG TO

	Low Income	MARs	Average Middles	High Educa-tion Middles	Affluents
Church or synagogue	66%	68%	69%	67%	79%
Church connected group	26%	26%	23%	33%	38%
Labor union	6%	21%	21%	7%	5%
PTA organizations	7%	19%	21%	28%	47%
Fraternal lodges or veterans organizations	13%	17%	21%	28%	47%
Social groups	10%	13%	13%	22%	39%
Civic groups	4%	12%	11%	19%	33%
Professional groups	7%	12%	11%	40%	53%
Sports teams	3% −	10%	14%	11%	20%
Youth oriented groups	5% −	9%	11%	12%	20%
Charitable organizations	4% −	8%	6%	16%	20%
Community centers	4%	7% +	4%	6%	11%
Neighborhood improvement associations	2% −	6% +	4%	9%	19%
Political groups	2%	6% +	3%	13%	10%
Social action groups	2%	4%	4%	13%	18%
Ethnic groups	2%	1%	2%	4%	6%

TABLE 17

TYPES OF PAST ORGANIZATIONAL CONTACTS

	Low Income	MARs	Average Middles	High Education Middles	Affluents
Local Police	31%	46%	41%	51%	66%
Local School Official	13% −	33%	32%	48%	56%
Business Officials	11%	28%	25%	44%	55%
Religious Groups	18%	26%	23%	40%	47%
U.S. Government Official	18%	25%	20%	45%	55%
Other Local Official	16%	25%	20%	31%	44%
State Government Official	15%	25%	20%	42%	45%
Influential People	13%	23% +	14%	27%	31%
Contact with the Media	12%	21%	19%	45%	43%
Unions	4% −	21%	18%	13%	14%
Neighborhood Assoc.	4% −	11%	8%	21%	37%
Civic groups	5% −	11%	10%	23%	38%
Social Action Groups	5%	6%	4%	27%	24%
Ethnic Organizations	3%	2%	2%	15%	11%

TABLE 18

NUMBER OF ORGANIZATIONAL CONTACTS

	Low Income	MARs	Average Middles	High Education Middles	Affluents
Six or more	8%	21% +	14%	41%	48%
Four - Five	10%	16%	17%	20%	23%
Two - Three	20%	24%	22%	14%	13%
One	19%	13%	17%	8%	9%
No Contact	43%	26%	29%	17%	8%
Total	100%	100%	100%	100%	100%
Mean	1.7	2.9	2.5	4.4	5.2

TABLE 19

STAGES OF GROUP DEVELOPMENT: RACE

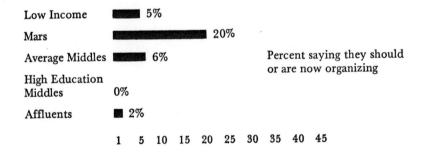

Low Income ▬▬ 5%
Mars ▬▬▬▬▬▬ 20%
Average Middles ▬▬ 6%
High Education Middles 0%
Affluents ▪ 2%

Percent saying they should or are now organizing

1   5   10   15   20   25   30   35   40   45

TABLE 20

INTERCORRELATIONS AMONG PARTICIPATION AND MOBILIZATION VARIABLES FOR MIDDLE AMERICANS AND OTHER WHITE RESPONDENTS

	Number of Organization Memberships	Number of Past Organization Contacts	Number of Past Political Actions	Legitimation of Direct Protest Actions	Legitimation of Busing Protest Actions
MIDDLE AMERICAN Number of Organizational Memberships	—				
Number of Past Organizational Contacts	+.47	—			
Number of Past Political Actions	+.42	+.58	—		
Legitimation of Direct Protest Actions	+.06	+.12	+.15	—	
Legitimation of Busing Protest Actions	+.01	+.21	+.18	+.27	—

TABLE 20 — *Continued*

	Number of Organization Memberships	Number of Past Organization Contacts	Number of Past Political Actions	Legitimation of Direct Protest Actions	Legitimation of Busing Protest Actions
OTHER WHITE RESPONDENTS					
Number of Organizational Memberships	—				
Number of Past Organizational Contacts	+.50	—			
Number of Past Political Actions	+.09	+.61	—		
Legitimation of Direct Protest Actions	+.01	+.05	+.17	—	
Legitimation of Busing Protest Actions	+.00	+.14	+.21	+.26	

TABLE 21

ATTITUDE ABOUT THIRD PARTY IN THE
1972 PRESIDENTIAL ELECTION

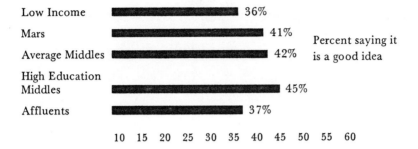

Low Income	36%	
Mars	41%	
Average Middles	42%	Percent saying it is a good idea
High Education Middles	45%	
Affluents	37%	

10 15 20 25 30 35 40 45 50 55 60

TABLE 22

REPORTED VOTING IN THE
PRESIDENTIAL ELECTION OF 1972
1975 SURVEY
(WHITE RESPONDENTS ONLY)

	MARs	*Others*
Nixon	46%	45%
McGovern	30%	29%
Didn't Vote	15%	19%
Don't Remember	4%	3%
Too Young	5%	4%
Total	100% (N=409)	100% (N=912)

TABLE 23

WHO WOULD YOU LIKE TO SEE THE
DEMOCRATS NOMINATE FOR
PRESIDENT?
1975 SURVEY
(DEMOCRATIC RESPONDENTS ONLY)

	MARs	Others
Kennedy	19%	18%
Wallace	17% +	12%
Jackson	9%	8%
Humphrey	8%	5%
Muskie	4%	3%
McGovern	3%	3%
Others*	9%	11%
Don't Know	28%	39%
"Nobody"	2%	1%
Total	100% (N=191)	100% (N=415)

*Includes Morris Udall, Birch Bayh, Sargent
Shriver, Frank Church, Walter Mondale, Lloyd
Bentson, William Proxmire, Terry Sanford,
Jimmy Carter, Fred Harris, Milton Shapp—each
of whom received no more than 2 percent of
the preferences.

TABLE 24

ATTITUDES REGARDING NATIONAL HEALTH
INSURANCE

"Some people have proposed a national medical and
health care system. I'm going to read you four
different proposals and I'd like you to tell me which
one you most support."

	MARs	Others
A totally nationalized system where not only is everyone guaranteed as much health care as he or she needs but doctors and hospitals are taken over by the government and fees, salaries and prices are regulated	20%	18%
A system of national health insurance where everyone is guaranteed as much health care as he or she needs	34%	35%
A small system where poor people are given medical insurance and everyone is protected against a sudden major illness.	26%	24%
Keeping things as they are today	16%	13%
Not sure	4%	10% +
Total	100%	100%

TABLE 25

DEALING WITH THE CRIME PROBLEM:
1975 SURVEY
'Which of these statements is closest
to your opinion?"

	MARs	Others
The best way to deal with crime is to impose stiff penalties and punish the criminal severely	53%	39%
The best way to deal with crime is to clean up the social and economic problems that cause it.	39%	54%
Don't Know	8%	7%
Total	100%	100%

TABLE 26

PATTERNS OF RELATIVE DEPRIVATION: SELF SOCIETY CONGRUENCES
1972 SURVEY

	Low Income	MARs	Average Middles	High Education Middles	Affluents
Country not doing as well as self in the last five years	25%	45%	40%	33%	39%
Country in next year will not do as well as self in next five years	16%	13%	16%	11%	19%
Shift	− 9%	−32%	−24%	−22%	−20%

TABLE 27

FAMILY INCOME AND MAR IDEOLOGY:
1972–1975

	1972	1975	Difference
$0–6,999	32%	36%	+ 4%
$7,000–9,999	33%	22%	−11%
$10,000–12,999	31%	35%	+ 4%
$13,000–14,999	25%	30%	+ 5%
$15,000–19,999	28%	35%	+ 7%
$20,000–24,999	24%	29%	+ 5%
$25,000–34,999 } 15%		28% }25%	+10%
$35,000 +		21%	

TABLE 28

AGE IN RELATION TO MAR IDEOLOGY:
1972–1975

	1972	1975	Difference
Age: 18–25	25%	31%	+ 6%
25–29	29%	27%	− 2%
36–45	30%	27%	− 3%
46–55	28%	39%	+11%
56–65	33%	32%	− 1%
Over 65	29%	33%	+ 4%

TABLE 29

EDUCATION IN RELATION TO MAR IDEOLOGY:
1972–1975

	1972	1975	Difference
Education Level: 0–8		32%	− 4%
9–11	36%	31%	− 5%
12	33%	35%	+ 2%
Technical: 1–3		41%	
College:	20%	24%	+ 4%
College Graduate:	18%	25%	+ 7%
Graduate School:	13%	27%	+14%

TABLE 30

RELIGIOUS GROUPS IN RELATION TO
MIDDLE AMERICAN RADICAL IDEOLOGY
(PERCENT QUALIFYING AS MARs)

	1972 Survey	1975 Survey
Protestant	28% (N=1139)	31% (N=693)
Catholic	35% (N=397)	31% (N=415)
Jewish	34% (N=056)	33% (N=073)
Other	13% (N=016)	25% (N=075)
No Preference	19% (N=072)	33% (N=090)

TABLE 31

ATTITUDES TOWARD PARENTAL
CONTROL OVER SCHOOL BOOKS:
1975 SURVEY

"Recently there has been a lot of controversy in West Virginia about school books. Some parents have argued that the books are immoral or contrary to religion. Others say teachers should be given freedom to choose books and it would be impossible to have books that satisfied everyone. Ignoring the specifics of this issue, do you think a majority of parents at school ought to be able to prevent a book from being used even if the teachers support it?"

	MARs	Others
Parents should be able to prevent it	54% +	45% −
Not Sure	15%	16%
Parents should not be able to prevent it.	31% −	39% +
Total	100%	100%

APPENDIX B

QUESTIONS USED TO CONSTRUCT
THE MIDDLE AMERICAN RADICAL INDEX

As you see it, is the idea that "we need tax reforms to make taxes fair for everyone" one which rich people support more than you do or do they give it less support?

1. Rich Support More
3. Same
5. Rich Support Less

8. Don't Know
9. NA (Not Ascertained)

How about the poor; do you feel that they support the idea that "we need tax reforms to make taxes fair for everyone" *more* or *less* than you do?

1. Poor Support More
3. Same
5. Poor Support Less

8. Don't Know
9. NA

Here is another statement: "People should raise their children with discipline and respect for authority." How much do you support this idea, a great deal, some, a little, or not at all?

1. A Great Deal
2. Some
4. A Little
5. Not At All

8. Don't Know
9. NA

Thinking about the help different kinds of people get from the government, do the following groups get the right amount of help, less than the right amount of help, or more than the right amount of help from the government?

Black Workers

1. Less
3. Right Amount
5. More

8. Don't Know
9. NA

Middle Income Blacks

1. Less
3. Right Amount
5. More

8. Don't Know
9. NA

Rich People

1. Less
3. Right Amount
5. More

8. Don't Know
9. NA

White Workers

1. Less
3. Right Amount
5. More

8. Don't Know
9. NA

Middle Income Whites

1. Less
3. Right Amount
5. More

8. Don't Know
9. NA

Would you say that over the last five years or so that the people who are rich are moving up *faster than you,* the *same,* or *slower* than you?

1. Faster
3. Same
5. Slower

8. Don't Know
9. NA

Would you say that over the last five years or so poor people are moving up *faster than you,* the *same,* or *slower* than you?

1. Faster
3. Same
5. Slower

8. Don't Know
9. NA

For the following things, would you tell me, in your opinion, whether blacks have more chance, the same chance, or less chance than people like yourself?

1. More
3. Same
5. Less

8. Don't Know
9. NA
0. INAP,

To get into colleges

1. More
3. Same
5. Less

8. Don't Know
9. NA
, 0 INAP

To get good housing at reasonable cost

1. More
3. Same
5. Less
8. Don't Know
9. NA
0. INAP

To get fair treatment in the courts

1. More
3. Same
5. Less

8. Don't Know
9. NA
0. INAP

To get help from the government when they are out of work

1. More
3. Same
5. Less

8. Don't Know
9. NA
0. INAP

To get a good education

1. More
3. Same
5. Less

8. Don't Know
9. NA
0. INAP

Here is a list of statements you sometimes hear about blacks. For each one would you tell me if you think it is very true, somewhat true, not very true, or not at all true.

Blacks have too much power or influence in politics.

1. Very true
2. Somewhat true

4. Not very true
5. Not at all true

8. Don't Know
9. NA
0. INAP

Blacks show off and act like they're better than anyone else.

1. Very true
2. Somewhat true
4. Not very true
5. Not at all true

8. Don't Know
9. NA
0. INAP

Blacks are taking jobs that should go to whites.

1. Very true
2. Somewhat true
4. Not very true
5. Not at all true

8. Don't Know
9. NA
0. INAP

How much responsibility do white people today have to make up for wrongs done to blacks in the past? A lot, some, little, or none?

1. A lot
2. Some
3. Little
5. None

8. Don't Know
9. NA

Here are several steps that some people feel could help solve the problem of race tensions. Would you favor:

Investigating to see if there is racism in the local schools?

1. Favor
5. Not Favor

8. Don't Know
9. NA

Black control over black neighborhoods?

1. Favor
5. Not favor
8. Don't Know
9. NA

Government job training programs for blacks?

1. Favor
5. Not Favor
8. Don't Know
9. NA

Giving blacks a chance ahead of whites in promotions where they have equal ability?

1. Favor
5. Not favor
8. Don't Know
9. NA

Here is a list of statements you sometimes hear about the rich. For each one, would you tell if you think it is very true, somewhat true, not very true, or not at all true?

The rich have too much power or influence in politics.

1. Very true
2. Somewhat true
4. Not very true
5. Not at all true

8. Don't Know
9. NA

Being rich is more than money, it's a whole different way of thinking and acting.

1. Very true
2. Somewhat true
4. Not very true
5. Not at all true

8. Don't Know
9. NA

The rich show off and act like they're better than anyone else.

1. Very true
2. Somewhat true
4. Not very true
5. Not at all true

8. Don't Know
9. NA

The rich pay less than their fair share of taxes.

1. Very true
2. Somewhat true
4. Not very true
5. Not at all true

8. Don't Know
9. NA

Rich people's children get into universities more easily than others.

1. Very true
2. Somewhat true
4. Not very true
5. Not at all true

8. Don't Know
9. NA

If you're rich you get better treatment in the courts.

1. Very true
2. Somewhat true
4. Not very true
5. Not at all true

8. Don't Know
9. NA

The rich give into the demands of the poor, and middle income people have to pay the bill.

1. Very true
2. Somewhat true
4. Not very true
5. Not at all true

8. Don't Know
9. NA

Now we would like to get an idea of how well you think other people are doing. Would you say over the last five years that (OPPOSITE RACE) are moving up *faster* than you, the *same*, or *slower* than you?

1. Faster
3. Same
5. Slower

8. Don't Know
9. NA

NOTES

Introduction

1. For a recent biography of the radio priest of the "Shrine of The Little Flower" see Sheldon Marcus, *Father Coughlin* (Boston: Little, Brown and Company, 1973).

2. There have been several analyses of the political movement that Coughlin spearheaded. Among the most significant of these is Daniel Bell's *The Radical Right* (Garden City: Doubleday, 1964).

Chapter 1. What Is a Middle America Radical?

3. The acronym MAR first appeared in an article in *Nation* magazine of August 17, 1974, entitled "The Middle American Radical."

4. For a more complete discussion of this question see E. Litwak, N. Hooyman and D. Warren, "Ideological Complexity and Middle American Rationality," *Public Opinion Quarterly*, 37 (Fall 1973): 317–32.

5. Some survey data on this point were obtained from a two-city sample of respondents participating in a longitudinal study of media usage. Using items similar to the MAR index, attitudes of "warm" or "cold" toward Ralph Nader were obtained. Results showed that MARs were more toward the cool end of the "feeling thermometer" device used to measure attitudes. See D. Warren and Beth Egnator, "Is There a Middle American?: Some Clues from Archie Bunker and the 1973 Meat Boycott," unpublished paper, University of Michigan, 1974.

6. For a very thorough exploration of these belief system distinctions see Nancy M. Hooyman, *The Proble: : Definitions and World Views of Working Class Whites* (Ph.D. diss., University of Michigan, 1974).

Chapter 2. Who Are the Middle American Radicals?

7. Referred to in a report by Basil Whiting, "The Alienated Middle American," Ford Foundation paper circulated in April, 1970.

8. Rosow's now famous "leaked memorandum" on "The Problems of the Blue Color Workers" further stated that:

*In 1968, 34 percent of all minority-group families were in the $5,000
to $10,000 income category. Of course, on the average, most black
families are still not anywhere as well off as white families: the median
income of all Negro families was $5,590, that of all white families
$8,937. But the point is that both these groups have essentially
"working class" economic and social problems related to wage, tax
and government benefit structure for the nonpoor—a fact not given
adequate recognition by the media, which, to the extent it emphasizes
only the black ghetto, perpetuates a stereotype. Quoted in Whiting,
p. 25.*

9. Ibid., p. 26.

10. Exceptions include the work by William Kornblum, *Blue Collar
Community* (Chicago: University of Chicago Press, 1974); Arthur M.
Shostak, *Blue Collar Life* (New York: Random House, 1969) and John
Musick, *Interaction with Black People: White Working Class Perspectives*
(Ph.D. diss., University of Michigan, 1974).

11. Quoted in Whiting, p. 27.

12. The concept of "alienation" has a number of different meanings
and conceptual bases. For a summary of the literature and a useful review
of the pertinent sociological issues regarding this idea see Mary H. Lystad,
Social Aspects of Alienation, (National Institute of Mental Health, Publication No. (CHSM) 72—9107, U.S. Government Printing Office, 1969).

13. In the 1975 Cambridge survey, which included measures of the
MAR ideology, the identical percentage differences between men and
women occurred—32 percent and 28 percent respectively fell into the
classification indicated.

14. Appendix Table 28 shows that the more recent 1975 survey finds a
higher proportion of persons age 18—25 with the MAR perspective than
was true in 1972.

15. In the 1975 Cambridge sample retired persons were an even larger
proportion of the MAR group than had been the case in 1972. Unemployed persons were not disproportionately found in the ranks of the
MAR group.

16. In the less extensive 1975 survey those with no religious preference
were about as likely as other groups to partake of the MAR ideology—a
marked shift from three years earlier.

17. Once again the pattern manifested in the 1975 survey showed in
relation to total family income a pattern replicated by other variables; the
MAR perspective was more widely dispersed than in 1972. The main
change was in the higher income groups at $25,000 or more.

Chapter 3. The Concerns of the Middle American Radical

18. In the 1975 Cambridge survey a similar question was asked, "Is
your income now higher, lower, or about the same as it was three years

ago?" This provides a basis for longitudinal comparison; among the MAR group 25 percent indicated income decline.

19. This pattern of neighborhood is one in which limited linkage to the outer or larger community occurs—either formally or informally. There is high internal cohesion and local identification. For an analysis of neighborhood types see D. Warren, *Black Neighborhoods*: An Assessment of Community Power (Ann Arbor: University of Michigan Press, 1975), and D. Warren and R. Warren, "Six Types of Neighborhoods," in *Psychology Today*, June, 1975, pp. 66–68.

20. The same survey also indicates that 62 percent of MARs and 73 percent of other white respondents feel that less racial tension is present now than there was a few years ago.

Chapter 4. The World of Work and the MAR

21. Quoted in the *Detroit Free Press*, November 4, 1972.

22. Sar A. Levitan, *Blue Collar Blues* (New York: McGraw Hill, 1971).

23. Seymour M. Lipset, *The Politics of Unreason* (New York: Harper and Row, 1970), p. 509.

24. Patricia and Brendan Sexton, *Blue Collars and Hard Hats: The Working Class and the Future of American Politics* (New York: Random House, 1971.

25. Ibid., p. 196.

26. Harold L. Sheppard and Neal Q. Herrick, *Where Have All the Robots Gone*? Work Dissatisfaction in the '70's (New York: The Free Press, 1972).

27. Edward H. Ransford and Vincent Jeffries, "Blue Collar Anger: Reactions to the Students and Black Protest Movements," Paper read at the 66th Annual Meeting of the American Sociological Association, 1971.

Chapter 5. Organizational Criticisms:
Major Targets and Grievances

28. In the 1975 Cambridge Report the belief that government was unresponsive was a distinctive MAR attitude. In response to the statement "Most politicians don't really care about people like me," 65 percent of MARs compared to 46 percent of other whites said that they agreed with this indictment.

29. A comparable measure of government deceit was derived from answers to the statement: "Over the last ten years this country's leaders consistently lied to the American people." In the 1975 survey 76 percent of MARs and 64 percent of other whites agreed with this statement. This reflects the generally higher alienation from government leaders that has

permeated American society between 1972 and 1975. This personalized rejection of the political process as it has been functioning in our society should not be interpreted as a desire to restructure basic institutions; the evil is seen to lie with individuals, not the system. This is indeed the MAR perspective.

30. The *Detroit Free Press,* May 3, 1975. A series of legal suits and countersuits has followed in a bewildering sequence of reactions to Mayor Young's initial stance. At this writing the special cases brought to protest female police officers in the one hand, black policemen on the other hand, and the police sargeants and the Detroit Police Officers' Association itself have yet to receive definitive court action.

Chapter 6. Social Participation and Political Mobilization

31. Andrew Greeley, *Why Can't They Be Like Us?* (New York: Dutton, 1971).

32. In the 1972 presidential race the role of Ronald Reagan was a muted one. By late 1975, Reagon had become one of the leading potential candidates. In assessing the response of the MAR to his emergence as a leading "conservative" ideologue, the similarity of his style to that of Wallace has been frequently noted—his attack on dishonest and corrupt politicians and the directness of his rhetoric. Yet the content of the two presidential aspirants' philosophies is markedly different. This separation is one fundamentally tied to the uniqueness of the MAR perspective. Such a distinction was effectively captured by Remer Tyson, political writer for the Knight Newspapers:

> *Wallace wants to change the people who run the government; Reagan wants to shrink the government's size.*
>
> *Wallace's rhetoric is a mixture of populist liberalism and social conservatism; Reagan wants to repeal the New Deal, to impose fiscal conservatism.*
>
> *Wallace takes on the moneyed capitalists, Reagan speaks their praise.*
>
> *The two would have difficulty writing a platform to meet the satisfaction of both.*
>
> *Detroit Free Press, 5/11/75*

Reagan's stand on issues of the day fly in the face of many programs that MARs are dependent on and wish to strengthen. Thus, on social security, Reagan has indicated that he believes it should be made voluntary. On labor unions, he states that "organized labor exerts a force on government that wouldn't be tolerated for a minute if it were attempted by management." On the economic squeeze situation in the mid-1970s Reagan remarked, "Only by enduring a market adjustment—a recession if you will—can we stop the inflation and restore the stability of the dollar."

Only with regard to the Viet Nam war issue might Wallace and Reagan appeals respond to the MAR concern over ineffective military action and domestic dissent in the early years of the involvement.

33. *Newsweek,* April 21, 1975, p.43.

34. The Wallace remarks that aroused so much commentary were bannered by leading newspapers around the country. On the thirtieth anniversary of V-E Day, Wallace provided a rather direct link to the Coughlin movement of the 1930s when he asserted:

> *I think we were fighting the wrong people, maybe, in World War II. Our true foreign policy . . . ought to have been cultivating the friendship of the Japanese and the Germans instead of being antagonistic.*
>
> *Detroit Free Press, 5/8/75*

In confirmation of MARs' distrust of media and newspaper reporting, *Newsweek* on June 23, 1975, reported that the *Washington Post* story from which the Wallace quotes were taken involved "quote juggling." The story indicated that Charles B. Seib of the *Post* criticized his own paper for linking two statements together (as noted in the *Free Press* citation above) which in fact appeared 48 pages apart in a transcript of Wallace's appearance in a press conference with a group of foreign journalists.

SELECTED BIBLIOGRAPHY

1. Anson, Robert Sam. "Southie Is My Home Town." *New Times* (15 November 1974): 16–24.
2. Binzen, Peter. *Whitetown, U.S.A.* New York: Random House, 1970.
3. Coles, Robert. *The Middle Americans.* Boston: Little, Brown & Co., 1971.
4. Friedman, Murray, ed. *Overcoming Middle-Class Rage.* Philadelphia: Westminster Press, 1971.
5. Greeley, Andrew M. *Why Can't They Be Like Us?* New York: E.P. Dutton & Co., Inc., 1971.
6. Hamill, Peter. "The Revolt of the White Lower Middle Class." *New York* (14 April 1969): excerpts.
7. Harris, Fred R. *The New Populism.* New York: Saturday Review Press, 1973.
8. House, James S., and Mason, William M. "Political Alienation in America, 1952–1968." *American Sociological Review* 40, no. 2 (April 1975): 123–47.
9. Howe, Louise Kapp, ed. *The White Majority: Between Poverty and Affluence.* New York: Random House, 1970.
10. Hooyman, Nancy, and Musick, John. "The Busing Controversy: Working Class Patterns of Adaption." Paper. School of Social Work, University of Michigan, Feb. 1972.
11. Kornblum, William. *Blue-Collar Community Structures of Urban Society.* Chicago: University of Chicago Press. 1974.
12. Krickus, Richard J. "The White Ethnics: Who Are They and Where Are They Going?" *City* (May-June 1971): 23–31.
13. Lahart, Kevin. "Ethnics '71: What Happens When the Melting-Pot Fire Goes Out." *Newsday* (5 June 1971).
14. Lane, Robert E., and Lerner, Michael. "Why Hard Hats Hate Hairs." *Psychology Today* (November 1970): 45–50, 104–6.
15. Lemon, Richard. *The Troubled American.* New York: Simon and Schuster, 1970.
16. Levine, Irving M. "The White Working American." *Catholic Mind* (January 1971): 3–10.
17. Levine, Irving, and Herman, Judith. "Search for Identity in Blue-Collar America." *Civil Rights Digest* (Winter 1972): 1–6.

259

18. Levitan, Sar A. *Blue Collar Blues.* New York: McGraw-Hill, 1971.
19. Lipset, Seymour Martin. *The Politics of Unreason: Right-Wing Extremism in America, 1970–1970.* New York: Harper and Row, 1970.
20. Lipset, Seymour Martin, and Raab, Earl. "The Wallace Whitelash." *TransAction* (December 1969: 1–12.
21. Litwak, Eugene, Hooyman, Nancy and Warren, Donald. "Ideological Complexity and Middle-American Rationality." *Public Opinion Quarterly* 37, no. 3 (Fall 1973): 317–32.
22. Magidson, Judith. "The Reacting Americans; An Interim Look at the White Ethnic Lower Middle Class." Material quoted from position papers and discussion at the National Consultation on Ethnic America, Fordham University, 20–21 June 1968 and the Philadelphia Conference on the Problems of White Ethnic America, University of Pennsylvania, 25 June 1968.
23. Pettigrew, Thomas F., Riley, Robert T., and Vanneman, Reeve D. "George Wallace's Constituents." *Psychology Today* 5, no. 9 (February 1972): 47–49, 92.
24. Ransford, H. Edward, and Jeffries, Vincent. "Blue Collar Anger: Reactions to the Student and Black Protest Movements." Paper read at the American Sociological Association meetings, 1971.
25. Scammon, Richard, and Wattenberg, Ben J. *The Real Majority.* New York: Coward, McCann and Geoghegan, 1970.
26. Sexton, Patricia, and Sexton, Brendon. *Blue-Collars and Hard Hats; The Working Class and the Future of American Politics.* New York: Random House, 1971.
27. Sheppard, Harold L., and Herrick, Neal Q. *Where Have All the Robots Gone? Worker Dissatisfaction in the 70's.* New York: Free Press, 1972.
28. Warren, Donald I. "Anomia and Middle Americans: Some Observations of Normative Flexibility." Proceedings of the 24th Annual Meeting of the Industrial Research Association (December 1971): 371–79.
29. Warren, Donald I. "Middle American Radicals." *Nation* (17 August 1974): 107–10.
30. Wenk, Michael, Tomasi, S.M., and Baroni, Geno, eds. *Pieces of a Dream: the Ethnic Worker's Crisis with America.* New York: Center for Migration Studies, 1972.
31. Wille, Lois. "The Anxious Majority, Chicago's Working Class." Chicago Daily News (reprinted New York: American Jewish Committee, May 1970).
32. Wright, James D. "The Working Class, Authoritarianism, and the War in Vietnam," *Social Problems* 20, no. 2 (Fall 1972): 133–50.